COMMANDING SENTENCES

A Charted Course in Basic Writing Skills

Helen Mills
American River College

Consulting Editor
Wayne Harsh
University of California, Davis

Scott, Foresman and Company   Glenview, Illinois · Brighton, England

ISBN: 0-673-07917-1

Regional offices of Scott, Foresman and Company are located in Dallas, Texas; Glenview, Illinois; Oakland, New Jersey; Palo Alto, California; Tucker, Georgia; and Brighton, England.

ACKNOWLEDGMENTS
Illustrations in this book are taken from *1800 Woodcuts by Thomas Bewick and His School,* edited by Blanche Cirker and the Editorial Staff of Dover Publications (New York: Dover Publications, Inc., 1962); *Graphics AD LIB,* by Tony Hinwood (London: Business Books Limited, 1969); *Old Engravings and Illustrations, Volume One: People* and *Old Engravings and Illustrations, Volume Two: Things,* compiled, edited, and published by the Dick Sutphen Studio (Minneapolis: Dick Sutphen Studio, 1965).

TO THE INSTRUCTOR

Commanding Sentences lends itself equally well to individualized instruction in sentence writing, to instruction in a learning lab, to modular scheduling, and to lecture-discussion classes. Its detailed index makes it a quick reference in composition courses. It is suitable for students who need a step-by-step descriptive study of language functions and characteristics and experience in writing a wide variety of sentences, or for those who need a rapid review before beginning a composition course. Most students, including those who have some reading difficulties, can move through the *Commanding Sentences* program easily in nine to twelve weeks. Highly motivated students with good vocabularies and good reading skills can finish the program in four to six weeks. Those who read poorly may take eighteen to thirty-six weeks, but they can complete the program if they are given supplementary exercises and reading instruction as well.

Based on the mastery concept and instructional objectives, the *Commanding Sentences* package consists of nine units of sequential, single-concept lessons, exercises for each lesson to test application, answers for immediate feedback, and X-TRAS (additional unit exercises) for open-book quizzes, all found in this book. A separate test package available from the publisher contains the Unit Reviews (Forms A and B), a diagnostic Pretest, a *Writing Pretest*, and a Posttest. An instructor may choose to use only the first six units, which cover basic sentence patterns, modifiers, coordination, and subordination. For modular scheduling an instructor may divide the text into these logical segments: Units One, Two and Three —basic sentences and modifiers; Units Four, Five, and Six—coordination and subordination; Units Seven, Eight, and Nine—verbals, punctuation review, and sentence editing. In addition, by administering the Pretest or Writing Pretest, which are keyed to the nine units, an instructor may assign only those units the student needs to fill his information gaps.

Although most of the exercises are objective, there are many in which the student generates his own sentences. As a result, the instructor can see whether the student really comprehends the lessons and can apply what he has learned to his own writing. Another way of discerning student comprehension is to use the Unit Reviews as an inventory of what the student knows. If he scores at least 85 percent on Form A, he is ready for the next unit. If he scores less, the student should study the whole unit or parts of it with help from the instructor or tutors and take either all or part of Form B of the Unit Review.

With individualized instruction, an instructor will find that students who qualify for a composition course or who have a good grammar background can work as tutors very effectively with only an introduction to the *Commanding Sentences* program and with a supervisor present during class meetings to clarify or elaborate on some points.

If you have any questions about individualizing instruction or the *Command Sentences* program, please write to me at American River College, 4700 College Oak Drive, Sacramento, California, 95841. Send me your phone number and hours you are available. I will either write or call you.

Helen Mills

TO THE STUDENT WRITER

Most of us can talk comfortably with others. We may even write an occasional friendly letter easily —or some class assignments. But when we are faced with writing an essay or a research paper, we dread the hours we have to spend on the assignment. Even though we know what we want to say, we cannot seem to put the words on paper. What we finally write is not really good, and often the more we revise it, the more confusing and awkward it seems to become. Even as we hand it in, we know it will come back covered with notes and meaningless symbols marked in red.

CAN WE EVER LEARN
TO WRITE ESSAYS EFFECTIVELY?

Yes. It is possible that we can learn the writing style for essays. Although writing is more than putting words on paper—it is both an art and a discipline—we can acquire the necessary discipline even if we cannot always be artistic. Here are some ways we can help ourselves:
1. Read with understanding.
2. Develop an adequate vocabulary and understand the effect of words.
3. Understand sentence structure and the system of language—its characteristics and functions.
4. Learn to diagnose and overcome weaknesses in writing.
5. Develop flexibility in writing style. Learn to use a style appropriate to the demands of the piece to be written.

We must be patient with ourselves and realize that we cannot acquire these skills all at once. As we gain insight, we will see more complexities to explore and appreciate, and then even more. It is somewhat like looking into a kaleidoscope. We can observe one pattern and become familiar with its parts. Then one small shift makes the parts move into a new pattern, and still more new patterns develop, seemingly without end. Although we may admire these patterns, we may not be able to understand how they evolve and how to produce them ourselves, but we can begin by studying a small unit—the sentence, not only its basic patterns, but also the characteristics of the words that make up the patterns—in *Commanding Sentences*.

Because this book is a style manual—a description of the written sentence—we will not discuss the characteristics of oral language. And although we recognize that there are many kinds of language, we will limit our discussion to the writing style for reports, essays, and research papers. We will not talk about what is correct or incorrect, but rather about what is appropriate for a particular style.

In this exploration of language function we will use labels, a limited number of familiar terms, to talk about the sentence parts, just as we use names of parts in discussing an automobile engine or the characteristics of music. However, these labels will serve primarily as a means to talk about language, a way of discussing how language works. Their specific names, then, are of no great importance. We need them only in order to understand the patterns of language and to use language to our purpose and advantage.

COMMANDING SENTENCES AS
SELF-INSTRUCTIONAL UNITS

Whether you are using *Commanding Sentences* in a class, in a workshop, or on your own, you can complete this book if you follow these steps:
1. Read each lesson and try to apply the information given by working with the examples.
2. To test your understanding of the lessons and your ability to apply information, complete the exercises following the lessons.
3. Check your answers with those in the Answer Key in the back of the book.

4. Correct any errors by finding the related explanation in the lesson. Mark corrections above your original answers in the exercises.
5. When you have completed all the lessons in a Unit, review the lessons and the corrected exercises.
6. Complete the X-TRAS exercises at the end of each unit to test your accomplishment. Answers for these are also in the Answer Key.
7. If you are enrolled in a course or attend a workshop where the *Commanding Sentences* program is used, your instructor or supervisor will have a set of Unit Reviews for you to take. The instructor will also have the Pretest and the Posttest.

If you are working in this book on your own and want to do the Unit Reviews which instructors give to students in their classes, you may obtain the Unit One Review, Form A, by writing to the author: Helen Mills, American River College, 4700 College Oak Drive, Sacramento, California, 95841. When you have completed it, return the Review to the author. It will be graded and returned to you with items marked for further study. If you pass it, you will also receive a copy of the Unit Two Review, Form A. If you do not pass, you will receive Form B of the Unit One Review to Complete.

GRADING
GUIDELINES

Completing exercises in this book and checking your answers immediately afterward with the key is one way you can learn whether or not you are acquiring knowledge, understanding, and the ability to apply what you learn as you complete the lessons and units. If you miss only one or two items in an exercise, you are doing well. If, however, you miss five, six, seven, or more, you may have problems in one or more of these areas:

1. You may not have really understood the lesson.
2. You may not have understood the directions for the exercise.
3. You may not have read the lesson before you did the exercise.
4. You may not be able to understand fully the words in the lesson or exercise.
5. You may try to do as little work as possible; as a result, you skim over both the lesson and the exercise and miss important details.
6. You learn only enough to complete the exercise, and you allow yourself to forget what you have learned in preceding lessons. The result is that you lose an overall view and cannot associate new information with what you have already learned.

Help yourself by trying to be methodical. Information in Units One, Two, and Three provide the basis for understanding Units Four, Five, and Six. And the first six units furnish the basis for understanding Units Seven, Eight, and Nine. Even with careful study you may find that you do not understand every bit of each lesson. Do not be discouraged; language is intricate. Although trying to understand its patterns may frustrate you now, you will find yourself becoming fascinated by the details as you acquire understanding during the rest of the book and the rest of your life.

To evaluate your progress, to discover what you know and what you still have to learn, complete the Unit Reviews, which consist of several parts, each worth a specific number of points. Even though tests make you nervous and you think grades are absurd, this objective approach is a quick way to complete an inventory of what you have learned and to find out what you need to study in more detail. Although you should get 85 percent before going on to the next unit, a score of 60 or 70 percent reveals that you need only a little more work to give yourself a firm foundation for subsequent units.

To weight the kinds of problems that may occur in sentence writing exercises, we will deduct points according to the following chart. In the Unit Reviews, sentences may be worth 10 or 20 points. Both the point values and percentages are listed.

As an example, if you use only a comma between two independent clauses, you will receive no credit for the sentence because you still have to learn what a compound sentence is. If you omit a comma, you will lose 10 percent (1 or 2 points), but if you insert a comma where it does not belong, you will lose 25 percent (3 or 5 points). The total score, then, gives you a indication of your strengths and weaknesses in writing.

	Total Points for Sentence		
	20	10	
Problem	Points deducted		Percentage deducted
Comma fault Fragment Run-On Misused semicolon	10	10	100%
Sentence wordy, awkward, not clear	5–10	2–5	25–50%
Subject-verb agreement Pronoun-antecedent agreement Reference Misplaced modifier Dangling modifier Lack of parallelism	4	2	20%
Misused comma	5	3	25%
Spelling Comma omitted Idiom Word usage	2	1	10%

Remember that this scoring is only a way for us to communicate, to reach a common understanding of what you know about written Standard English. It indicates where you need more practice or more study.

Helen Mills

CONTENTS

unit ONE

Sentence Patterns One and Two, Nouns, Verbs

lesson 1 Heading for a Goal

Let's explore.

How do we reach our goal?

Some of us can set our course and arrive at our destination without much practice or planning.

Others of us need a carefully mapped route with signposts along the way.
But we can all arrive at our goal even though some of us need more detailed help and take longer than others.

To build a ship, for example, we need a frame construction—the ribs—first, and then we can add the hull planking, the fittings, and the sails. To make a ship operate, we must know how to sail it.
If the ship is not built carefully and sailed carefully—

Similarly, to make an engine work, we have to know something about its individual parts, like the carburetor, the pistons, the spark plugs, and how they function together to produce power. We can then repair the engine or make adjustments if it does not work.

If we want to write effectively, we have to prepare ourselves. In order to revise what we have written, we have to be familiar with the framework of language. With this knowledge we can add words to basic sentences to give our readers explicit information:

Basic Sentence: The crew boarded the ship.

Expanded Sentence: The well-trained, energetic crew quickly boarded the seaworthy sailing ship.

OR

The crew—unshaven, ill-tempered, mutinous—slowly boarded the battered, unpainted sailing ship.

We can learn how to combine short sentences by eliminating unnecessary words; we can learn to show relationships of ideas by using a variety of constructions:

Basic Sentences: The crew boarded the ship.

The captain boarded the ship.

The ship set sail.

They searched for the treasure.

Combined Sentences: The crew and the captain boarded the ship and set sail to search for the treasure.

OR

After the crew and captain had boarded the ship, they set sail and searched for the treasure.

The key to this kind of revision lies in our understanding of how language functions. As we work our way through this book, we must come to understand each step thoroughly, especially those parts marked with keys; each key provides the basis for understanding the next part. If we omit any of them—

This book will become our charted course to the understanding of language. As we get detailed training, we will gain the control and the confidence we need to write economically, convincingly, and forcefully.

SIMPLE SENTENCE

In writing, the SENTENCE is a key unit we use to communicate our thoughts to readers. It can convey one thought or several, depending on how we choose to write it. The basic English sentence, a simple declarative statement, has two parts—SUBJECT and PREDICATE. The subject appears first, and the predicate follows:

Sentence =	Subject (S)	Predicate (P)	We can compare sentence patterns to mathematical equations:
	John and Mary	met.	$10 = 5 + 5$
	John	loves Mary.	$10 = 12 - 2$
	Mary	loves John.	$10 = 6 + (1 + 3)$
	John and Mary	became engaged.	$10 = 15 + 4 - 9$
	The young couple	will be married soon.	$x = y + z$

SUBJECT AND PREDICATE

The SUBJECT, either a single word or several words, tells who or what the sentence is about. If it is a group of words, it frequently consists of modifiers plus the NOUN HEAD, a noun around which its modifiers cluster.

The PREDICATE, either a single word or several words, tells something about the subject. It may consist of a single-word verb or verb phrase, and it may have completers and modifiers.

ALL OF THESE TERMS WILL BE EXPLAINED IN THE FOLLOWING LESSONS.

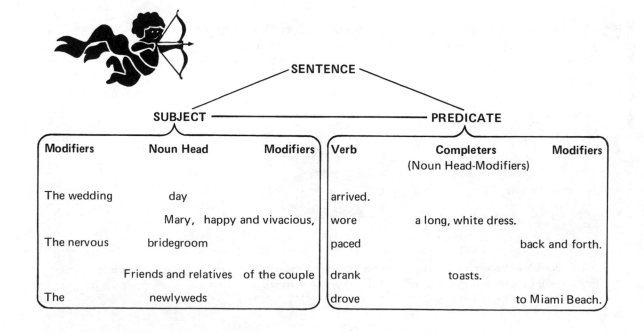

SENTENCE

SUBJECT ——————————————— PREDICATE

Modifiers	Noun Head	Modifiers	Verb	Completers (Noun Head-Modifiers)	Modifiers
The wedding	day		arrived.		
	Mary,	happy and vivacious,	wore	a long, white dress.	
The nervous	bridegroom		paced		back and forth.
	Friends and relatives	of the couple	drank	toasts.	
The	newlyweds		drove		to Miami Beach.

*SUGGESTION—Memorize these ways to decide whether
a word functions as a verb or a noun.*

VERB TEST

1. Place *I* or *they* before the word if it does not end in *-s.*

   v   v   v
   I *call.*   They *answer.*   I *smile.*

   Place *he* or *she* before words ending in *-s.*

   She *calls.*   He *answers.*   She *helps.*

2. Notice whether the word ends or can end in the suffix *-ed.*

   We inquir*ed.*   They respond*ed.*

   She call*ed.*   He answer*ed.*

   She *called* her boyfriend this morning and *smiled* when he *answered.*

3. Notice whether auxiliary (helping) verbs like *have* and *would* can be used before the verb.

   He *has arrived.*   They *have departed.*

   She *had called.*   He *would have answered.*

NOUN TEST

1. Place *the, a, an, my, our, your, her* or *some, several,* or *two* before the word. Or notice whether one of these words may be used before the word being identified.

   the call   *my* answer   *a* smile   *some* help

   The call came late, but *John's polite answer* brought *a smile* to Mary's face.

   Two girls requested *some* help.

2. Add *-s (-es)* to make the word plural.

   the call*s*   their answer*s*   our smile*s*

   Notice that the words *call, answer, smile,* and *help,* like many other words, can be both nouns or verbs, depending on their function in the sentence.

   PRONOUNS, words used in place of nouns, will be labeled nouns (N), but they cannot be identified by using the Noun Test; they have to be learned. Here are some of them: *I, you, he, she, it, we, they, me, him, her, us, them, mine, yours, his, hers, ours, theirs, this, that,* plus words like *each, some, all,* and *two.*

EXERCISE 1A

Use the Verb Test and Noun Test to examine each
of these words. If the word can function as a verb,
write V in the first blank. If it can function as a
noun, write N in the second blank.

1. head	_____ _____	11. did	_____ _____
2. map	_____ _____	12. go	_____ _____
3. pan	_____ _____	13. kiss	_____ _____
4. bat	_____ _____	14. net	_____ _____
5. pit	_____ _____	15. peck	_____ _____
6. cup	_____ _____	16. music	_____ _____
7. rub	_____ _____	17. back	_____ _____
8. hat	_____ _____	18. bell	_____ _____
9. pick	_____ _____	19. pet	_____ _____
10. chill	_____ _____	20. shell	_____ _____

EXERCISE 1B

Using the Noun and Verb Tests, determine whether the word in boldface (heavy) type functions as a
N or V in the following sentences. Write N or V in
the blank at the right.

Example: Dogs **bark** loudly. _V_ (they **bark**)

Owls hoot at **night**. _N_ (the **night**)

1. Bruce fell down the **stairs**. _____

2. Jon **called** early. _____

3. **Bells** ring at five o'clock. _____

4. He rode the **bus**. _____

5. The **baker** made cakes. _____

6. The dentist attended a **convention**. _____

7. At noon the chairman **spoke**. _____

8. The birds **sang** at daybreak. _____

9. Open the **window**. _____

10. Morgan **wrote** a letter. _____

EXERCISE 1C

Write V above each verb and N above each noun in these sentences. Use the Verb Test and the Noun Test.

1. Vines covered the fence.

2. The fence concealed the warehouse.

3. Lightning struck the warehouse at midnight.

4. The fire spread rapidly.

5. Quickly the flames enveloped the building.

6. The firemen arrived promptly.

7. They stretched hoses everywhere.

8. They broke windows and entered the warehouse.

9. The furniture, papers, books, and carpeting burned.

10. A fireman found a cat and carried it outside.

11. The cat ran away and hid.

12. Firemen climbed ladders and inspected the roof.

13. Suddenly the roof collapsed and the walls caved in.

14. Still the fire raged.

15. At dawn the ruins still smoldered.

lesson 2   Sentence Pattern One

In English, we have our choice of at least five basic sentence patterns. Each pattern varies according to the type of verb used. Certain verbs require completers; others do not. Verbs that we will consider under SENTENCE PATTERN ONE do not need completers. We begin by matching SENTENCE PATTERN ONE to the general pattern of the sentence.

Sentence	=	S	P
Sentence Pattern One	=	NS	Vi
		Flowers	bloom.

SUBJECT AND VERB IN SENTENCE PATTERN ONE

SENTENCE PATTERN ONE consists of the SUBJECT, which we will always designate as NS, and of an INTRANSITIVE VERB, labeled Vi. NS, the subject, tells what the sentence is about, and Vi, the verb (the PREDICATE), states something about the subject.

NS   Vi
John called.

NS   Vi
Mary answered.

In SENTENCE PATTERN ONE, the PREDICATE may consist of the VERB ALONE. The verb is INTRANSITIVE, requiring no noun, adjective, adverb, or adverbial phrase to serve as a completer. We will always label this type of verb Vi. The symbol *Vi* (or *vi* or *v intr*) is used in dictionaries before definitions of a word which can function as a complete or intransitive verb:

Example: *call*—Vi.   1. To communicate by telephone

2. To pay a short visit

3. To summon

COMMANDS

For a COMMAND, the complete verb (Vi) can stand alone as a sentence. The subject (NS) is *you* understood:

Vi   NS   Vi   Vi   NS   Vi
Stop.   (You) stop.   Run.   (You) run.

ADVERBS

The verb may be modified by an ADVERB (Adv), a single word or a word group that tells *when*, *where*, *why*, or *how*.

NS   Vi   Adv
The boat sank *rapidly*.

NS   Vi   Adv
John called *frantically*.

NS   Vi   Adv--------------------
The boat disappeared *under the water*.

NS Vi   Adv C Adv   Adv------------
He bobbed *up and down like a cork*.

sentence keys

By learning a definite sequence to analyze what we write, we will be able to examine each word group systematically and determine whether we write acceptable sentences. Use these keys to analyze Pattern One.

1. Find the verb by using the verb tests. Write V above the verb.

           V   V
    The wind blew.   The leaf fell.   (I *fell*. It *fell*. I *blew*. They *blew*.)

2. Ask *who* or *what* plus the verb. Label the word that answers the question NS (subject).

    What blew?

    What fell?

        NS
    The wind blew.

        NS
    The leaf fell.

3. Read subject (NS) + verb (V). If the verb makes a complete predicate (that is, if it requires no other word or words to complete it), label it Vi.

        NS   Vi
    The wind blew.

        NS Vi
    The leaf fell.

4. Read NS + Vi and ask *when, where, why,* or *how*. Label the word that answers the question *Adv.*

        NS   Vi Adv
    The wind blew *forcefully*. (how)

        NS Vi Adv
    The leaf fell *slowly*. (how)

    Adv   NS Vi
    Yesterday the leaf fell. (when)

        NS Vi Adv----------------
    The leaf fell *to the ground*. (where)

EXERCISE 2A

Examine these word groups to determine whether
they are sentences or fragments (parts of sentences). If the word group is not a sentence, write
F (fragment) in the first blank. If the word group
is a sentence, write the word or words which make
up NS in the first blank at the right and the word
or words which make up the verb in the second
blank. If NS is understood, write (you) in the first
blank.

		NS	Vi
Example:	Camels bite.	Camels	bite
	Lonely wanderer.	F	

1. Walked quickly. _____ _____

2. Butterflies and birds fly. _____ _____

3. Earth tremor. _____ _____

4. Fish swim. _____ _____

5. Sit. _____ _____

6. Cocks crow. _____ _____

7. Golden opportunity. _____ _____

8. Betty phoned. _____ _____

9. Stars twinkle. _____ _____

10. People fish and hunt. _____ _____

COMPOUND SUBJECTS AND COMPOUND PREDICATES

In most of the examples given in this lesson, NS and Vi have each consisted of a single word—simple
subject and simple predicate. Exceptions are Sentence 2 (*Butterflies and birds . . .*) and Sentence 10
(*. . . fish and hunt.*) in Exercise 2A. These exceptions illustrate how two or more nouns or verbs may be
joined with CONJUNCTIONS (C) like *and* or *or* to form a COMPOUND SUBJECT or COMPOUND
PREDICATE. It is one way of combining two sentences.

Simple Subjects

NS Vi
Nancy swims.

Jane swims.

Compound Subject

NS   C   NS   Vi
Nancy and Jane swim.

Simple Predicates

NS   Vi
Nancy swims.

Nancy dives.

Compound Predicate

NS   Vi   C   Vi
Nancy swims and dives.

(Notice that with only two items
NO PUNCTUATION is used before *and*.)

EXERCISE 2B

Write these paired sentences as a single sentence by
omitting duplicate words and using conjunctions
(C). Make either the subject or the verb compound.

1. Diane yawned.

    Joe yawned.

2. The flowers blossomed.

    The flowers died.

3. The door banged.

    The shutters banged.

4. Marilyn writes.

    Marilyn paints.

WRITING SENTENCES

Here are a few suggestions to help you learn to write sentences to match Sentence Pattern One. Begin
by writing a word that can function as a verb. Write V above it:

V
arrived

V
put

Then ask *who* or *what* performed the action of the verb. The word that answers the question is the
subject (NS):

NS   V
The guests arrived

NS   V
The guests put

Read *NS* and *V* together. If the verb is complete, place a period after it, and label the verb Vi.

NS   Vi
The guests arrived.

If the verb needs a noun to complete it, try another verb and subject.

The guests put (?) *Put* is not a complete verb.

To add adverbs (Adv), read NS + Vi and ask *when*, *where*, *why*, or *how*. Add words which answer any of these questions:

NS	Vi	Adv		NS	Vi	Adv--------

The guests arrived *yesterday.*   (when)   The guests arrived *by train.*   (how)

EXERCISE 2C

Write sentences to match the patterns given. If you do not know how to begin, reread Writing Sentences above. Label parts.

Example: NS   Vi   Adv
                                    NS   Vi   Adv
                                    The women laughed loudly.

               Compound   NS   Vi
                                    NS   C   NS   Vi
                                    The men and boys applauded.

1. NS Compound Vi

2. Command

3. NS Vi Adv

4. Compound NS Vi

5. NS Vi

lesson 3   Sentence Pattern Two

The second basic sentence pattern consists of at least two nouns and a verb.

Sentence	=	S	P	

Sentence Pattern Two	=	NS	Vt	Ndo

The carpenter bought lumber.

SUBJECT, VERB, AND DIRECT OBJECT

Sentence Pattern Two consists of the SUBJECT (NS) and the PREDICATE which contains both a TRANSITIVE VERB (Vt) and a DIRECT OBJECT (Ndo).

   NS   Vt   Ndo
The carpenter built a cabin.

The verb is INCOMPLETE or TRANSITIVE (Vt). It must be followed by a noun, a DIRECT OBJECT (Ndo), which completes the predicate. If we placed a period after *built*, the sentence would be confusing; the reader would ask *what* the carpenter had built.

  *The carpenter built. (What did he build?)

The INTRANSITIVE verb (Vi), on the other hand, can serve as the complete predicate in Pattern One.

   NS   Vi
The carpenter worked.

The direct object (Ndo) after the verb gives the reader the information he needs. A sentence with a transitive verb (Vt) always has a direct object (Ndo). The direct object, which represents a person or thing different from the subject (NS), can be said to receive the action stated by the verb.

    Example: The carpenter smashed his thumb.

                    NS   Vt
             The carpenter smashed what?   his thumb

*The asterisk (*) indicates word groups that form ungrammatical English sentences.

He called his doctor immediately.

NS Vt   **Ndo**   **Adv**
He called whom?   his doctor   When?   immediately

Notice that certain verbs like *called, wrote, spoke,* and *read* can be either Vi or Vt.

NS Vi   **NS Vt**   **Ndo**
He called.   He called his doctor.

sentence keys

   To analyze Pattern Two sentences, we follow the same procedure as for Pattern One and then add one more step:

1. Find the verb. Label it V.

2. Ask *who* or *what* plus the verb. Write NS (subject) above the word that answers the question.

3. Read NS + V together and ask *whom* or *what.* Write Ndo (direct object) above the word that answers the question. Label the verb Vt.
    If there is no noun answering *whom* or *what,* the verb is complete.
    Label it Vi.

4. Write Adv above the words that tell *when, where, why,* and *how.*

COMPOUND DIRECT OBJECT

The direct object (Ndo) may consist of two or more words joined by a conjunction:

NS   Vt   Ndo   C   Ndo
The doctor used a splint and bandages.

It is a way of combining two sentences:

NS   Vt   Ndo
The doctor used a splint.

The doctor used bandages.

Notice that *splint* and *bandages* represent *two different items.*

EXERCISE 3A

Label the words in the following sentences with
NS, Ndo, Vt, Adv, C by using the Sentence Keys.
If you have difficulty, review the Noun Tests and
Verb Tests in Lesson 1.

Example:
      NS   Vt   Ndo Adv
    The beaver built a dam carefully.

1. Maxine bought a coat and hat yesterday.

2. The athletes carried torches.

3. Robins and blue jays ate the cherries.

4. The bricklayer hurt his back badly.

5. Tim chews gum and eats popcorn.

EXERCISE 3B

Label the words in the following sentences with
NS, Vi, Vt, Ndo, Adv, C by using Sentence Keys.

Example:
    NS   Vi
    The moon shines.

    NS Vt   Ndo C   Ndo
    Dan lost his comb and toothbrush.

1. The wind tore the flag to shreds.

2. Ice and snow completely covered the road.

3. Colors flashed brightly.

4. The trees swayed and creaked in the wind.

5. Paper littered the sidewalk.

6. Ellis and Brian agree.

7. The collie quickly herded sheep.

8. Ashley bought paints and brushes.

9. The pendulum swung.

10. Sarah knits sweaters and sews skirts.

WRITING SENTENCES

To write sentences to match Sentence Pattern Two, begin by writing a word that can function as a
verb:

V
read

V
wrote

Then ask *who* or *what* performed the action of the verb. The word that answers the question is the
subject (NS):

NS   V
The editor read

NS   V
The explorer wrote

Read NS and V together. If a noun, a direct object (Ndo), must be added to complete its meaning, the verb is incomplete (Vt). Write Vt over the verb and Ndo over the direct object.

NS   Vt   Ndo
The editor read the novel.

NS   Vt   Ndo
The explorer wrote reports.

The verb is complete (Vi) if there is no noun to complete its meaning.

NS   Vi
The editor spoke.

NS   Vi
The explorer wrote.

To add adverbs, read NS Vt Ndo or NS Vi and ask *when, where, why,* or *how.* Add words which answer these questions, and label them Adv:

The editor *eagerly* read the novel.   (how)

The editor read the novel *last week.*   (when)

The editor spoke *at the convention.*   (where)

The explorer wrote reports *quickly.*   (how)

The explorer wrote reports *daily.*   (when)

The explorer wrote reports *concisely.*   (how)

EXERCISE 3C

Write sentences to match these patterns. Label each word with one of these symbols: NS, Ndo, Vi, Vt, Adv.

1. NS Vi

2. NS Vt Ndo

3. NS Compound verb Adv (p. 7)

4. Compound NS Vt Ndo (p. 7)

5. NS Vt Ndo Adv

lesson 4 **Nouns**

Words can be identified as nouns by their MEANING (naming a person, place, or thing, a concept, an act), by their FUNCTION (serving as subjects or direct objects), by their FORM (the endings they have or may have), and by the NOUN DETERMINERS (words like *a*, *the*, *two*, *some*) that may precede nouns.

Meaning: Nouns name persons, things, places, actions, concepts.

       N   N   N   N

The *actor* liked the *scene* about the *discovery* of *truth* through

      N   N

the *medium* of a *dream.*

Function: Nouns function as subjects, direct objects, objects of prepositions (and other sentence parts that will be discussed later).

     NS   Ndo   Nop

The *manufacturer* took the *order* from the *government.*

Form: Most nouns change form to show plural number (that they represent more than one).

     N   N   N

The *boy* asked three *girls* to his *party.*   *Boy* and *party* are singular (one); *girls* is plural (more than one).

Noun Determiners: Most nouns can be preceded by words like *a, an, the, two, some,* and *my.*

The men asked for *two* representatives from *the* clubs.

(See Lesson 13, pp. 61-63, for a more complete description of noun determiners.)

PRONOUNS

PERSONAL PRONOUNS, used in place of nouns, are words like *I*, *you*, and *they*, which undergo a complete spelling change for each of their forms. See Unit Five for a complete discussion. They represent three persons:

First Person—the person speaking: *I, we*

I told *my* story.   *We* added other details.

Second Person—the person spoken to: *you*

You were unaware of the confusion.

Third Person—the person spoken about: *he, she, it, they*

He became very curious, and *she* asked many questions. *They* wanted to know the facts.

Other types of pronouns, the DEMONSTRATIVES *(this, that, these, those)* and the INDEFINITE pronouns (words like *some, any, each*, and *all*) may also replace nouns.

The fabrics arrived.   *These* are cotton.   *Those* are polyester.

Some are expensive.   *All* are attractive.

PLURAL NOUNS

1. Many nouns can be made to represent more than one simply by adding the suffix *-s* to the singular form. It is a simpler, shorter form than writing *flower + flower + flower* when we talk about several flowers. The word *they* can be used instead of the plural noun. The verb used with the plural noun is plural.

Maps cover the wall.

They are colorful.

2A. Form plurals of nouns ending in *-s, -sh, -ch, -x, -z*, and -o[†] by adding *-es:*

miss/misses	desperado/desperadoes
sex/sexes	or desperàdos
Jones/Joneses	church/churches
bush/bushes	echo/echoes
potato/potatoes	

NOTE: quiz/quizzes—The final *z* is doubled before the suffix *-es.*

2B. Form plurals of musical terms ending in -o[†] by adding *-s:*

banjo/banjos
solo/solos
soprano/sopranos

3A. Form plurals of nouns ending in *-y* preceded by a consonant by changing the *-y* to *-i* and adding *-es:*

family/families
factory/factories
baby/babies

3B. Form plurals of nouns ending in *-y* preceded by a vowel by adding *-s:*

key/keys
valley/valleys
monkey/monkeys

4. Form plurals of some nouns ending in an *-f* sound by adding *-s* and also making an internal spelling change as well:

wife/wives
thief/thieves
knife/knives

For others ending in an *-f* sound add only *-s:*

belief/beliefs
chief/chiefs
roof/roofs

Some have two forms:

elf/elves or elfs
scarf/scarves or scarfs

5. Notice that *-en* and *-ren* are added to form the plural form of these nouns:

ox/oxen   child/children

6. Form the plural of these by changing internal spelling:

man/men   foot/feet
goose/geese   mouse/mice
woman/women   tooth/teeth

7. Some nouns have the same form in both singular and plural: *sheep, deer, fowl, bear, swine, bass, pike, quail.*

8. Some nouns are used primarily in their singular forms: *arithmetic, happiness, chaos.*

9. The words *barracks, bellows, goods, pants, scissors, slacks, trousers, vespers, oats, tidings* are rarely used as singulars. The verb is plural.
   Other words of this type include words ending in *ics: acoustics, athletics, civics, politics.* However, the verb may be singular or plural.

10. Certain foreign plurals are continued in English usage:

datum/data   stratum/strata
stimulus/stimuli   focus/foci
larva/larvae   alumna/alumnae
crisis/crises   thesis/theses
alumnus/alumni   phenomenon/phenomena
analysis/analyses   criterion/criteria

Sometimes some of the singular forms may also be made plural by adding *-s.* Check dictionary for current usage.

datum/datums   criterion/criterions
focus/focuses   phenomenon/phenomenons

11. Compound nouns usually require plurals at the end of the group or unit: *schoolhouse/ schoolhouses, cupful/cupfuls.*
   However, in hyphenated words the main word in the unit shows the plural form:

mother-in-law/mothers-in-law
passer-by/passers-by
man-of-war/men-of-war
hanger-on/hangers-on
lady-in-waiting/ladies-in-waiting

12. Plurals of figures, words, and letters are usually formed by adding *-'s:*

He misdialed the *2's.*
She mispronounced her *r's.*
Tom uses too many *so's* in his talking.

13. Proper names make their plurals by adding *-s* or *-es*, as do most regular nouns:

Smith/Smiths
Church/Churches
Jones/Joneses

However, proper names ending in *-y* add only *-s:*

Murphy/Murphys
Kelley/Kelleys

Never form the plural of a proper name by adding *-'s.*

NOT Smith/Smith's   BUT Smith/Smiths
NOT Brown/Brown's   BUT Brown/Browns

†*Other words ending in -o vary in forming their plurals and have to be remembered or looked up in the dictionary.*

EXERCISE 4A

Underline the nouns in these sentences. Then write
the plural forms of the nouns in the first two
blanks at the right. In the third blank write the
numbers of the explanations in the lesson which
tell why the plural is the one you have chosen.

Example:

The *scientist* studied the *phenomenon*. _____scientists_____   _____phenomena_____   _1, 10_

1. A committee organized the curriculum.   _____   _____   _____

2. The waitress broke a dish.   _____   _____   _____

3. The goose hissed at the passer-by.   _____   _____   _____

4. He completed his quiz and thesis.   _____   _____   _____

5. The man seized the valley.   _____   _____   _____

6. The thief carried a knife.   _____   _____   _____

7. The child bought a toy.   _____   _____   _____

8. The woman mispronounced *r.*   _____   _____   _____

9. The class found a larva.   _____   _____   _____

10. The mother-in-law faced the crisis.   _____   _____   _____

COUNT NOUNS AND MASS NOUNS

COUNT NOUNS include everything that can be counted. They have both a singular and a plural form:

horse   horses   owl   owls   idea   ideas

In the singular they are always preceded by a DETERMINER, a word like *the, a, an* (See Lesson 13):

a cabin   the mountain   this stream

In the plural they may or may not be preceded by a determiner:

the gears   these pistons   those cylinders
   gears   pistons   cylinders

MASS NOUNS include everything that cannot be counted. They have no plural form:

relaxation   advice   knowledge   dirt   air

They may or may not be preceded by determiners like *the* or *some*, but they cannot be preceded by *a (an):*

With *the: The advice* is worthless.

Without *the: Advice* is cheap.

NOT: **An advice* is worthless.

Some words can be mass nouns or count nouns, depending on how they are used:

Mass: My mother bakes *bread.*

Count: My mother bakes various *breads.*

Mass: Joe drinks *beer.*

Count: Joe drank two *beers.*

Mass: *Truth* is a virtue.

Count: Remember these *truths.*

COLLECTIVE OR GROUP NOUNS

Collective (or group) nouns such as *class, team, jury, crew, band, audience,* and *congregation* designate a group that may act either as one unit or act separately as individuals.

NS Vt---------- Ndo
The senior class is having a party.   (*The senior class* is acting as a unit, and the verb is singular.)

NS   Vt----------------
The senior class have ordered their   (Members of *the senior class* are acting as
Ndo   individuals; therefore, the verb is plural.)
graduation photos.

EXERCISE 4B

Determine whether the following nouns are count nouns or mass nouns. Place the determiner *a* or *an* before each count noun. Write the plural form after it. Leave the spaces before and after mass nouns blank.

Example: ___a___ question _____questions_____

_____ assistance _____

1. _____ soap _____   4. _____ belief _____

2. _____ information _____   5. _____ position _____

3. _____ sincerity _____   6. _____ wheel _____

GENDER

Some nouns refer specifically to male or female:

Masculine Gender	**Feminine Gender**
man	woman
boy	girl
father	mother

Some nouns change their spelling and add a suffix to show gender, especially those that come into our language from foreign languages:

major	**majorette**
fiancé	**fiancée**
chanteur	**chanteuse**
actor	**actress**

EXERCISE 4C

Fill in the blanks with the masculine or feminine form of the following nouns.

Example: _____equestrian_____ equestrienne

1. _____ empress   3. _____ blonde

2. waiter _____   4. protégé _____

NOUN-FORMING SUFFIXES (ENDINGS)

In English we can form new nouns by adding certain suffixes, or endings, to verbs, adjectives, and other nouns. Listed in the first column is a partial list of noun-forming suffixes. In the second column are Source Words followed by labels (Vi, Ndo, NS, Vt) which indicate how they function in the sentences given in the third column. In the last column the Source Word with suffix added appears as a noun in the sentence given.

Suffix	**Source Word**		**Noun**
-ance	perform (Vi)	The musician *performs* capably.	His *performance* is competent.

-ence	prominent (Adj)	J. Bailey is a *prominent* reporter.	Bailey's *prominence* deprives him of solitude.
-ment	commit (Vt)	The judge *committed* him to prison.	His *commitment* destroyed him.
-al	arrive (Vi)	The dancers *will arrive* tomorrow.	We await their *arrival*.
-ant	pollute (Vt)	Wastes *pollute* water.	Wastes are *pollutants*.
-ent	repel (Vt)	The fabric *repels* water.	She applied a water *repellent*.
-age	rampant (Adj)	The *rampant* river flooded the land.	The river's *rampage* was uncontrollable.
-tion	cooperate (Vi)	The students *cooperate* with us.	We appreciate their *cooperation*.
-cian	music (Ndo)	The trumpeter plays delightful *music*.	The trumpeter is a *musician*.
-ity	real (Adj)	Joe dislikes the *real* world.	Joe tries to avoid *reality*.
-ee	employ (Vt)	Ted and Matt *employ* plumbers.	Ted and Matt have seven *employees*.
-er	teach (Vt)	The Smiths *teach* golf.	The Smiths are *teachers*.
-eer	chariot (Ndo)	Brutus drove a *chariot*.	Brutus was a *charioteer*.
-dom	king (NS)	The *king* ruled Camelot.	Camelot was his *kingdom*.

EXERCISE 4D

Change each of the following words to a noun form by using an appropriate suffix. Use the list given in the lesson, or find the noun forms in your dictionary. It is possible in some cases to add the noun-forming suffix to the word given, as in the first example with the word *involve*. In other cases, it is necessary to drop a suffix before adding the noun-forming suffix, as in the second example.

Example: involve (V)   _____ involvement (N) _____

convenient (Adj)   _____ convenience (N) _____

1. participate _____   6. wise _____

2. pure _____   7. reverse _____

3. write _____   8. profit _____

4. industrial _____   9. govern _____

5. defend _____   10. solve _____

lesson 5   Verbs, Verb Phrases, Auxiliary (Helping) Verbs

When we use the term VERB, we are usually speaking about a single word. A VERB PHRASE, on the other hand, consists of two or more words functioning as a unit.

VERB PHRASE

The LAST word in the verb phrase is the MAIN VERB.

The words preceding are AUXILIARY (HELPING) VERBS.

We will label the entire verb phrase with one of these symbols if it is written as a unit:

Vi—complete (intransitive) verb (See Lesson 2)

Vt—incomplete (transitive) verb (See Lesson 3)

LV—linking verb (See Lesson 23)

Here are examples of the verb and verb phrase within sentences:

Verb	**Verb Phrase**
NS Vi Adv.	NS Vi------------------------ Adv
They talked loudly.	They should have talked softly.
NS Vt Ndo	NS Vt------------------ Ndo
They considered his offer.	He is considering theirs.
NS LV Adj-C	NS LV-------- Adj-C
They were uncooperative.	He is being patient.

AUXILIARY VERBS

Auxiliaries, or auxiliary verbs, are sometimes referred to as HELPING VERBS because they are used along with the main verb, or notional verb, to show condition, possibility, and probability of action and also to show something about time and duration of action. In addition, certain auxiliaries—like *do*—are used to form questions or to insert the *not*-negative in a sentence.

For convenience, we can divide auxiliaries into three classes or categories.

MODAL AUXILIARIES

MODAL Auxiliaries—words like *may, shall, will, must,* and *should*—do not take the verbal endings *-s, -ing,* or *-ed.* They are always used with a main verb, either stated or understood:

Vt	NS	Vt	Ndo
Will	you	attend	the meeting?

NS	Vt	Vt	Ndo
Yes, I	will.	(attend	the meeting)

Modals and the verbs *have* and *be* appear in these positions before the main verb, a word like *give:*

	Modal	*have*	*be*	**Parts 4 or 5 of the verbs (Lesson 8)**
I	will	have	been	given (giving)
I	must		be	given (giving)
I	should	have		given
I	could		be	giving
I	may	have		given

Modals can also be used with Part 1 of the verb (Lesson 7)

I	can	give (Part 1)
I	shall	give (Part 1)

HAVE AND *BE*

HAVE and BE in their various forms may be used either as the main verb or as the auxiliary verb in a verb phrase:

1. Main verb: Bill *is* here.   Sheila *has* contact lenses.

2. Auxiliary verb (to indicate stages of action or progression of action):

   Dick *had been working* for two hours.   Sheila *has worn* contact lenses.

DO

DO may be used as the main verb or to emphasize statements, to ask questions, and to insert the negative word *not:*

1. Main verb: Sue *did* her work quickly.   Brian *does* nothing.

2. Emphasis: Margaret *did plan* to attend.   Matt *does deserve* praise.

3. Question (*DO* and its forms appear before the subject, and the main verb follows.):

   Does Tom *play* the guitar?

4. Not (negative) (*NOT*, or its contracted form *n't*, always appears immediately after or joined to the first word in a verb phrase):

The teacher *does* not *require* attendance.

FORMS OF THE AUXILIARIES *HAVE, BE,* AND *DO*

have	has	had	had	having[†]
am, are	is	was, were	been[†]	being[†]
do	does	did	done[‡]	doing[‡]

QUESTIONS

The auxiliary verbs are also used to write questions. The verb phrase is divided because the auxiliary verb comes before the subject, and the main verb follows it:

Vt   NS   Vt   Ndo
Does Sheila have contact lenses?

Vi   NS   Vi   Adv--------------
Have the twins returned from France?

Vt   NS   Vt   Ndo
Should Sheila wear contact lenses?

Vt   NS   Vt   Adj   Ndo
Are they planning another trip?

NEGATIVE PHRASES—THE WORD *NOT*

The negative in English, *not* or its contracted form *-n't*, always appears immediately after or joined to the first word in a verb phrase. It is *not* part of the verb phrase; label it Adv.

Vt Adv
Mary *hasn't* time to attend.

Vi   Adv Vi
Tom *will not go* on the trip.

Vt Adv Vt
The jury *didn't award* any damages.

We can also form negative statements by using negative pronouns like *no one* and *nothing*:

No one knew the verdict.

Nothing can be done yet.

EXERCISE 5

Underline the verb or verb phrase in the following sentences.

[†] These forms must be used with other auxiliaries.
[‡] These forms are not used as auxiliaries.

1. Was the snow falling?

2. The dancer had sprained her ankle.

3. Murray does not like cabbage and carrots.

4. The cupboards are being painted.

5. Had the horses been given food?

6. The truck stalled.

7. The children should not have taken the other road.

8. The tailor ripped the seam.

9. Flowers have been blooming everywhere.

10. He had gathered driftwood.

lesson 6   Verb Forms

Verbs can be recognized by their form and by their function in sentences. As the predicate, or part of it, they help tell what the sentence is about. They make a statement or ask a question about the subject. Verbs may have three, four, or five forms, which are shown in the chart below.

For convenience, we can also arrange these forms under five headings—Part 1, Part 2, Part 3, Part 4, and Part 5. In Lessons 7 and 8 we will examine the characteristics and functions of each of these parts in detail.

VERB FORMS AND PARTS

Except for the highly irregular verb *be*, which has eight forms, verbs may have three, four, or five different forms. Verb forms change either by the addition of suffixes (endings) or by spelling changes within the words. They are regular or irregular in the way their forms change in Parts 3 and 4. PARTS 4 AND 5 MUST BE USED WITH AUXILIARY VERBS WHEN THEY FUNCTION AS THE VERB IN A SENTENCE.

	Part 1	Part 2	Part 3	Part 4	Part 5
Three forms	*set*	*sets*	set	set	*setting*
Four forms	*help*	*helps*	*helped*	helped	*helping*
Five forms	*break*	*breaks*	*broke*	*broken*	*breaking*
Verb *be*†	*am, are, be*	*is*	*was, were*	*been*	*being*

REGULAR AND IRREGULAR VERBS

Regular	*Irregular*
Suffixes: -s (or -es), -ed, -ing added to Part 1.	Suffixes: -s (or -es), -ing, added to Part 1; spelling changes in Parts 3 and 4.
Verbs are REGULAR when Parts 3 and 4 take the suffix -ed (sometimes spelled with a -t as in *dealt*).	Verbs are IRREGULAR when Parts 3 and 4 undergo spelling changes.

	Regular	Irregular
Part 1	The travelers arrive.	The concerts begin.
Part 2	The traveler arrives.	The concert begins.
Part 3	The travelers arrive**d**.	The concert beg**a**n.
Part 4	The travelers have arrive**d**.	The concert has beg**u**n.
Part 5	The travelers are arriv**ing**.	The concert is beginn**ing**.

†The verb *be* is discussed separately in Lesson 23.

DICTIONARIES and books on language list the forms of irregular verbs. They give Parts 3, 4, and 5 after the base word. If these are not listed in your dictionary, the verb is regular and Parts 3 and 4 end in *-ed.*

FORMS AND USES OF SOME VERBS

Drag, meaning *to pull,* is regular. Part 3 and Part 4 are *dragged,* not *drug,* which has the meaning *to administer medication.*

NOT: *He drug the huge log to the sawmill.

BUT: He dragged the huge log to the sawmill.

Hang is a regular verb when it means *to execute.* Part 3 and Part 4 are *hanged.* It is irregular when it means *to suspend* or *attach.* Part 3 and Part 4 are *hung.*

To execute: The executioner hanged the murderer.

To suspend: The artist hung his painting on the wall.

INFINITIVE—THE UNINFLECTED FORM

The uninflected, or unchanged, form of the verb is called the INFINITIVE, which means *unlimited.* It represents all the forms of a verb. The infinitive appears either with its "sign"—*to*—as in "She began *to work.*" or without it after certain verbs and auxiliaries: "You can *see* the harbor." or "I helped him *complete* his assignment."

to happen   *to want*   *to take*

The boys want *to ride* the horses.

Or it may be used with *to* and auxiliaries and Part 5 of the verb:

to be hoping   *to be thinking*

Nancy happens *to be thinking* about her final exam.

It may also appear as *to* plus auxiliaries and Part 4 of the verb:

to have chosen   *to have been chosen*

Harvey was *to have chosen* a partner.

Philip wished *to have been chosen* as Harvey's teammate.

Details about the infinitive as a VERBAL are given in Unit Seven.

EXERCISE 6A

Fill in the blanks by recalling what you learned

about regular and irregular verbs in this lesson.
Refer to the lesson if you need help.

1. List the parts of the verb that use the same inflections, or method of forming those parts, in both regular and irregular verbs.   _____

2. What parts of the verb can end in -ed?   _____

3. List the parts of the verb that have different spellings in the irregular and regular verbs.   _____

4. What part of the verb ends in -s or -es?   _____

5. What part of the verb ends in -ing?   _____

6. What books list parts of irregular verbs?   _____

SOME DIFFICULT VERBS

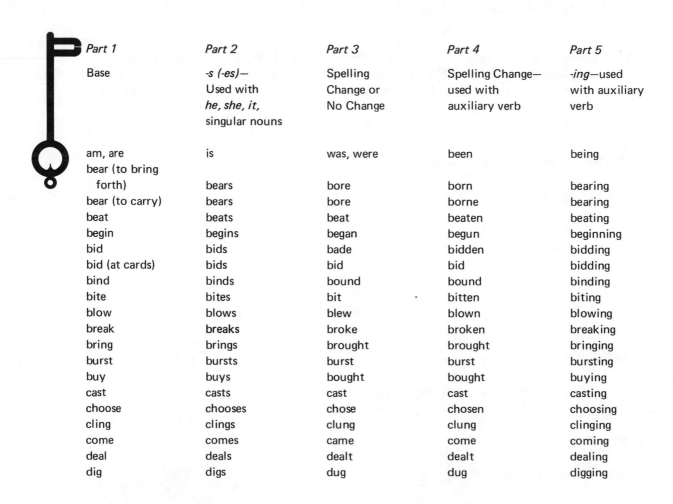

Part 1	Part 2	Part 3	Part 4	Part 5
Base	-s (-es)—Used with he, she, it, singular nouns	Spelling Change or No Change	Spelling Change—used with auxiliary verb	-ing—used with auxiliary verb
am, are	is	was, were	been	being
bear (to bring forth)	bears	bore	born	bearing
bear (to carry)	bears	bore	borne	bearing
beat	beats	beat	beaten	beating
begin	begins	began	begun	beginning
bid	bids	bade	bidden	bidding
bid (at cards)	bids	bid	bid	bidding
bind	binds	bound	bound	binding
bite	bites	bit	bitten	biting
blow	blows	blew	blown	blowing
break	breaks	broke	broken	breaking
bring	brings	brought	brought	bringing
burst	bursts	burst	burst	bursting
buy	buys	bought	bought	buying
cast	casts	cast	cast	casting
choose	chooses	chose	chosen	choosing
cling	clings	clung	clung	clinging
come	comes	came	come	coming
deal	deals	dealt	dealt	dealing
dig	digs	dug	dug	digging

do	does	did	done	doing
draw	draws	drew	drawn	drawing
drink	drinks	drank	drunk	drinking
drive	drives	drove	driven	driving
eat	eats	ate	eaten	eating
fall	falls	fell	fallen	falling
fight	fights	fought	fought	fighting
find	finds	found	found	finding
fly	flies	flew	flown	flying
forbid	forbids	forbade (forbad)	forbidden	forbidding
forsake	forsakes	forsook	forsaken	forsaking
forget	forgets	forgot	forgotten	forgetting
freeze	freezes	froze	frozen	freezing
give	gives	gave	given	giving
go	goes	went†	gone	going
grow	grows	grew	grown	growing
hang (suspend)	hangs	hung	hung	hanging
hang (execute) (regular)	hangs	hanged	hanged	hanging
have	has	had	had	having
hide	hides	hid	hidden (hid)	hiding
hold	holds	held	held	holding
know	knows	knew	known	knowing
lay (Vt)	lays	laid	laid	laying
lie (Vi)	lies	lay	lain	lying
lose	loses	lost	lost	losing
ride	rides	rode	ridden	riding
ring	rings	rang	rung	ringing
rise (Vi)	rises	rose	risen	rising
run	runs	ran	run	running
see	sees	saw	seen	seeing
shake	shakes	shook	shaken	shaking
shine	shines	shone (shined)	shone (shined)	shining
shoe	shoes	shod	shod	shoeing
shrink	shrinks	shrank (shrunk)	shrunk	shrinking
sing	sings	sang (sung)	sung	singing
sink	sinks	sank	sunk	sinking
sit (Vi)	sits	sat	sat	sitting
set (Vt)	sets	set	set	setting
slay	slays	slew	slain	slaying
slide	slides	slid	slid	sliding
sling	slings	slung	slung	slinging
slink	slinks	slunk	slunk	slinking
speak	speaks	spoke	spoken	speaking
spin	spins	spun	spun	spinning
spring	springs	sprang (sprung)	sprung	springing
stand	stands	stood	stood	standing
steal	steals	stole	stolen	stealing
stick	sticks	stuck	stuck	sticking

†Word change because of historical falling together of two verbs.

sting	stings	stung	stung	stinging
stride	strides	strode	stridden	striding
strike	strikes	struck	struck	striking
strive	strives	strove	striven	striving
swear	swears	swore	sworn	swearing
swim	swims	swam	swum	swimming
swing	swings	swung	swung	swinging
take	takes	took	taken	taking
teach	teaches	taught	taught	teaching
tear	tears	tore	torn	tearing
throw	throws	threw	thrown	throwing
wake	wakes	waked (woke)	waked	waking
waken (regular)	wakens	wakened	wakened	wakening
wear	wears	wore	worn	wearing
weave	weaves	wove	woven	weaving
win	wins	won	won	winning
wring	wrings	wrung	wrung	wringing
write	writes	wrote	written	writing

EXERCISE 6B

Determine whether each of these verbs is regular
or irregular. Write R for regular and I for irregular
in the blanks. Use the list of irregular verbs in this
lesson or your dictionary if you need help. Or try
adding -ed to each verb given. If the verb is regular,
-ed can be added; if the verb is irregular, -ed cannot
be added.

Example: *Regular*   *Irregular*

occupy   occupied   NOT: sing *singed   NOT: win *winned
stop   stopped   BUT: sing sang   BUT: win   won

1. drag   _____   4. sink   _____   7. shake   _____

2. reward _____   5. forget _____   8. swim   _____

3. accept _____   6. return _____   9. drink   _____

EXERCISE 6C

One part of a verb is given. Fill the blanks with the
other four principal parts. Examine the examples.
Notice the subject used with each part. Notice
whether the verb part is used with an auxiliary
verb. If you need help with irregular verbs, use the
chart in this lesson or your dictionary.

Example:

	Part 1	Part 2	Part 3	Part 4	Part 5
Regular:	I walk.	She walks.	He walked.	We have walked.	He is walking.
Irregular:	We drink.	He drinks.	They drank.	He has drunk.	She is drinking.

1. open
2. _____ takes
3. buy
4. _____ _____ _____ washed
5. _____ _____ saw
6. _____ _____ _____ _____ swimming
7. teach
8. _____ drives
9. _____ _____ _____ _____ coming
10. drag

IF YOU MISSED TWO OR MORE in the first part,
review regular and irregular verbs and complete the
second part.

11. hop
12. _____ _____ _____ _____ throwing
13. _____ _____ wrote
14. _____ _____ _____ given
15. qualify
16. _____ _____ _____ ordered
17. run
18. _____ _____ _____ _____ blowing

19. go   _____ _____ _____ _____

20. _____ freezes   _____ _____ _____

VERB-FORMING SUFFIXES (ENDINGS)

Another clue to identifying verbs is found in verb suffixes. If these endings are added to words which usually function as nouns or adjectives, a new form results which may then function as a verb.

bath	The warm *bath* (NS) relaxed the child.
bathe	Parents *bathe* (Vt) their children carefully.

Sometimes these suffixes are added to the bases of Latin and Greek words, and the form may function as a verb.

rotate—rot (Latin for *wheel*) + -ate

The huge globes *rotate* (Vi) slowly.

Here are verb-forming suffixes, source words, and verb forms:

Suffix	Source Word		Verb Form
-e	breath (NS)	Her *breath* smelled fresh.	*Breathe* deeply.
-ate	nomination (Ndo)	Jack received the *nomination.*	The voters *nominated* Jack.
-ify	liquid (NS)	Water is a *liquid.*	Blenders *liquify* vegetables.
-ize	harmony (NS)	The *harmony* of colors is pleasing.	The colors *harmonize* well.
-en	strength (NS)	His *strength* lies in his hands.	He *strengthens* his hands by exercising.

EXERCISE 6D

Change the following words to a verb form by adding an appropriate suffix. Use the list given in the lesson, or find words in your dictionary. For example, find the word *beauty*. Examine related words, and find the form labeled *V*.

Example: beauty (N)   beautify (V)

1. length   _____

2. operation   _____

3. sign   _____

4. motor   _____

5. sick   _____

6. generator   _____

7. simple   _____

8. solid   _____

9. colony   _____

10. population _____

lesson 7   Verb Parts 1, 2, and 3

The following verb parts can be used as single words. We use these parts to talk about the past, present, and future. As a result, they each have particular functions. Some, like Part 3, are used with either singular or plural nouns (Lesson 4) and pronouns (Lessons 4 and 29). Others, like Part 2, function only with singular nouns and pronouns, or, like Part 1, with plural nouns and pronouns.

As you will see, Part 2 is used only with singular nouns and singular third-person pronouns like *he, she,* and *it* (or *mine, each, everyone, this*) which represent the person or thing spoken about (Lessons 4 and 29). The verb endings *-s* and *-es* make the verb SINGULAR. Only nouns can be made plural by adding *-s* or *-es.*

	NS Vt Ndo		NS Vt Ndo
Singular	The dog wags his tail.	**Plural**	The dogs wag their tails.

Learn how to use each of the five parts by learning their function and by studying the examples in this lesson and in Lesson 8.

PART 1

Time	Function	Example
Present	Used with plural nouns (Lesson 4) plus *they, we, you, all, some, these.*	The *writers support* Hunter's platform. *They like* his views.
Present	Used with *to* to form the infinitive.	*to assist to anticipate to come*
Present or *Future*	Used after modals like *can, do, might, should* (Lesson 5).	He *can succeed.*
Future	Used after *will* and *shall.*	Don *will try.*
Present	Part 1 of *be*[†] is *am* and *are.*	I *am* confident. They *are* capable.

PART 2 (Part 1 + -s or -es)

Time	Function	Example
Present	Used after singular nouns.	Martin *does* (NOT *do*) his work every day.
Present	Used after *he, she,* and *it,* third person singular pronouns, and pronouns like *each, everyone, this,* or *mine.*	He *likes* (NOT *like*) his job. He *doesn't* (NOT *don't*) complain.
Present	Part 2 of *be*† is *is.*	He *is* reliable.

PART 3 (Part 1 + -ed or spelling change)

Time	Function	Example
Past	Used with singular and plural nouns and pronouns.	Gabriel *selected* a bright tie. He also *bought* a new shirt.
Past	Part 3 forms of *be*† are *was,* used with *he, she, it,* and singular nouns and *were,* used with *they* and plural nouns.	They *were* (NOT *was*) college freshmen.

†The verb *be* is discussed separately in Lesson 23.

EXERCISE 7A

Write answers for the following questions in the blanks. If you do not know an answer, reread Lesson 7.

1. What parts of the verb are used with singular nouns and third person singular pronouns? _____

2. What parts of the verb are used to write about the present—today? _____

3. What parts of the verb can be used with plural nouns and pronouns? _____

4. What is the ending of the verbs used with third person singular pronouns? _____

5. What is the ending of regular verbs used to write about the past? _____

EXERCISE 7B

Underline the verb in each sentence. Determine
whether its form is acceptable. If it is not, write
an acceptable form in the blank at the right. Use
only the forms of verb Parts 1, 2, or 3. If the verb
form is acceptable, write *A* in the blank.

1. Ted go to college.   _____

2. Mike don't want advice.   _____

3. The car struck the small child.   _____

4. Bob come here every day.   _____

5. Betty finish her new dress this morning.   _____

6. John call his brother last week.   _____

7. Tom and Lee knowed the owner.   _____

8. Yesterday Margaret painted the apartment.   _____

9. The storm begun early in the evening.   _____

10. The small child don't like bananas.   _____

EXERCISE 7C

Before each sentence there is a verb, or a verb and
auxiliary, in parentheses. Write the appropriate
form of this verb in the blank.

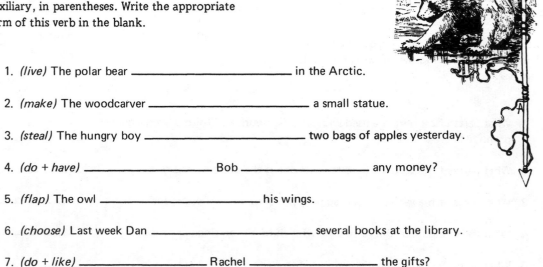

1. *(live)* The polar bear _____ in the Arctic.

2. *(make)* The woodcarver _____ a small statue.

3. *(steal)* The hungry boy _____ two bags of apples yesterday.

4. *(do + have)* _____ Bob _____ any money?

5. *(flap)* The owl _____ his wings.

6. *(choose)* Last week Dan _____ several books at the library.

7. *(do + like)* _____ Rachel _____ the gifts?

8. *(have)* Harold and Tom _____ the camera.

9. *(buy)* Alfred _____ a new coat last year.

10. *(do)* Becky _____ nothing all week.

lesson 8   Verb Parts 4 and 5

Verb parts 4 and 5 must be used with auxiliary (helping) verbs. These auxiliaries help form a verb phrase. IN A VERB PHRASE THE AUXILIARIES APPEAR FIRST; THE MAIN VERB ENDS THE PHRASE. The use of Parts 4 and 5 as nouns or adjectives is discussed in Lesson 43, Verbals.

PART 4 (Part 1 + -ed or spelling change)

Time	Function	Example
	Used with these auxiliaries (Lesson 5):	
Present	am, is, are	I *am comforted.* He *is troubled.* They *are influenced.*
Past	has (with singular nouns)	Bob *has arrived.*
	have (with plural nouns, compound subject) also with modals like *may, could, been*	The others *have left.* Bob *may have arrived.*
	had	They *had traveled* far. The winner *had been selected.*
	was (with singular nouns)	Roberts *was nominated.*
	were (with plural nouns, compound subject)	Bond and Davis *were elected.*
Future	will (shall) have	Hughes *will have chosen* a successor before tomorrow.
	will (shall) have been	The trees *will have been transplanted* by next week.
	Used alone, it may function as a noun. (See Lesson 43)	The *wounded* lay helpless.
	Used alone, it may function as an adjective. (See Lesson 43)	The *forgotten* man had his memories.

PART 5 (Part 1 + -*ing*)

Time	Function	Example
	Used with these auxiliaries (Lesson 5):	
Present	am, is, are	I *am listening.* Burt *is speaking.* They *are calling.*
Past	was, were	Dan *was trying.* Mary and Jane *were succeeding.*
Future	will (shall) be	They *will be waiting.*
	will (shall) have been	They *will have been waiting.*
	Used alone, it may function as a noun. (See Lesson 43)	*Fishing* is relaxing.
	Used alone, it may function as an adjective. (See Lesson 43)	*Boring* books make Joyce tired.

EXERCISE 8A

Underline the verb or verb phrase. If the form is not acceptable, write the form you think is preferable in the blank at the right. If the sentence is acceptable, write A in the blank.

1. The cowboys hung the cattle rustler at dawn. _____

2. Mark had drove all night. _____

3. Bob had drank the hot tea and burned his lips. _____

4. Ted seen his girlfriend yesterday. _____

5. Nan done nothing for a week. _____

6. The retired plumber has not boughten a new suit for two years. _____

7. Are I going with you to New York? _____

8. Will you choose cereal for breakfast? _____

9. Ted had wrote the contract. _____

10. We was invited to the party. _____

11. The Notre Dame Choir has sang in seven states.   _____

12. Mr. and Mrs. Holt was awarded first prize.   _____

13. She been here one hour.   _____

14. The landlord has spoke to the tenant five times about overdue rent.   _____

15. Elephants was captured for the circus.   _____

16. They gone to town.   _____

17. The general writ his message hurriedly.   _____

18. His parents teached reading and spelling.   _____

19. Bob teared his shirt accidentally.   _____

20. They was offered several choices.   _____

EXERCISE 8B

Before each sentence there is a verb, or a verb and
auxiliary, in parentheses. Write the appropriate
form of this verb in the blank.

1. *(have + weave)* The Indians _____ for tourists.

2. *(will + wash)* I _____ my hair tomorrow.

3. *(have + ride)* The conqueror _____ in triumph on his men's shoulders.

4. *(blow)* The musician _____ the trumpet.

5. *(had + give)* Ben _____ a tie to Jack.

6. *(ring)* The fire bell _____ three times.

7. *(burst)* The water pipe _____ , and the main floor was flooded.

8. *(have + hide)* The dog _____ the bone in the closet.

9. *(have + lose)* Cheryl _____ the key for the trunk.

10. *(bring)* The plumber _____ his own tools.

11. *(cast)* The frightened boy _____ his lot with the pirates.

12. *(have + blow)* _____ the wind _____ the television antenna down?

13. *(do + avoid)* _____ you _____ your responsibilities?

14. *(have + fall)* The tree _____ in the driveway.

15. *(had + mention)* _____ Dave _____ his accident?

16. *(come)* The kidnaper _____ for the ransom last night.

17. *(know)* Martha _____ Dale's family.

18. *(have + freeze)* The water _____ in the drinking fountain.

19. *(drink)* The hobo _____ the soup and made a peculiar noise.

20. *(wake)* Willis _____ before dawn.

lesson 9   **Verb Tense (Time)**

To decide what form of the verb to use in a sentence to tell time, watch for adverbs or adverbial phrases that indicate time:

last year   by this time

next week   for the past year

soon   yesterday

before   tomorrow.

The chart below shows the verb forms used to tell time in English; however, it is not necessary to learn all the names of the tenses. It is necessary only to know what forms of verbs and what auxiliaries are needed to indicate when an event took place. The forms given with the pronoun *I* may also be used with *you, he, she, it, we,* and *they* unless a definite form or an auxiliary are shown with one of these pronouns.

The past tenses indicate what happened yesterday or any other time in the past, and the future tenses indicate what will happen tomorrow or any time in the future. Although present tenses may indicate today's happenings, they may also indicate habitual action, future action, or timeless facts, such as an assumption or belief: *The world is round.*

YESTERDAY

Past perfect (past action or time before another past action or time)

Active   Passive (See Unit Seven)

I *had given* a lecture.   I *had been given* a topic.
They *had listened* attentively.   They *had been asked* to attend.

Past (definite time in past not extending to present)

Active   Passive

He *asked* a question.   He *was given* an answer.
                                              They *were told* the truth.

Present perfect (indefinite time in past, possibly extending to present)

Active   Passive

You *have opened* the window.   The papers *have been scattered.*
He *has closed* it.   The window *has been closed.*

Past progressive (definite action in past, not necessarily completed)

Active

I *was helping* my friend.
We *were signing* his cast.

Passive

He *was being carried* to his room.
Doctors *were being asked* about his condition.

TODAY

Present (moment of happening)

Active

I *dance;* I *sing.*

She *dislikes* me.

Passive

He *is intrigued.*
I *am pleased.*
They *are amused.*

Present progressive (action in progress at time of happening)

Active

I *am writing* a letter.
You *are helping* me.
He *is feeling* pleased.

Passive

He *is being sent* a request.
They *are being convinced.*

Present (timeless facts)

All men *are* mortal.
Rain *falls* on the land.

Present (habitual action)

She *meets* Mike every day.

Present (historical present)

Napoleon *meets* Wellington.
He *is* defeated.

Present (future action)

They *leave* for Europe next week.

TOMORROW

Future (future extending from present)

Active   Passive

You *will call* our friends.   They *will be pleased* with the invitation.

Future progressive (action in future with emphasis on continuing action)

Active   Passive

I *shall be leaving* town.   By this time tomorrow he *will have been traveling* six months.

Future perfect (future action completed before another future action)

Active   Passive

I *will have completed* the project.   We *will have been praised.*

EXERCISE 9

Fill in the blanks in the following sentences by writing in the appropriate form of the verb given in parentheses. Watch for adverbs indicating time.

Example: *(receive)* Margaret *will receive* her degree in June.

OR

Margaret *receives* her degree in June.

1. *(prefer)* Mabel _____ to do her laundry every day.

2. *(make)* Scott _____ his decision next week.

3. *(leave)* Last week Dale _____ for a trip to Europe.

4. *(complete)* By this time tomorrow I _____ seven exercises.

5. *(open)* For the past week Bartlett _____ the store in the morning.

6. *(arrive)* Martha _____ an hour ago.

7. *(try)* Meyer _____ the new printing press for several weeks.

8. *(prepare)* Jonathan _____ the food several hours before the party.

9. *(buy)* Silas _____ a new coat next fall.

10. *(join)* John _____ us at the convention.

IF YOU MISSED MORE THAN TWO sentences in
the first part, review verb tenses and complete the
second part.

11. *(run)* The frightened animals _____ through the forest.

12. *(swim)* The boy _____ in the river every day.

13. *(participate)* Morris _____ in the debate next week.

14. *(argue)* Mary _____ with Michael since her arrival.

15. *(travel)* Stewart _____ around the world before retiring.

16. *(return)* Sharon _____ the book before Rita needs it.

17. *(meet)* The officers gather in the conference room, and the delegates _____
In the auditorium.

18. *(creep)* Cars _____ slowly on the freeway during the rush hour.

19. *(plunge)* The airplane _____ to the earth.

20. *(move)* Ivan _____ out of town a year ago.

lesson 10   Troublesome Verbs

Although differentiating between *sit* and *set*, *rise* and *raise*, and *lie* and *lay* causes writers enormous confusion, the usage of these verbs is not difficult if we place them into two groups. Remember that transitive (Vt), or incomplete, verbs must be followed by a direct object (Ndo).

COMPLETE VERBS					INCOMPLETE VERBS				
Pattern 1: NS Vi Adv					*Pattern 2: NS Vt Ndo*				
1	2	3	4	5	1	2	3	4	5
sit	sits	sat	sat	sitting	set	sets	set	set	setting
lie†	lies	lay‡	lain	lying	lay‡	lays	laid	laid	laying
rise	rises	rose	risen	rising	raise	raises	raised	raised	raising

All of these examples follow the same sentence patterns:

NS	Vt	Ndo	Adv----------		NS	Vi	Adv-----------
He	*set*	the glass	on the table	while	he	*sat*	on the porch.
He	*raised*	the window	easily	after	he	*rose*	from his chair.
He	*lays*‡	the book	down	before	he	*lies*	on the couch.
He	*laid*	the book	down	before	he	*lay*‡	on the couch.

Set, *lay*, and *raise* usually need a noun to complete them: *He set* what? *the glass* where? *on the table*. However, there are a few exceptions: *The sun set. The pheasant hen wants to set. Sit, lie,* and *rise* are complete. They do NOT need a noun to complete them. They may be modified by an adverb: *he sat* where? *down.*

---

†The principal parts of the verb *to lie,* meaning to tell an untruth, are *lie, lied, lied.* The word *lye* names an alkaline solution made from wood ashes.

‡Notice that *lay* is a form for both the complete and the incomplete verb, but one form is used to talk about the present as in the third example, and the other is used to talk about the past as in the fourth example. We may confuse these because we have difficulty hearing whether the speaker is saying *lay* or *laid.* They sound similar.

EXERCISE 10A

Label the sentence parts. Then fill in the blanks
with one of the two verbs given. Begin by determining whether the verb should be complete (Vi)
or incomplete (Vt) by using Sentence Keys.

Example:

Vi	Vt	NS	Vi	Adv Adv-----------
rose	*raised*	The sun ____ rose (complete) ____		late that morning.

	Vi	Vt	
	Vi	Vt	
1.	*sat*	*set*	The hen _____ on her eggs for three weeks.
2.	*rose*	*raised*	The farmer _____ corn in his fields.
3.	*rises*	*raises*	The farmer's wife _____ early every morning.
4.	*lie*	*lay*	She cannot _____ in bed until noon.
5.	*sits*	*sets*	The farmer _____ in his favorite chair in the evening.
6.	*sat*	*set*	The farmer's wife _____ the table for dinner.
7.	*sat*	*set*	She _____ her hair at night.

EXERCISE 10B

In the following sentences, find the verb and label
it V. Then find the subject and label it NS. Read
NS + V and ask what or whom. If there is no
answer, label the verb Vi. If a noun answers the
question, label it Ndo, and label the verb Vt.
Check the form given with the one needed by
looking at the verb chart in this lesson. If the form
given in the sentence should be changed, write the
appropriate form in the blank at the right and
label it Vi or Vt. If the form is acceptable, write A
in the blank.

Example:
          NS   Vt   Ndo Adv--------------
The plumber *sat* the pipe on the ground.   set (Vt) _____

          NS Vi Adv---------------
The dog *laid* on the sidewalk.   lay (Vi) _____

1. The seasick sailor laid in his bunk all day.   _____

2. The sun had rose at six o'clock.   _____

3. Squashes and pumpkins lay in the field.   _____

4. Set the suitcase on the rack.   _____

5. The exhausted man had laid there for two hours.   _____

6. Bob had set down in the broken rocker.   _____

7. Lie the baby in her crib.   _____

8. Divers raised the sunken treasure.   _____

9. The fishing net had risen to the surface.   _____

10. The cat lay on the soft pillow in the sun.   _____

lesson 11   **Contractions**

Contractions of pronouns with verbs or of verbs with *not* are usually written as one word, and the apostrophe indicates the omitted letter or letters.

I'm/I am

he can't/he cannot

they won't/they will not

he's/he is

it's/it is

they're/they are

you shouldn't/you should not

we'd/we would

> Although contractions appear in all kinds of prose, they are found most often in informal writing. Many college instructors, therefore, prefer that their students avoid using contractions in college compositions unless the composition is informal.

The contraction *it's* always means *it is*. The word *its* (without the apostrophe) can be used before a noun as a modifier (See Lesson 13, DETERMINERS).

Contraction: *It's* (it is) an enormous bird.

Modifier: The eagle flapped *its* wings.

The contraction *they're* is sometimes confused with two other words—*their* and *there*.

Contraction: They're *(they are)* friends.

Modifier: They offered *their* help.

Adverb: They were needed *there*.

EXERCISE 11

Write the full form of the following contractions:

Example: They're   they are _____

1. They shouldn't _____

2. I can't _____

3. He won't _____

4. He's _____

5. I'll _____

6. They'd _____

Now that you have completed the last exercise in this unit, YOU ARE READY FOR THE UNIT ONE REVIEW. If you need additional practice, complete the X-TRAS which follow.

UNIT ONE

UNIT ONE REVIEW will consist of exercises like the ones in Lessons 1 through 11. To prepare for the REVIEW, read the lessons and go back over the exercises. Note any corrections you have made. Be especially familiar with Exercises 2C, 3A, 3B, 3C, 4A, 5, 6A, 6B, 6C, 7A, 7B, 7C, 8A, 8B, 9, 10A, 10B, 11. If you do not thoroughly understand any part of the exercises, ask your instructor for help. Make sure that you understand the directions for each exercise because those on the REVIEW will be very similar.

Complete these exercises only if you want additional practice before you attempt the UNIT ONE REVIEW, Form A or Form B. Answers for these are in Answer Key.

I.   Write in the blanks the symbol that completes
     each sentence pattern. Use these symbols: NS,
     Ndo, Vi, Vt, Adv

1. NS _____   3. NS _____ Ndo   5. _____ Vi Adv

2. NS Vt _____   4. NS _____ Adv   6. NS _____ Ndo Adv

II. Write sentences to match these patterns.
     Label parts.

1. NS Compound Vi

2. NS Vt Compound Ndo

3. NS Vi Adv

4. NS Vt Ndo

5. Compound NS Vt Ndo

III. Label the words in these sentences by writing
     NS, Ndo, C, Vi, Vt, or Adv above each word
     to indicate its function.

1. Marie is not being help with homework.

2. The car stalled.

3. The cowboy wore a gun and spurs.

4. The cat licked its paws.

5. Coins and jewels filled the chest.

6. The fire burned brightly.

7. Children sang and hummed.

8. Carl ordered shoes yesterday.

9. Bob and Jane visited Hawaii last year.

10. The mule sat down.

IV. Write the plural form of each of these words. Review Lesson 4, NOUNS, and use your dictionary. If more than one form is given, list both.

1. waltz _____

2. medium _____

3. mouse _____

4. mouthful _____

5. party _____

6. datum _____

7. desperado _____

8. paper _____

9. gulf _____

10. alumnus _____

11. theory _____

12. kiss _____

13. wreath _____

14. wolf _____

15. foot _____

16. leaf _____

17. appendix _____

18. formula _____

19. nucleus _____

20. key _____

21. memorandum _____

22. piano _____

23. potato _____

24. cafeteria _____

V. Underline the verb or verb phrase. If the form is not acceptable, write the form you think is preferable in the blank at the right. If the sentence is acceptable, write A in the blank. Use your dictionary or Lesson 6 if you do not know the principal parts of the verb.

1. Marie not being help with homework. _____

2. Bill has take the test today. _____

3. Bob make a model airplane. _____

4. The medicine has stop the infection. _____

5. He require a car for the job. _____

6. What the man say to John? _____

7. Bert need that letter tomorrow. _____

8. The house was being clean carefully. _____

9. Nancy has obtain a new driver's license. _____

10. Joe and Jim has deposit money in the bank. _____

11. Margaret want new shoes. _____

12. The tractor has drag the log away. _____

13. Russell have little hope of winning the race. _____

14. Ben had purchase a new suit. _____

15. The newspaper carry the story about the accident. _____

16. Joe have memorize the long poem. _____

17. The dentist has extract two of Sally's teeth. _____

18. Gale like oranges and pears for lunch. _____

19. Has Ruth mention her concern for Jody's safety? _____

20. Have Ted call Mary recently? _____

VI. Before each sentence there is a verb, or an
auxiliary and verb, in parentheses. Write the
appropriate form of this verb in the blank.

1. *(begin)* The Johnson family _____ moving into the house today.

2. *(will + become)* Eventually Ted _____ accustomed to his new job.

3. *(could have been + tear)* The wall _____ out long ago.

4. *(had + know)* Jeff _____ Tina for years.

5. *(have + ring)* The chimes _____ not _____ all day.

6. *(should be + throw)* Some of those papers _____ away.

7. *(have + choose)* The supervisor _____ not _____ a partner for Bob.

8. *(had + break)* Sue _____ a long fingernail.

9. *(dig)* The workmen _____ a trench yesterday.

10. *(blow)* The wind _____ the door shut.

11. *(had + drag)* The boys _____ the sacks of potatoes inside.

12. *(had + ride)* Don _____ horses for several years.

13. *(must have + sink)* The leaky boat _____ in the lake.

14. *(see)* No one _____ the jockey fall off the horse.

15. *(do)* Dick _____ the same thing over and over.

16. *(drag)* The two boys _____ the empty barrel down the road an hour ago.

17. *(had + eat)* He _____ all the ice cream.

18. *(draw)* The artist _____ an excellent sketch of the house.

19. *(had + rise)* The water _____ ten feet.

20. *(have + take)* Dan _____ Dale's hat.

unit TWO

Modifiers—Adjectives, Adverbs, Prepositional Phrases

lesson 12   Modifiers— Adjective Forms

MODIFIERS are ADDITIONS to basic sentence patterns, which consist of NOUNS and VERBS. Modifiers give the reader additional information by further describing both nouns and verbs.

These modifiers—ADJECTIVES (Adj) and ADVERBS (Adv)—can be single words or word groups. They can be identified by their form, their position, and their function in sentences.

ADJECTIVE FORM

Words that can take the suffixes *-er* and *-est* usually function as adjectives. Often these same words can function as adverbs by adding the suffix *-ly*, or they can function as nouns by adding the suffix *-ness*:

Adj	Adj	Adj	Adv	Noun
	-er	*-est*	*-ly*	*-ness*
sweet	sweeter	sweetest	sweetly	sweetness

close	closer	closest	closely	closeness
high	higher	highest	highly	highness

Some of the most common adjective-forming suffixes are listed below. The symbol following each source word indicates its functions in the sentence following:

Suffix	Source Word		Adjective
-ed	carve (Vt)	Eskimos *carve* animals.	They sell *carved*[†] animals.
-ic	artist (NS)	The *artist* painted a mural.	His *artistic* talent is obvious.
-ish	child (Ndo)	Boyd watched the *child.*	He enjoyed his *childish* pranks.
-y	stick (Vt)	Stamps *stick* on the envelope.	The glue is *sticky.*
-ar	pole (Ndo)	Ice covers the North *Pole.*	The *polar* bear has white fur.
-ary	imagine (Vt)	He *imagines* he sees elves.	*Imaginary* ghosts trouble him
-ory	compensate (Vt)	He *compensates* his workers.	*Compensatory* education aids the deprived.
-less	hope (Ndo)	She always has *hope.*	No situation is *hopeless.*
-esque	picture (NS)	The *picture* attracts attention.	The *picturesque* scenery is relaxing.
-ous	humor (Nop)	He has a good sense of *humor.*	The *humorous* incident made everyone laugh.
-ful	power (Ndo)	The turbine generated electric *power.*	The *powerful* bulldozer leveled the hill.
-ive	create (Vt)	Soft colors *create* a peaceful atmosphere.	The *creative* artist uses colors effectively.
-ent	depend (Vi)	He can *depend* on his father.	He has one *dependent* child.
-able	respect (Vt)	They *respect* the law.	He is a *respectable* citizen.
-ible	force (NS)	The *force* pushed the rocket upward.	*Forcible* ejection sent the pilot into space.
-al	exception (NS)	There is no *exception* to the rule.	His *exceptional* talent was recognized.
-ant	repent (Vt)	They *repent* their wrong-doing.	The *repentant* man was forgiven.

[†]See Lesson 43 on VERBALS.

EXERCISE 12

Change the following words to an adjective form
by adding an appropriate suffix. Use the list given
in the lesson or find words in your dictionary.

		N	**Adj**
Example:		truth	*truthful*

1. read _____

2. please _____

3. peace _____

4. act _____

5. region _____

6. fragment _____

7. love _____

8. fool _____

9. rhythm _____

10. prohibit _____

lesson 13 **Determiners (Adj)**

A DETERMINER is a word that precedes a noun and functions as a pointer by further identifying the noun. Determiners indicate that a noun is to follow just as auxiliary verbs indicate that a verb is to follow. Notice that many determiners serve as other parts of speech, like the pronouns *her*, *their*, *all*, and *every*. Here are some determiners. In this text we will label them *Adj*.

SOME DETERMINERS

the	my	our	all	many	two	Tom's[†]
			any	much	four	youth's[†]
a	your		both	more	several	*Any possessive*
			each	most	thirty-one	*form of a noun*
an	her	their	every	no	a hundred	
	his		few	other		
	its		either	some		
			neither			
	this	these				
	that	those				

Adj N
his proposal

Adj Adj   N
his straightforward proposal

Adj   N
today's[†] news

Adj   Adj   N
today's shocking news

The determiner individualizes general terms like *truth* and *beauty* to a particular person or situation:

N   Adj N
Truth is a virtue.   The truth he speaks . . . .

NS   **Adj NS**
Beauty can be only skin-deep, but her beauty radiates from within.

If the determiner *the* is used with a singular noun, it can make that noun represent a large group:

Adj   NS   **Adj NS**
The dog is usually more devoted to his master than the cat is.

Dogs are usually more devoted to their masters than cats are.

[†]See Lesson 14, POSSESSIVES.

The determiner *a* (spelled *an* before a word beginning with a vowel) is a form evolved from the word *one* and usually indicates *one* or *one of* a group.

a man   a house   an idea   an owl

Without a determiner before a noun, the word group might be ambiguous (have two possible meanings). Sometimes newspaper headlines are difficult to understand because they are written without determiners:

MENTAL HEALTH SERVICES STUDY NOTES
GAINS, AREAS OF CONCERN

Do we read it like this?

Mental Health Services study the notes, the gains, the areas of concern.

Or like this:

The Mental Health Services study notes the gains, the areas of concern.

NOUN SUBSTITUTES

Notice that some of the determiners and the possessives may also function as noun substitutes:

                Adj   **Ndo**
The decorator chose these paintings.

             Ndo
He does not want those.

Ndo
Some he dislikes.

         Ndo
He prefers his.

EXERCISE 13

Indicate whether the bold-faced word functions as a determiner or a noun substitute in the following sentences by writing Adj for determiner and N for noun substitute in the blank at the right.

To test whether the bold-faced word is a determiner, substitute the word *the*. If the bold-faced word can be replaced with *the*, the word is a determiner.

        Example: **Men's** ties are colorful.

                The ties are colorful.   **Men's** is a determiner (Adj).

Those are very attractive.

*The are very attractive.   **Those** is a noun substitute (N).

1. **These** cherries taste sour. _____   6. Who owns **that** castle? _____

2. Meg will deliver **theirs**. _____   7. They examined **their** property. _____

3. Others respect **his** opinion. _____   8. The trip takes **an** hour. _____

4. **This** is Carol's hat. _____   9. **Those** are inadequate. _____

5. **Women's** fashions change   10. **Betty's** illness is serious. _____
   constantly. _____

lesson 14   Possessives— Apostrophe (')

The POSSESSIVE forms of nouns may be used either as nouns or as another kind of modifier. To form the possessive we add -'s or -s' to a noun and place it before another noun as a modifier, or we use it as we would use a noun. When it functions as a modifier, we will label it *Adj* in this text.

Noun: captain

             Adj   **N**
Possessive: captain's hat

             Adj   **NS**
            The captain's hat was missing.

             NS
            The captain's was missing.

It is also a way of rewriting a word group beginning with *of* which functions as an adjective (See Lesson 19):

Adj N   **Adj**--------------------
the benefits *of the employees*

First, cross out *the* before *benefits* and *of* following it:

t̶h̶e̶ benefits o̶f̶ the employees

Next, add an apostrophe to *employees* and place *the employees'* before *benefits*:

benefits   the employees'   the employees' benefits

t̶h̶e̶ news o̶f̶ today   today's news

t̶h̶e̶ left paw o̶f̶ the dog   the dog's left paw

SUFFIXES FOR POSSESSIVES

1. Add -'s to words not ending in -s:

    boy's   women's   kitten's

4. Add the suffix to the second noun when two nouns show joint ownership:

    Jane and Jill's parents (Jane and Jill are sisters).

2. Add only the apostrophe to words ending in -s:

   boys'   coaches'

3. Exception: Some writers add -'s to singular words of one syllable ending in -s:

   bus's   Jones's

5. Add the suffix to the end of hyphenated nouns:

   sister-in-law's   passer-by's

6. Words representing inanimate (not living) objects sometimes do not take the possessive form:

   the paint of the house
   NOT the house's paint

Instead we may use the noun *house* as a modifier:

   Adj   N
   house paint

EXERCISE 14A

Write the possessive form of the following nouns:

1. children _____ games

2. doctor _____ instruments

3. Bruce and Dick _____ uncle
   (Bruce and Dick are brothers.)

4. father-in-law _____ occupation

5. dog _____ collar

6. Charles _____ necktie

7. men _____ decision

8. jury _____ verdict

9. fox _____ face

10. Thomas _____ attitude

EXERCISE 14B

Rewrite each of the bold-faced phrases as a possessive modifier of the noun. Be sure to use the apostrophe (') in the right place.

Example:

The news **of today** is reported nightly.   *today's news*

1. The sister **of Jay** and the brother **of Susan** are engaged.

   _____

2. The equipment **of the skiers** is buried under snow.

   _____

3. The paws **of the kitten** are pink.

   _____

4. The house **of Bert Jones** is newly painted.

   _____

5. The store **of Burton and Washborn** opened this week.

   _____

6. Ghosts, goblins, and demons fill the dreams **of many children.**

   _____

7. The energy **of a small boy** sometimes gets him into trouble.

   _____

8. The response **of the attorney** was brief.

   _____

9. Dick borrowed the boat **of his father-in-law.**

   _____

10. The conference **of the football coaches** was cancelled.

    _____

lesson 15 Modifiers— Adjective Function and Position

Adjectives modify (describe or further designate) nouns and pronouns. They cluster about the word called the NOUN HEAD, which they modify. They help to make a general term—like *tree*—more specific by telling something about a given tree that distinguishes it from other trees:

the bent, gnarled, wind-swept tree

the towering, dark-green pine tree

the pine, towering and dark green

KINDS OF ADJECTIVES

1. The DETERMINER (Lesson 13), which acts as a pointer, is one kind of noun modifier. When it is used, it comes before the noun and before any other adjective:

Determiner		Noun Head
the	(native)	costumes

2. The POSSESSIVE (Lesson 14) is a second kind. It may function as a determiner in some sentences, or it may appear between the determiner and noun head:

Determiner	Possessive	Noun Head
his		costume
the	gypsy's	costume

3. NOUN ADJUNCTS are words that usually function as nouns, but they may precede a noun head, often a general term, and make it specific:

Determiner	Noun Adjunct	Noun Head
several	gypsy	costumes

4. ADJECTIVES, words that can show comparison either by adding *-er* or *-est* or by being preceded by *more*, *most*, *less*, or *least*, precede noun adjuncts:

Determiner	Adjective	Noun Adjunct	Noun Head
several	colorful	gypsy	costumes

Or adjectives may follow the noun head:

Determiner	Adj	Noun Adjunct	Noun Head	Adj	Adj
several	colorful	gypsy	costumes,	attractive and	decorative

5. V-ED (Part 4 of the verb) and V-ING (Part 5 of the verb) may also function as adjectives, coming either before or after the noun head. (See Lesson 8, Verb Parts 4 and 5.):

Determiner	Adj/V-ed	Noun Adjunct	Noun Head	Adj/V-ed	Adj/V-ing
	V-ed			**V-ed**	**V-ing**
the	decorated	gypsy	costumes,	embroidered and	glistening

6. NUMBERS and AMOUNTS precede Adj:

Determiner	Determiner (Number)	Adj/V-ed/ V-ing	Noun Adjunct	Noun Head	Adj/V-ed/ V-ing	Adj/V-ed/ V-ing
		Adj			**V-ed**	**V-ing**
several	hundred	colorful	gypsy	costumes,	embroidered and	glistening
		Adj			**Adj**	**V-ed**
Mark's	one	warm	wool	shirt,	threadbare and	worn

PUNCTUATION

NO PUNCTUATION is used between adjectives *before* the noun if they are consecutive adjectives and fill each of the positions given above.

COMMA is used between COORDINATE ADJECTIVES. It replaces the word *and* between two adjectives (Lesson 26).

>   **Adj**   **Adj**   **N**
> The comfortable ~~and~~ attractive recliner . . . .
>   **comfortable**   **attractive**

COMMAS enclose adjectives following the noun they modify:

>   **Adj**   **NS**   **Adj**   **Adj**   **Vt**   **Ndo**   **Adv----------**
> The leather recliner, *comfortable* and *attractive,* added warmth to the den.

ADJECTIVES AS PARTS OF SENTENCE PATTERNS

Adjectives may be substituted for nouns in Pattern 4 (Lesson 21) and Pattern 5 (Lesson 23). They are still modifiers, but they are part of the pattern itself.

In Pattern 4 (NS Vt Ndo Noc) the object complement may be an adjective which modifies the direct object (Ndo):

               NS   **Vt**   **Ndo**   **Adj**

Pattern 4: Jackson labeled the foreman *incompetent.*

In Pattern 5 (NS LV Nsc) Adj-c can be used as the completer following the linking verb:

              NS   **LV**---------- **Adj-c**   **Adj-c**

Pattern 5: The foreman had been *careless* and *negligent.*

             NS LV   **Adj-c**

             He seemed *indifferent.*

In Pattern 5 (NS LV Nsc) Adj-c can be used as the completer following a form of the verb *be:*

             NS LV Adj-c

Pattern 5: She was *attractive.*

EXERCISE 15A

Indicate the kind of adjective or determiner each bold-faced word is by writing in the blank at the right one of the following abbreviations:

D	(Determiner)	*NA*	(Noun Adjunct)
D—(Num)	(Number)	*V-ing*	(Part 5 of verb)
Adj	(Adjective)	*V-ed*	(Part 4 of verb)
Poss	(Possessive)		

1. **ten** jobs   _____

2. a **silk** scarf   _____

3. **frozen** water   _____

4. **the** entire staff   _____

5. **Harry's** only opportunity   _____

6. **shining** silver pitcher   _____

7. light tan **leather** purse   _____

8. **cheerful** apartment manager _____

9. a **hundred** antelope   _____

10. **skillful** auto mechanic   _____

EXERCISE 15B

Arrange the modifiers given in a meaningful order before or after the bold-faced noun. Include commas or the word *and* if needed.

Example: cheerful yellow **paint** house bright

cheerful, bright yellow house **paint**

or yellow house **paint,** bright and cheerful

1. **drivers** five brawny truck

2. snow-covered the fir magnificent **trees**

3. pink **blossoms** violet purple African blue

4. Hawaiian inviting warm secluded **beach** a sunny

5. hundred pecking **chickens** several cackling hungry

EXERCISE 15C

Write Adj above all the adjectives in the following
sentences. Include determiners (See Lesson 13).
Begin by labeling the basic sentence patterns—NS
Vi and NS Vt Ndo—above each sentence. The
remaining words should be Adj.

                      Adj Adj   Adj   **NS**   **Vt**   **Adj Adj**   **Ndo**
Example: The large, enthusiastic crowd applauded his stirring speech.

1. The short fat man opened the creaking cabin door.

2. Little boys and big boys like custard pie and chocolate cake.

3. His dark, dingy office needs bright carpeting.

4. The gray stone house occupies the entire city lot.

5. The church soloist, well-trained and poised, sang the difficult aria.

6. The American team won three prizes.

7. The four-year-old boy broke the valuable antique clock.

8. The exhausted men reported an overwhelming victory.

9. Orange, red, and yellow flowers filled the antique vase.

10. The fourteen musicians, satisfied and relaxed, had given an outstanding performance.

EXERCISE 15D

Rewrite these sentences by adding modifiers for
each of the nouns.

                           NS   Vt   **Ndo**
        Example: The dog chased the cat.

        The *black, short-haired* dog chased the *Persian* cat.

1. The man carried a package.

2. The car hit the embankment.

3. The messenger delivered the letter.

4. The woman combed her hair.

5. Coins filled the chest.

lesson 16   Modifiers— Adverbs

FORM AND FUNCTION

ADVERBS (Adv), like adjectives, are modifiers. They add further information about VERBS, ADJECTIVES, OTHER ADVERBS, or SOMETIMES MODIFY A COMPLETE SENTENCE. Sometimes they can be identified by their form when they end in -ly; however, not all words ending in -ly are adverbs:

V
rely on him

Adj
holy city

V
comply with his wishes

Friendly and *daily* can function as both adjectives and adverbs:

   Adj   **Adv**
The friendly dog acts friendly.

   Adj   **Adv**
The daily paper arrives daily.

Identifying adverbs sometimes seems very difficult, but if we ask WHEN, WHERE, WHY, and HOW, and if we see whether the word will fit a test frame for adverbs, we will find that words or word groups answering these questions function as adverbs:

When (time)	—	The college directors chose the library site *last year.*
Where (place)	—	Construction began *there.*
How (manner)	—	The architect supervised construction *carefully* . . .
Why (reason)	—	. . . *because he had accepted the responsibility.*

The test frame for adverbs shows that normally the adverb can be placed at the end of the sentence.

Words that modify adjectives and adverbs qualify them by telling *how:*

                  Adv   **Adj**   **Adj**   **N**
Modifier of adjective: The *deliriously* happy Olympics winner . . .

       Adv   **Adj**   **N**   **Adv**   **Adj**
The *delicately* flavored pastries, *richly* filled . . .

       Adv **Adj** **N**   **Adj**   **Adv**
The *very* hot fire, burning *brightly* . . .

       Adv   **Adj**   **N**
The *extremely* delicate blossom . . .

Modifier of adverb: *very* loudly   *increasingly* loudly
                          Adv Adv   Adv   Adv

Words or word groups that may have other functions can also function as adverbs:

Noun: *home*   He went *home*.   (where)
                             Adv

Adj: *high*   He leaped *high*.   (how)
                              Adv

Adj-Noun: *this year*   He received his degree *this year*.   (when)
                                                     Adv--------

Preposition: *down*   Come *down*.   (where)
                               Adv

POSITION

Although most adverbs can be fitted into an adverb test-frame, the positions adverbs can take in a sentence cannot be plotted as precisely as those of adjectives. An adverb can modify more kinds of words than an adjective can. It can modify a whole sentence as well as a verb, an adjective, or another adverb. It can also modify a word from which it is separated; sometimes a double meaning results if it can also modify another word closer to it. Notice the positions the word *soon* can take:

Sentence modifier: *Soon* he will return.

Modifier of verb: He *soon* will return.

Modifier of verb: He will *soon* return.

Modifier of verb: He will return *soon*.

QUALIFIERS

Note that certain words traditionally classed as adverbs—words like *very, extremely, rather*—will not function as an adverb in the adverb test-frame.

He read the paper quickly.

He read the paper *very* quickly.

NOT: *He read the paper *very*.

Words like these are often designated as qualifiers since they qualify adjectives and adverbs. For convenience we can designate them Adv in marking sentence parts.

EXERCISE 16A

Write Adv above each word functioning as an adverb. Begin by labeling the basic sentence patterns
NS Vi or NS Vt Ndo.

                                              Adv   NS   Adv
                         Example: The *poorly* built house fell *down*.

1. The badly frightened child cried loudly.

2. Gradually the temperature rose higher and higher.

3. The menacing hawk soared silently.

4. Quickly he fastened the safety belt.

5. The aromatically scented incense filled the very small room.

6. The watch repairman worked slowly but precisely.

7. The eager, young pilot carefully plotted his course.

8. The astronaut touched the moon's surface hesitatingly.

9. Apprehensively the freshman took his first final exam.

10. The carefully designed garden pleased visitors from many countries.

EXERCISE 16B

Add adverbial modifiers to the bold-faced words;
write the adverb in the blank at the right.

               Example: The **raging** wind fanned the roaring fire.   **violently.**

                         The **violently raging** wind fanned the roaring fire.

1. The carpenter **hammered** the nails.   _____

2. The wolf howled **mournfully.**   _____

3. The **fragrant** white flowers grow in the spring.   _____

4. Blossoming succulents **covered** the hill.   _____

5. The projectile hit the **moving** target.   _____

lesson 17   **Overworked Modifiers**

Sometimes it seems easier to use a word that comes quickly to mind than to find a synonym. But if these words turn out to be *awful, fine, great, nice, rotten, swell, wonderful, terrible, fierce,* and *lovely,* try finding other words. Good sources, especially while one is revising a written piece, are the dictionary and Roget's *Thesaurus,* and other books of this kind. Here are a few examples:

NOT: He paid an *awful* price for the fur coat.

BUT: He paid an *exorbitant* price for the fur coat.

NOT: The *rotten* weather spoiled a *swell* vacation.

BUT: The *rainy* (or *stormy*) weather spoiled a *well-planned* (or *exciting*) vacation.

NOT: Marvin did a *real nice* job painting the house.

BUT: Marvin did a *very competent* (or *professional*) job painting the house.

EXERCISE 17

The following sentences contain overworked mofi-
fiers. Underline the word or words to be replaced
and write your choice in the blank at the right.
Use your dictionary or Roget's *Thesaurus.*

1. We had a nice trip through the mountains   _____

2. This geometry course is terrible.   _____

3. I have never seen such awful tall buildings.   _____

4. They treated him rotten in the job interview.   _____

5. In such awfully crowded streets people should drive slowly.   _____

6. The heat in the desert was terrible.   _____

7. There are some wonderful freeways across the country.   _____

8. The tourists found a fine camping place.   _____

9. There was a nice lake not far away.   _____

10. Dick and Mary saw a swell movie last night.   _____

lesson 18   Misused Modifiers

SOME MISUSED WORDS

We should be aware that words like *real* and *sure* function as adjectives and should not be used as adverbial modifiers before adjectives:

NOT: *He looked *real* handsome.

               NS LV   Adv   Adj-C
BUT: He looked *really* handsome.

NOT: *He *sure* gave a successful party.

               NS Adv   Vt   Adj   Ndo
BUT: He *surely* gave a successful party.

Words like *good*, *bad*, and *fine* are adjectives and should not be used to modify verbs:

NOT: *They did *fine* on the test.

               NS   Vi Adv Adv-----------
BUT: They did *well* on the test.

NOT: *He treated the children *bad*.

               NS Vt   Ndo   Adv
BUT: He treated the children *badly*.

NOT: *The men worked *good* together.

                  NS   Vi   Adv Adv
BUT: The men worked *well* together.

THE WORDS *ONLY* AND *ALMOST*

The words *only* and *almost* can function either as adjectives or adverbs. Because they can modify different words in a sentence, they must be placed carefully *before* the word they modify. Be sure to distinguish between the words *most* and *almost*. Each has a distinctive meaning: *almost* means *nearly*; *most* means *greatest in number*.

Adj: *Almost* all of the apples are rotten.

Adv: He *almost* (not *most*) ate a worm.

Pronoun: *Most* of the apples are rotten.

THE WORD *NOT*

In using the word *not* as an adverb, we must watch the other adverbial modifiers which also appear in the sentence. If we want to express the negative, the word *not* alone is sufficient.

NS   Vt   Adv Vt   Ndo
George does *not* want the grapes.

If, however, we include another negative word in the same sentence, we might change the meaning or find that the second negative word is unnecessary.

In this example, the word *never* is not needed:

NOT: *Manuel can *not never* agree with Rick.

BUT: Manuel can *not ever* agree with Rick.

MORE USUAL: Manuel can *never* agree with Rick.

EXERCISE 18

The following sentences contain misused modifiers.
Underline the word or words to be replaced and
write the preferred form in the blank.

1. Linda's new outfit looks real attractive. _____

2. Ben can't hardly hear Marcia. _____

3. He most fell down the stairs. _____

4. The boxer was sure fast on his feet. _____

5. Did they get a real good opportunity to buy the house? _____

6. The men talked bad about all the labor trouble. _____

7. He threatened to beat her up good if she ran away again. _____

8. He most got his hand chewed off in the grinder. _____

lesson 19 Modifiers— Prepositional Phrases

Modifiers may be either single words or word groups. One kind of word group that functions either as an adjective or an adverb modifier is the PREPOSITIONAL PHRASE.

> The PREPOSITIONAL PHRASE begins with a PREPOSITION (P), a word like *in, of,* or *to,* and is followed by a noun or pronoun functioning as the object of the preposition (Nop).

to the party   *in the house*

The prepositional phrase offers a way to combine two ideas by embedding one in another. For example, we can write two sentences:

There are voters.

Seventy-five percent cast their ballots yesterday.

By making the word *voters* the object of the preposition *of,* we can combine the two sentences into one:

P   Nop

Seventy-five percent *of the voters* cast their ballots yesterday.

~~There are~~ voters.

A LIST OF PREPOSITIONS

If we are able to recognize words that may function as prepositions, we will be able to identify the noun object and see the word group as a unit. Moving modifying phrases about in a sentence becomes much easier if we recognize them quickly. Here is a partial list of prepositions:

aboard	beneath	in	to
after	beside	inside	up
about	besides	into	toward

above	between	near	under
across	beyond	of	until
against	but	off	upon
along	by	on	via
amid	concerning	out	with
among	despite	outside	within
around	down	over	contrary to
as	due to	past	in spite of
at	during	per	in place of
because of	except	round	in addition to
before	for	since	along with
behind	from	through	according to
below	like	throughout	

CAUTION

IF THESE WORDS APPEAR ALONE IN A SENTENCE, THEY MAY FUNCTION AS ADVERBS:

        NS   Vi   Adv   NS   Vi   Adv
The host came *out.*   Then the guests went *in.*

I never saw him *before.*   Look *up.*

Go *aboard* now.   The lamp fell *down.*

ADJECTIVE PREPOSITIONAL PHRASES (Adj)

If the prepositional phrase functions as an adjective, IT FOLLOWS THE NOUN OR PRONOUN IT MODIFIES. We label the whole phrase *Adj.*

              Adj
NS   P   Nop   Nop   Vt   Ndo
No one / *except George and Don* \ heard the news.

               Adj
  NS   P   Adj Nop   Vi   Adv
The members / *of the sales staff* \ met yesterday.

The same word group may be used as an adjective phrase in one sentence and an adverbial phrase in another sentence, depending on what each word modifies:

              Adj
The man / *with a cane* \ walks slowly.

                          Adv
The man walks slowly / *with a cane.* \

ADVERBIAL PREPOSITIONAL PHRASES (Adv)

Prepositional phrases that function as adverbs answer the questions *when, where, why,* and *how,* just as the single-word adverbs do.

The phrase may follow the verb:

NS   Vi   **Adv** ——— **P**   **Nop**
Dave walked / *into the kitchen.*   (where)

It can precede the verb it modifies or fit between the auxiliary and verb:

NS   **Adv** ——— **P**   **Nop**   Vt -------------- Ndo
Don / *by that time* \ had finished the job.   (when)

NS   Vt   **Adv** ——— **P**   **Nop**   Vt   Ndo
Don had / *by that time* \ finished the job.   (when)

It can follow Ndo even though it modifies the verb:

NS   Vt   Ndo   **Adv** ——— **P**   **Nop**
Don placed the chair / *behind the desk.*   (where)

Two phrases, one following the other, may modify the same verb:

NS   Vi   **Adv** ——— **P**   **Nop**   **Adv** ——— **P Adj Nop**
Sarah ran / *down the street* \ / *to Jane's house.*   (where)

If the second phrase can modify either the Nop or the verb, it may have two meanings. Sentences like this have to be rewritten to eliminate ambiguity:

Jack called / **Adv** ——— *to his friend* \ / **?** ——— *with a loud voice.*

Does the phrase tell how Jack called? Or does it identify his friend? Which one has the loud voice?

Jack called / **Adv** ——— *with a loud voice* \ / **Adv** ——— *to his friend.*

Jack called / **Adv** ——— *to his friend* \ / **Adj** ——— *who has a loud voice.*

The adverbial phrase can modify an adjective:

Adj   **Adv** --------------
Her complexion was delicate *as a rose petal.*

Or it can modify an adverb:

Adv Adv --------------
The hikers wandered far *into the forest.*

One sentence may contain several prepositional phrases, used both as adjective and adverbial modifiers:

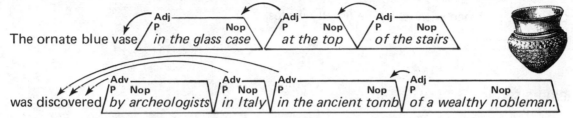

The ornate blue vase / *in the glass case* \ / *at the top* \ / *of the stairs* \

was discovered / *by archeologists* \ / *in Italy* \ / *in the ancient tomb* \ / *of a wealthy nobleman.* \

PUNCTUATION WITH PREPOSITIONAL PHRASES

Because most prepositional phrases are necessary to the meaning of the sentence, they are NOT enclosed in commas. However, adverbial prepositional phrases at the beginning of a sentence may be followed by a comma, particularly if the phrase is very long or if it serves as a connective with the preceding paragraph or sentence:

She received vocational training for five years.

Adv-----------------------------------
During that entire time, she worked diligently.

INCLUSION OF NECESSARY PREPOSITIONS

When two words which require different prepositions for completion of a thought are used, both prepositions should be expressed:

NOT: *She showed loyalty and pride *in* her fiancé.

BUT: She showed loyalty *to* and pride *in* her fiancé.

END-OF-SENTENCE PREPOSITIONS

Sentences may end in prepositions if the usage is natural and avoids stilted language:

NOT: *Tell me what it is *to which* you object.

BUT: Tell me what you object *to.*

NOT: *From where* do you come?

BUT: Where do you come *from?*

In addition, avoid needless repetition of prepositions:

NOT: He let me use the pen *with* which he usually writes *with.*

BUT: He let me use the pen he usually writes with.

OR: . . . the pen with which he usually writes.

EXERCISE 19A

Write prepositional phrases by adding a noun with any necessary modifiers (Nop) after each of the prepositions given:

Example: in _____the sky_____

1. to _____   4. below _____

2. by _____   5. above _____

3. of _____   6. for _____

EXERCISE 19B

Write sentences using the prepositional phrases you wrote in Exercise 19A.

1.

2.

3.

4.

5.

6.

EXERCISE 19C

Find a preposition and its Nop (it may be more than one word) in the following sentences. Write the preposition in the first blank and the word functioning as Nop in the second blank. If the word that appears to be a preposition functions as another part of speech in the sentence, write it in the first blank and write X in the second blank. Do not list infinitives (to + verb) (Lesson 7).

Example:

	Prep	Nop
Inf----- P Nop The mechanic tried *to find* the oil leak *in the engine*.	in	engine

	Prep	Nop
1. The troops marched aboard the transport ship.	_____	_____
2. When are you coming over?	_____	_____
3. Jack drives within a three-mile circle each day.	_____	_____
4. Under the bridge sat a troll.	_____	_____
5. Both of the boys bought guns.	_____	_____
6. Between you and me I have no opinion.	_____	_____
7. The train came round the bend.	_____	_____
8. He intends to arrive at nine o'clock.	_____	_____
9. Look inside to find the trouble.	_____	_____
10. From this point I can see three states.	_____	_____

IF YOU MISSED TWO OR MORE SENTENCES
in the first part, review the lesson on prepositions and complete the second part.

11. The girl with the dog fell down.	_____
12. The girl fell with the dog.	_____
13. Have you seen New Orleans before?	_____

14. Slowly he walked around the block.   _____

15. She gave him two baskets of apples.   _____

16. Why did you buy a car like that?   _____

17. She took money to the bank.   _____

18. A moment of silence preceded the explosion. _____

19. After heavy rains the town was flooded.   _____

20. He built a house of brick.   _____

EXERCISE 19D

Label the prepositional phrases with Adj or Adv
and write the words they modify in the blanks. If
a word appears to be a preposition but functions
as another part of speech, write an X in the blank.
Begin by labeling the basic sentence patterns—NS
Vi or NS Vt Ndo. The remaining words may be
prepositional phrases.

                 NS Adj-------------Vt   Ndo
Example: The sign on the corner shows the temperature.   _____ sign _____

1. The members of the club signed the pledge.   _____

2. Walker chose two of his friends to help him. _____

3. Her ring fell into the well.   _____

4. He came home late at night.   _____

5. The flowers grew in abundance.   _____

6. Bill arrived from New York yesterday.   _____

7. The woman in the blue dress said hello.   _____

8. The safety patrol helped the boy across the street. _____

9. Look out the window.   _____

10. Has Henry brought the load of hay?   _____

IF YOU MISSED TWO OR MORE SENTENCES
in the first part, review the lesson on prepositions
and complete the second part.

11. Come out this minute.   _____   _____

12. The dog leaped into the lake.   _____   _____

13. Don went across town this morning.   _____   _____

14. The flowers filled the garden below.   _____   _____

15. The campers arrived home after dark.   _____   _____

16. How can you study amid the confusion?   _____   _____

17. The baby looks like him.   _____   _____

18. I will meet you at the fair.   _____   _____

19. Come to my house tonight.   _____   _____

20. Open the gates for the horsemen.   _____   _____

EXERCISE 19E

In the following sentences a prepositional phrase
modifier may be misplaced. Underline the phrase
and write the word it should modify in the blank
at the right.

1. Last week Dick fell and injured himself on the back
   porch.   _____

2. I wrote a letter while riding to San Francisco on a
   scrap of paper.   _____

3. A violent storm broke and quickly filled rivers and
   streams with great fury.   _____

4. Becky was transferred to the island where the hotel
   was situated in a small boat.   _____

5. A piano was offered for sale by a man going to the
   Orient with carved legs.   _____

6. Some people think that my walnut chair is an
   antique with a knowledge of furniture.   _____

7. Barbara will sell this old table before she moves
   with one leg gone.   _____

Now that you have completed the last exercise in this unit, YOU ARE READY FOR THE UNIT TWO
REVIEW. If you need additional practice, complete the X-TRAS which follow.

UNIT TWO

UNIT TWO REVIEW will consist of exercises like the ones in Lessons 12 through 19. To prepare for the
REVIEW, read the lessons and go back over the exercises. Note any corrections you have made. Be
especially familiar with SENTENCE KEYS and Exercises 12, 13, 14A, 15D, 16B, 18, 19A, 19B, 19C,
19D, 19E. If you do not understand any part of the exercises thoroughly, ask your instructor for help.
Make sure that you understand the directions for each exercise because those on the REVIEW will be
very similar.

Complete these exercises only if you want additional practice before you attempt the UNIT TWO
REVIEW, Form A or Form B. Answers for these are in the Answer Key.

I.   Write Adj above each word functioning as an
     adjective. For this practice consider deter-
     miners and noun adjuncts as Adj.

   1. Very few people know Mark's last name.

   2. Recent research quickly disclosed many unidentified, contaminating agents.

   3. Thoroughly sterilized surgical instruments should not carry disease-producing bacteria.

   4. Unidentified flying objects frequently arouse many people's concern and fear.

   5. Reliably trained observers have photographed "flying saucers."

   6. Unfortunately the fear-ridden, trembling man would not recall his recent activities.

   7. Any radically new, complex phenomenon arouses keen interest.

8. The hungry and thirsty two-year-old boy eagerly ran home.

9. The colonel's privately owned plane, damaged and scorched, landed safely.

10. Weekly field trips offered unusually good travel opportunities.

II. Write Adv above each word functioning as an adverb in the sentences above. Consider qualifiers, like *very*, as adverbs.

III. Write five of your own sentences and label each word functioning as an Adj or Adv. Keep the sentences uncomplicated. Begin by writing a sentence to match one of the basic sentence patterns. Then add modifiers—either adjectives or adverbs.

1.

2.

3.

4.

5.

IV. Underline the prepositional phrases and draw arrows to the words they modify. If a word appears to be a preposition but functions as an adverb, write X above it.

1. Most of the skaters huddled around the camp fire.

2. All of the cabins were piled high with snow.

3. Tom backed his car down the steep driveway and swerved into the fence.

4. The captains of the teams shouted angrily at each other.

5. Two of the chairs needed a coat of paint.

6. Sarah stood at the window and looked out.

7. By nightfall most of the hunters had returned to camp.

8. Lilies in the field swayed in the gentle wind.

9. The flock of geese flew in formation over the quiet forest.

10. Tons of concrete filled the forms for the bridge pillars.

11. At home Dana waited anxiously for a telephone call.

12. At the end of the play the actors greeted members of the audience.

13. The soprano soloist from New York fainted and collapsed on the stage.

14. Marge handed Tom a dish of ice cream.

15. Dave moved the piano from one corner of the room to the other.

V. Write five prepositional phrases: P + Nop.
   Then use them in sentences.

   1.

   2.

   3.

   4.

   5.

VI. Write sentences to match these patterns.

   1. NS Vi Adv

   2. NS Vt Compound Ndo

   3. Compound NS Vt Ndo

   4. NS Compound Vi Adv

   5. NS Vt Ndo

unit THREE

Sentence Patterns
Three, Four, Five

lesson 20 Sentence Pattern Three

Sentence Pattern Three is similar to Pattern Two because both consist of a subject (NS), transitive or incomplete verb (Vt), and direct object (Ndo), but Pattern Three also has an INDIRECT OBJECT (Nio).

THE INDIRECT OBJECT (Nio) tells **TO WHOM** or **FOR WHOM** something is done and appears BEFORE the direct object (Ndo). In English we can also indicate the person to whom or for whom something is done by using a prepositional phrase, and placing the phrase *after* the direct object.

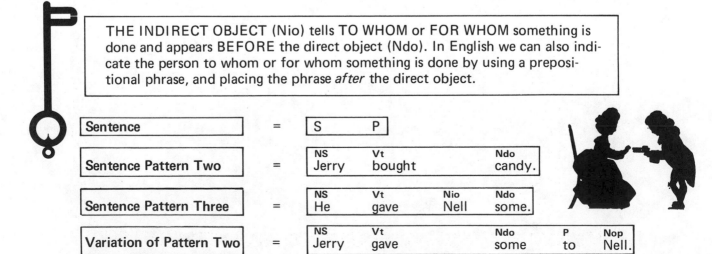

Sentence	=	S	P			

Sentence Pattern Two	=	**NS** Jerry	**Vt** bought		**Ndo** candy.	

Sentence Pattern Three	=	**NS** He	**Vt** gave	**Nio** Nell	**Ndo** some.	

Variation of Pattern Two	=	**NS** Jerry	**Vt** gave	**Ndo** some	**P** to	**Nop** Nell.

Remember that the direct object (Ndo) in both patterns can be COMPOUND: it can consist of two nouns joined by *and:*

NS	Adv	Vt	Ndo	C	Ndo
Jerry	also	bought	popcorn	and	sandwiches.

NS	Vt	Nio	Ndo	C	Ndo	Adv
He	offered	Nell	gum	and	soda pop	besides.

EXERCISE 20

Label the words in the following sentences with NS, Ndo, Nio, Vt, Adv, Adj by using Sentence Keys.

1. The florist sold Brian a white orchid.

2. He raised orchids and other tropical flowers..

3. Maria enjoyed her first orchid corsage.

4. She gave Brian a kiss.

5. They met Barbara and Don at the dance.

6. Afterward they had a midnight supper at Petit Pierre's.

sentence keys

To analyze Pattern Three sentences, we follow the same sequence as for Pattern Two and then add one more step:

1. Find the verb. Label it V.

2. Ask *who* or *what* plus the verb. Label the word that answers the question NS (subject).

3. Read NS + V together and ask *whom* or *what.*
   Label the word that answers the question Ndo (direct object).
   Label the verb Vt.

4. Label the words that tell *when, where, why,* and *how* Adv.

5. Label the word that tells to whom or for whom something is done Nio (indirect object).

lesson 21 Sentence Pattern Four

Sentence Pattern Four is also similar to Pattern Two because it consists of a subject (NS), a transitive verb (Vt), and a direct object (Ndo). Added to this pattern is an object complement (Noc).

> The OBJECT COMPLEMENT (Noc) is a word or words that either serve to rename or describe the DIRECT OBJECT (Ndo) or an ADJECTIVE (Adj) that modifies the direct object. It *follows* the direct object. Usually the object complement can be joined to the direct object by the phrase *to be.*

Sentence = | S P |

Sentence Pattern Two =

NS	Vt	Ndo
Members	held	an election.

Sentence Pattern Four =

NS	Vt	Ndo		Noc
They	elected	Beckett		president.
They	elected	Beckett	(to be)	president.

NS	Vt	Ndo	Adj C Adj
They	considered	him	capable and energetic.
They	considered	him (to be)	capable and energetic.

sentence keys

The first four steps of the Sentence Keys are the same for Pattern Three and Pattern Four, but the fifth step is different.

5. After labeling the direct object (Ndo), find the noun that renames the direct object. It always follows the direct object. Label it Noc (object complement).

If an adjective follows the direct object, label it Adj.

EXERCISE 21

Label the words in the following sentences with NS, Ndo, Noc, Vt, Vi, Adv, Adj by using Sentence Keys.

1. The sales manager resigned last week.

2. Myron Holt wanted the position desperately.

3. Mr. Farnsworth considered Myron a candidate.

4. He also considered Evan Watts and Joe Steele.

5. Finally he named Ruth Olson sales manager.

6. The men opposed his decision angrily.

7. Mr. Farnsworth would not change his mind.

lesson 22   Comparison of Pattern Three and Pattern Four

Pattern Three—NS Vt Nio Ndo

This sentence with an INDIRECT OBJECT (Nio)—

      NS   Vt   Nio   Ndo
The president sent Barclay a telegram.

is another way of writing these sentences:

    The president sent a telegram to Barclay.

    The president sent _____ a telegram.
                 t̸ø Barclay

Nio (INDIRECT OBJECT) appears BEFORE Ndo (direct object).

Nio is a person or thing different from NS and Ndo. It tells to whom or for whom something is done, or to whom something is given, told, or shown.

    Nio—Barclay   Ndo—telegram

Nio can appear in sentences after verbs like *give, find, send, bring, buy, sell, make, write, ask, play, build, teach, assign, feed, offer, throw, pass, pay.*

Pattern Four—NS Vt Ndo Noc

This sentence with an OBJECT COMPLEMENT (Noc)—

    NS Vt------------------ Ndo   Noc
He had appointed Barclay dean.

is a revision of these sentences:

    He had appointed Barclay _____.
                      Bár̸clá̸y ı̸s dean

Noc (OBJECT COMPLEMENT) appears AFTER Ndo (direct object). There is NO connector between them.

Noc (object complement) is a person or thing the same as Ndo (direct object).

    Ndo—Barclay   Noc—dean

Noc (object complement) can appear in sentences after verbs like *call, appoint, choose, name, select, elect, make, consider, find.*
Adj, serving to further describe what happens to the Ndo, can follow verbs like *consider* and *find* and also verbs like *paint, wash,* and *color.*

EXERCISE 22A

Fill in these patterns with the symbol that
belongs in the blank. Use NS, Ndo, Noc, Nio,
Vi, Vt, Adv.

1. NS _____ Ndo

2. NS Vt _____ Ndo

3. NS _____ Ndo Noc

4. NS Vt Nio _____

5. NS _____ Adv

6. _____ Vi Adv

7. NS Vt _____

8. _____ Vt Ndo Noc

EXERCISE 22B

If there is an indirect object (Nio) or object complement (Noc) in these sentences, write the word
in the first blank and the symbol in the second
blank. If there is none, write X in the first blank.

Example:

NS   Vt   Nio   Ndo
The reporter told the editor the story.   ____editor____   ____Nio____

NS   Vt   Ndo C Ndo
The widow sold the house and furniture.   ____X____   _____

NS   Vt   Ndo Noc
The settlers named the town Bridgeport.   ____Bridgeport____   ____Noc____

1. The caravan brought the ruler jewels.   _____   _____

2. The mouse fed its babies grain.   _____   _____

3. The people called him king.   _____   _____

4. The car needs gas and oil.   _____   _____

5. The hunters named the foundling Ruth.   _____   _____

6. The cashier gave Margaret the change.   _____   _____

7. Mary named Rita bridesmaid.   _____   _____

8. The pilot flew planes and helicopters.   _____   _____

9. Paul sent Jenny some roses.   _____   _____

10. Don offered the boy a pear.   _____   _____

11. Alice declared Tom the winner.   _____   _____

12. Candidates gave voters no choice.   _____   _____

EXERCISE 22C

Write sentences to match these patterns. Label
each word with one of these symbols: NS, Ndo,
Nio, Noc, Vi, Vt, Adv.

1. NS Vt Nio Ndo

2. NS Vt Compound Ndo

3. NS Vi Adv

4. NS Vt Ndo Noc

lesson 23 Sentence Pattern Five

Here is the fourth sentence pattern:

Sentence	=	S	P	

Sentence Pattern Five	=	NS	LV	Nsc

It may also be written like this:

NS	LV	Adj-c

NS	LV	Adv-c

This pattern has certain characteristics that make it easy to recognize:

1. It contains a linking verb (LV)

2. The noun completer (Nsc) following the linking verb renames the subject. It is often called a subject complement or predicate noun.

3. An adjective (Adj-c) following the linking verb modifies the subject. Like a noun, it serves as subject completer.

LINKING VERBS (LV)

Linking verbs include the verb *be* (discussed separately below because it has an unusual number of forms and has various functions) and verbs that—like *be*—can link or bind together the subject (NS) with a word or phrase that renames or describes the subject or tells where the subject is located (adverb of place). A noun, an adjective, or an adverb or adverbial phrase can be used as completers after *be:*

Noun completer:
NS   LV Nsc
Jane is a *senior.*

Adj completer:
NS LV Adj-c
She is *attractive.*

Adv completer:
NS LV Adv-c   NS LV Adv-c------
She is *here.*   She is *at college.*

After other linking verbs—words like *seem, remain, become, appear, grow,* and *turn*—either nouns or adjectives can be used as completers:

Noun completer: NS LV Nsc
Jane remained a *student*.

Adj completer: NS LV Adj-c
She seemed *happy*.

Remember, if a noun follows a linking verb, it renames the subject (NS) or tells what the subject *became, appears, remains*, etc. If an adjective follows a linking verb, it describes the subject (NS). If the verb *be* is followed by an adverb or adverbial phrase, it usually answers the question *where* about the subject (NS).

THE VERB *BE*

The verb *be* is the only English verb which has more than five separate forms. It has eight forms, used as follows:

	Singular			Plural		
		Present	*Past*		*Present*	*Past*
First person	I	am	was	we	are	were
Second person	you	are	were	you	are	were
Third person	he	is	was	they	are	were
	she	is	was			
	it	is	was			
Nouns	boy	is	was	boys	are	were
	Betty	is	was	women	are	were

Be verb forms, as you learned in Lesson 5, are used frequently as auxiliary forms. However, each function is distinctive. Consider the following examples:

As linking verbs they are the main verb in the sentence.

NS LV Nsc
Davis was the chairman.

NS LV Nsc
A rose is a flower.

As auxiliary verbs they are part of the main verb:

NS Vt------------ Ndo
Davis was asking a question.

NS Vi------------------------ Adv
Roses had been blooming a week.

The verb *be* also has the following forms:

Part 1: *be*—infinitive or uninflected form

Part 4: *been*—the *V-ed* form used in verb phrases

Part 5: *being*—the *V-ing* form used in verb phrases

Part 4 of the verb *be* cannot be used as an adjective as can Part 4 of most verbs.

NOT: *The *been* leaves were colorful.

BUT: The *fallen* leaves were colorful. (Part 4 of the verb *fall*)

(Exceptions are such phrases as "a *has-been* performer," in which the complete phrase *has* plus *been* is needed.)

Part 5 of the verb can be used as an adjective or noun only if it has completers:

NOT: *Being,* she could do more work.

BUT: *Being* happy, she could do more work.

NOT: *His *being* pleased everyone.

BUT: His *being* happy pleased everyone.

SHIFT IN VERB TYPE

A number of verbs—like *sound, appear, look, grow*—may function as either linking verbs or as intransitive (Vi) or transitive (Vt) verbs. Look at the following sentences:

NS Vt   Ndo
She grew roses.

NS LV   Adj-c
She grew lonely.

NS   Vt   Ndo
The visitor sounded the bell.

NS   LV   Adj
The bell sounds loud.

NS   Vi   Adv-----------
The butler appeared at the door.

NS LV   Adj
He appeared angry.

NS   Vt   Ndo
The visitor smelled the cooking food.

NS   LV   Adj
The food smelled good.

Some sentences containing the same words can have two meanings. They probably should be rewritten.

NS   LV   Adj
The detective looked hard. (His physical features were rugged.)

NS   Vi   Adv
The detective looked hard. (He searched diligently.)

THERE IS . . . , IT IS . . . , HERE IS . . .

In sentences beginning with *there is* or *it is*, the subject (NS) follows the verb. The words *there* and *it* are introductory words in these sentences:

LV   NS
There is the needle.

LV   NS
It is the sheriff.

The words *there* and *here* can also function as adverbs:

<table>
<tr><td>Adv</td><td>NS</td><td>Vi</td></tr>
</table>

Adv   NS   Vi
There the men stand.

Adv   Vi   NS
Here come their wives.

sentence keys

To analyze a Pattern Five sentence, follow this sequence:

1. Label the verb V.

2. Write NS above the word that answers *who* or *what* plus the verb.

3. Read NS + V and ask *who* or *what.*
   a. Label the word that answers the question *who* Nsc if it is a noun that renames the subject.
   b. Label the word that answers the question *what* Adj-c if it is an adjective which modifies the subject.
   c. Label the word that answers the question *how* Adj-c if it is an adjective following a verb like *become, seem, feel.* (See explanation above in this lesson.)
   d. Label the word that answers the question *where* Adv-c if it follows and completes the meaning of the verb *be.*

4. Label the verb LV.

EXERCISE 23A

Identify the function of the words in the following sentences by labeling them NS, Nsc, LV, Adj-c, or Adv-c.

                   NS LV Adv-c   NS   LV   Nsc
Examples: Ben is inside.   Mr. Briggs will be a teacher.

1. Dale is home.

2. The sea appears calm.

3. The music sounds pleasant.

4. The fabric feels soft and warm.

5. The sky looks threatening.

6. The sailor seems apprehensive.

7. There is the champion.

8. The mansion was elegant.

9. Margery is a pianist.

10. The bear looked vicious.

EXERCISE 23B

Identify the words in the following sentences by labeling them NS, Ndo, Nsc, Vi, Vt, LV, Adj-c, Adv-c.

1. The cart is standing in the hall.

2. The paintings look restful.

3. The fawn tasted the milk.

4. Mr. Danton became a counselor.

5. The runner appeared exhausted.

6. The watchman appeared suddenly.

lesson 24   Sentence Keys for All Patterns

The five sentence patterns discussed in preceding lessons illustrate the parts and word order of simple sentences written in English. They are summarized here together with definitions of the symbols:

	SUBJECT			PREDICATE	
One	NS	Vi			
Two	NS	Vt		Ndo	
Three	NS	Vt	Nio	Ndo	
Four	NS	Vt		Ndo	Noc
Five	NS	LV		Nsc	
Five	NS	LV		Adj-c	
Five	NS	LV		Adv-c	

SYMBOLS

NS — Subject tells what the sentence is about.

Nsc — Subject completer or complement always follows LV and renames subject (NS).

Ndo — Direct object always completes Vt.

Noc — Object complement follows direct object (Ndo) and renames object (Ndo).

Nio — Indirect object precedes direct object (Ndo) and tells to whom or for whom something is done, or to whom something is given, shown, or told.

Vi — Intransitive (complete) verb is the complete predicate. It can stand alone as a sentence with subject *(you)* understood.

Vt — Transitive (incomplete) verb is a part of the predicate and is followed by a direct object (Ndo) which completes the predicate.

LV — Linking verb is followed by subject completer (Nsc) which renames the subject or by an adjective (Adj-c) which modifies subject. *Be* verbs are sometimes completed by an adverb or adverb phrase (Adv-c).

Adj — Adjective, modifier of nouns and pronouns, precedes or follows the word it qualifies or describes.

Adj-c — Adjective completer follows LV and modifies NS.

Adv — Adverb, modifier of verbs, adjectives, other adverbs, or clauses and sentences, answers *when, where, why,* or *how.*

Adv-c — Adverb completer following verb *be.*

These patterns are our keys to determining whether the word groups we write are sentences. If we can find one of these patterns and the word group can stand alone, we can call the word group a sentence. Understanding these patterns can also help us improve reading comprehension because we can learn to read meaningful word groups rather than single words.

To find the patterns we can use a step-by-step sequence which was developed in preceding lessons. It is summarized here.

sentence keys

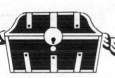

1. Find the verb. (Use verb tests given in Lesson 1, p. 5.)

   The mask *covered* his face.   The monster *chased* the scientist.
   <small>Vt</small>   <small>Vt</small>

   The monster *is* the scientist's creation.   The monster *looks* evil.
   <small>LV</small>   <small>LV</small>

   The scientist *gave* the monster life.
   <small>Vt</small>

2. Ask *who* or *what* plus the verb. The word that answers the question is NS (subject).

   The mask covered his face.   What covered?   The *mask (NS)* covered . . .
   <small>Vt</small>

   The monster looks evil.   Who looks?   The *monster (NS)* looks . . .
   <small>LV</small>

3. Say NS + verb + *who(m)* or *what.*

   a. The word (or word group) that answers the question can be Ndo following a transitive verb (Vt):

NS   Vt
The monster chased the scientist.   The monster chased whom?
The scientist (Ndo)

b. Or it can be Nsc following a linking verb (LV):

NS   LV
The monster is the scientist's creation.   The monster is what?
Creation (Nsc)

c. Or it can be Adj-c following a linking verb (LV). (Notice that Adj-c might also seem to answer the question *how* in some cases.)

NS   LV
The monster looks evil.   The monster looks what?   *Evil (Adj-c)*

d. If there is no noun answering *whom* or *what,* the verb is complete. Label it Vi.

NS   Vi   Adv
The monster shrieked menacingly.

These three steps will identify the verbs—Vi, Vt, and LV—and the nouns—NS and Ndo—in the basic sentence patterns. To identify Nio (indirect object) and Noc (object complement) which may appear after certain verbs, these additional steps are needed.

INDIRECT OBJECT (Nio)

First, examine the verb. If it is incomplete, is it one which can be completed by an indirect object (Nio) as well as direct object (Ndo)? (See list given with Pattern Three.)

Second, after labeling the direct object (Ndo), find the word that tells TO WHOM or FOR WHOM something is done. It always precedes Ndo. Label the word Nio.

NS   Ndo
The scientist gave the monster life.   The scientist gave life to whom?
The monster—Nio

OBJECT COMPLEMENT (Noc)

First, examine the verb. If it is incomplete (Vt), is it one which can be further completed by an object complement (Noc) as well as a direct object (Ndo)? (See list given with Pattern Four.)

Second, after labeling the direct object (Ndo), find the word that renames or further describes the direct object. It always follows the direct object. Label it Noc (object complement).

NS   Ndo   Noc

The scientist named the monster Gorgos.   *Gorgos* is object complement.

MODIFIERS

Although adjectives (Adj) and adverbs (Adv) may be a required part of Pattern Five, they may also be optional modifiers of the nouns and verbs in the sentence patterns.

ADJECTIVES

Single words or word groups that qualify or modify nouns and pronouns are adjectives (Adj). They may precede or follow the noun they modify:

The *grotesque* monster, *looming large* and *threatening,* frightened everyone *who saw him.*

ADVERBS

Single words or word groups that answer the questions *when, where, why,* and *how* are usually adverbs. They modify verbs, adjectives, other adverbs, and also clauses and sentences. They precede adjectives and adverbs they modify, but they may precede or follow the verb they modify, or they may even be separated from it.

Late at night (when) the monster traveled *stealthily* (how) *through the small town* (where) *in search of the scientist* (why).

Remember that an adjective following a linking verb may answer the question *how.* We can tell that the word is an adjective because it modifies NS:

NS LV Adj-c	Adj N
The food smells appetizing.	appetizing food
NS LV Adj-c	**Adj N**
The hostess looks relaxed.	relaxed hostess

An adverb following a *be* verb usually tells *where.*

NS   LV Adv-c
The traveler is home.

NS   LV Adv-c
Snow was everywhere.

(The word *home* is not used as a noun in this sentence because it does not rename *traveler;* it is not an adjective because it does not modify *traveler. Home* functions as an adverb completer because it tells *where* the traveler is.)

EXERCISE 24A

Label the sentence parts using NS, Ndo, Nio, Noc,
Nsc, Vi, Vt, LV, Adj, Adv, Adj-c, Adv-c, and C.

1. Louis Agassiz was a naturalist.

2. He studied European and American animals.

3. He observed many species.

4. He worked constantly.

5. He described recent and fossil fish forms.

6. These descriptions were invaluable.

7. Agassiz labeled Darwin's theories false.

8. He established a zoological laboratory.

9. An island was the site.

10. Harvard appointed him zoology professor.

IF YOU MISSED MORE THAN ONE SENTENCE
in Exercise 24A, review SENTENCE KEYS and
complete Exercise 24B.

EXERCISE 24B

1. The gypsy danced.

2. The marshal arrested the thief.

3. Gilbert handed Jonas the medal.

4. Douglas is an instructor.

5. The antenna fell down.

6. The food is delicious.

7. The truck lost a wheel.

8. The hostess looked attractive.

9. The hawk swooped downward.

10. Malcolm has been here.

Now that you have completed the last exercise in this unit, YOU ARE READY FOR THE UNIT THREE
REVIEW. If you need additional practice, complete the X-TRAS which follow.

UNIT THREE

UNIT THREE REVIEW will consist of exercises like the ones in Lessons 20 through 24. To prepare for the REVIEW, read the lessons and go back over the exercises. Note any corrections you have made; if you do not understand any part of the exercises thoroughly, ask your instructor for help. Make sure that you understand the directions for each exercise because those on the REVIEW will be similar.

Complete these exercises only if you want additional practice before you attempt the UNIT THREE REVIEW, Form A or Form B. Answers for these are in the Answer Key.

I. Write in the blank the symbol that completes each sentence pattern. Use one of these symbols: NS, Nsc, Ndo, Nio, Noc, Vt, Vi, LV, Adj, Adv.

1. NS _____ Nsc

2. NS _____ Adv

3. NS Vt Ndo _____

4. NS LV _____ (noun)

5. NS Vt _____ Ndo

6. NS _____ Ndo

7. NS Vi _____ (verb modifier)

8. NS LV _____ (modifier of subject)

9. _____ LV Adv-c

10. NS _____ Nio Ndo

11. NS Vt _____ Noc

12. NS Vt _____

II. Write in the blanks the BASIC SENTENCE PATTERN of each sentence. Begin by writing V above each verb and NS above each subject. Next, identify complements: Ndo, Nio, Noc, Nsc, Adj, Adj-c, and Adv-c. Determine whether verbs are Vi, Vt, or LV. Finally, write the Basic Sentence Pattern in the blank.

        Adj NS Vt   Adj Adj Ndo Adv
Example: The goat chewed the tin can vigorously.   Omit Modifiers   NS Vt Ndo

1. The camel caravan made frequent stops along the route.   _____

2. Red and brown leaves covered the trees.   _____

3. Autumn is a relaxing season.   _____

4. The modern camera takes remarkable pictures.   _____

5. Bruce Bennett is an amateur photographer.   _____

6. He is extremely talented.   _____

7. The skydivers awarded John the trophy.   _____

8. Last year Tom traveled extensively in Africa.   _____

9. Dan Baker named Dale Walker chairman of the board.   _____

10. Baker and Adams own the new dress shop on First Street.   _____

11. The college president gave graduates their diplomas.   _____

12. The pilot's fiancée christened the plane Orion.   _____

13. Bob gave Dick and Ellen copies of his new book.   _____

14. Bob titled the book *Adventures of the Spirit.*   _____

15. The walls of the lighthouse needed extensive repairs.   _____

16. The muddy water filled the shallow ditch completely.   _____

17. The cornered dog growled and snapped viciously.   _____

18. The film projectionist is very capable and energetic.   _____

19. The highly agitated man banged the closed office door.   _____

20. The brightly shining lights blinded the baseball players.   _____

III. Write sentences to match each of the patterns
given below. Label parts.

1. NS Vt Ndo

2. NS LV Nsc

3. NS Vi

4. NS Vt Nio Ndo

5. NS LV Adj-c

6. NS Vt Ndo Noc

7. NS LV Adv-c

8. NS Vi Adv

9. NS Vt Ndo Adv

10. NS LV Nsc

IV. When we use Sentence Keys, we follow a step-by-step procedure, and we identify sentence parts with these symbols: NS, Nsc, Ndo, Nio, Noc, Vi, Vt, LV, Adj, Adv. Answer the following questions by circling ONE OR MORE of the symbols or words at the right.

1. What symbol identifies words or word groups that modify nouns?   NS Adj Adv Vi·Vt

2. After we identify NS Vt in a sentence, we ask what or whom. What symbol do we use to identify the word that answers the question?   Ndo Vi Adv LV

3. What symbol do we use to label words like *taste, sound, smell* when they function as verbs of the senses?   Adv Vi LV Vt

4. What symbol is used to label determiners—words like *the* and *a?*   NS Noc Adj Adv

5. What symbols represent the subject and the direct object?   NS Nsc Ndo Nio Noc

6. In analyzing a sentence, what part do we identify first?   NS Vi-Vt-LV Adj Adv

7. What symbol represents words that answer the questions *when, where, why,* and *how?*   Adv NS Adj Nio

8. What three symbols may be used to label the word that
   follows a linking verb (LV)?   NS Adj Nsc Adv Ndo

9. After we have found a verb in a sentence, we ask *what* or
   who. What symbol do we use for the word that answers this
   question?   Ndo Nio NS Noc Adv

10. Which of the following questions does Ndo answer in a   When? Whom? Where? Why?
    sentence?   What? How? For whom?

unit FOUR

Coordination

lesson 25 **Coordination**

COORDINATING CONJUNCTIONS

To show that two ideas are of equal importance, we can join them with connectors called COORDI-NATING CONJUNCTIONS (C):

and, so	show addition
but, yet	show contrast
for, so	show cause
or, nor	show alternatives

For example, these two simple sentences can be joined with *but* to show that the ideas are both related to each other and in contrast to each other:

Simple Sentence:
NS   Vt   Adj Ndo
Jerry completed his experiment.

Simple Sentence:
NS Vt Adv Vt   Adj Adj Ndo
He did not write his final report.

The combined simple sentences become a compound sentence consisting of two independent clauses.

> An INDEPENDENT CLAUSE has a subject
> and predicate and can stand alone as a sentence.
>
> The word *independent* means *free* or *self-sufficient,* like an *independent* adult
> or an *independent* nation.

Compound Sentence = | Independent clause | | , C | OR | ; |

| **Independent clause**
| Jerry completed his experiment | | , but | OR | ; |

| Independent clause |

| **Independent clause**
| he did not write his final report |

> A COMPOUND SENTENCE consists of at least two NS-V combinations
> joined by a comma and conjunction or a semicolon alone.

PARALLEL STRUCTURES

Words or word groups of the same grammatical construction, called parallel structures, can be joined by the connectors:

Nouns:	house *and* lot, sea *and* sky
Verbs:	rises *and* shines, pouted *and* cried
Phrases:	at home *or* at play, in water *and* on snow
Dependent clauses:	who called *and* who came
Independent clauses:	Jack opened the door, *and* he saw the comet.

The connectors act as the point on which the two structures are balanced. To show this balance, we can rewrite sentences to point out the parallel structures. (The parallel structures are also called compound elements.)

Mary and
Jim   went swimming.

Hazel drove *up the hill and*
              through the tunnel.

Michael rented the dance hall, and
Joan planned the party.

To show relationship to a preceding sentence, connectors may be used to begin a sentence.

Charles worked hard to win.   *And* then he finally succeeded.

Ethel agreed.   *Or* did she?

EXERCISE 25

Determine whether the following word groups are
sentences. Write S in the blank if the word group is
a simple sentence, C if it is a compound sentence,
F if it is a fragment (part of a sentence). Write
basic sentence patterns above the appropriate
words.

          NS   Vi

Example: The horses race down the track and around the bend.   S

1. Many kinds of animals are facing extinction, and future generations will not be
   able to see living examples of some species.   _____

2. Some men have slaughtered animals needlessly; other men have protected them.   _____

3. Animal farms in many parts of the world are a haven for several species.   _____

4. The animals and their offspring live together on the farms in safety and later will
   be transported to wilderness areas.   _____

5. Eskimos in the Arctic changing their ways of living.   _____

6. Many Eskimos now live in conventional houses along paved roads, and they have
   jobs.   _____

7. Eskimo children probably will not build igloos in the future.   _____

8. The art of woodcarving may gradually disappear.   _____

9. Eskimos have carved animals and other figures from walrus tusks.   _____

10. Eskimos have survived for many years by using the meat and furs of the seal,
    walrus, and other animals, but now they are gradually acquiring the ways of
    western people.   _____

lesson 26 Punctuation with Coordinate Constructions

COORDINATE ADJECTIVES

If two adjectives modify a noun equally and separately, they are coordinate or of equal rank. To determine whether they are coordinate, place *and* between them. Also try reversing their order. They should function in either position as in the following sentence:
A COMMA is used between COORDINATE ADJECTIVES.

The *tall, willowy* blonde dived into the pool.

The *tall* and *willowy* blonde dived into the pool.

The *willowy, tall* blonde dived into the pool.

CONSECUTIVE ADJECTIVES

Adjectives derived from nouns (Lesson 15) immediately precede the nouns they modify, and the two words function as a unit:

putty knife   *science* teacher   *silver* pitcher

An adjective placed before these word combinations modifies the unit:

broken putty knife   *qualified science* teacher   *shining silver* pitcher

The adjectives are consecutive; therefore their positions cannot be reversed. NO COMMA is used between them. We can NOT write this word group in the following ways:

The *broken and putty* knife . . .

The *putty broken* knife . . .

NO COMMA is used between CONSECUTIVE ADJECTIVES.

EXERCISE 26A

Examine the modifiers preceding each noun, and
insert commas only between those which are coordinate adjectives.

Example: *beautiful, melancholy* song

blooming cherry tree

1. old-fashioned sewing machine

2. rusty broken screen door

3. dedicated trustworthy attorney

4. meek anxious patient

5. colorful house plant

6. brilliant flashing neon sign

COMPOUND SUBJECTS AND COMPOUND PREDICATES

No punctuation is used with COMPOUND SUBJECTS and COMPOUND
PREDICATES (Lesson 2):

Compound subject:
$\overset{\text{NS}}{\textit{The job coordinator and}}$

$\overset{\text{NS}}{\textit{the company treasurer}}$ $\overset{\text{Vt}}{\text{reached}}$ $\overset{\text{Ndo}}{\text{an agreement.}}$

Compound predicate:
They $\overset{\text{Vt}\text{-----------------}}{\textit{had discussed}}$ $\overset{\text{Ndo}}{\textit{several proposals and}}$

$\overset{\text{Vt}}{\textit{finally found}}$ $\overset{\text{Ndo}}{\textit{·two}}$ $\overset{\text{Adj}}{\textit{acceptable.}}$

COMPOUND SENTENCES

NO punctuation is used if two independent clauses are short:

$\overset{\text{NS Vi}}{\text{He works}}$ $\overset{\text{C}}{\textit{and}}$
he plays.

_____ and _____.

A COMMA (,) is used before the coordinate conjunction (C) if the independent clauses are of average length:

The merchant opened the store at nine o'clock, *and* he waited for the customers.

_____ , and _____ .

A SEMICOLON (;) is used alone in place of the COMMA AND CONJUNCTION:

He bought merchandise for the store; he displayed it attractively.

_____ ; _____ .

A SEMICOLON AND CONJUNCTION are used if the independent clauses have commas within them or if they are long clauses:

The customers eagerly bought *scented candles, incense, and place mats; but* they could not buy dinnerware.

_____ _____ , _____ , _____ ; _____ .

By late afternoon the merchant had sold most of his stocks; (and) he was pleased by the empty display counters.

_____ ; and _____ .

EXERCISE 26B

Punctuate only those sentences which need either a comma or semicolon. Begin by labeling each subject-verb combination; then determine whether the sentence is simple or compound and whether punctuation is needed.

Example:	NS V NS V Vivian likes to travel she has no money.
	Vivian likes to *travel; she* has no money.

1. Martha and Bob own a house they have a new car.

2. Jim and his father flew to Reno last weekend.

3. The elm trees give shade and they are graceful and picturesque.

4. Mr. Copeland ordered a new car and cancelled the order the next day.

5. Jennifer can style hair artistically but she cannot comb and set wigs.

6. Mrs. Hicks can buy a mink coat or she can spend the money for a swimming pool.

7. Kevin and Bob dislike the chemistry teacher and refuse to attend class.

8. Bert does not like foreign films or variety shows.

EXERCISE 26C

Write three compound sentences.

1.

2.

3.

Write a sentence with a compound subject.

4.

Write a sentence with a compound predicate.

5.

CONJUNCTIVE ADVERBS

Another way to connect two independent clauses is by using connectors called CONJUNCTIVE
ADVERBS (C). Here is a partial list:

accordingly	furthermore	likewise	then
besides	however	moreover	still
consequently	indeed	namely	hence
as a result	in addition	therefore	similarly

These connectors ARE PRECEDED BY A SEMICOLON AND FOLLOWED BY A COMMA when they
join two independent clauses:

┌─Independent clause ──────────────────────────┐   ┌─c ────┐
│ He planned to hunt and fish the whole weekend │   │; *however,* │
└──┘   └───────┘

┌─Independent clause ──────────────────────────────────────┐
│ he had forgotten shells for the gun and hooks for the fishing line. │
└──┘

The short connectors like *then, still, hence* are preceded by a semicolon, but NO comma follows:

                     c

He locked the car; *then*
he walked to the dock.

These connectors are valuable because they help the writer achieve coherence within paragraphs. They may indicate contrast of one sentence with another, the addition of one idea to another, or the consequences of one action in relation to another; however, they should be used with discretion because they tend to make writing rigid and weighty. Sometimes substituting a dependent clause (see lesson on Subordination, Unit Six) or a phrase for one of the independent clauses gives variety to the writing style.

┌─Dependent clause ──────────────────────────────────────┐
│ Although he had planned to hunt and fish the whole weekend, │
└──┘

┌─Independent clause ──────────────────────────────────────┐
│ he had forgotten shells for the gun and hooks for the fishing line. │
└──┘

CONJUNCTIVE ADVERBS AS PARENTHETICAL OR TRANSITIONAL WORDS

These same words can appear at the beginning of a sentence or within a sentence. They provide transition from one idea to another.

┌─ONE independent clause ─────────────────┐
│ He had, *in addition,* no gasoline for the boat. │
└───┘

COMMAS enclose the conjunctive adverb within the sentence.

┌──┐
│ *Finally,* he decided to go home and read a book. │
└──┘

A COMMA follows the conjunctive adverb at the beginning of the sentence.

Finally, he decided to go home and read a book.

EXERCISE 26D

Combine the two simple sentences after each number into one compound sentence. Use the connector indicated in the parentheses and use appropriate punctuation. Make a slash line (/) through capital letters to indicate they are to be small.

Example: *(Conjunctive adverb)* The science club members planned to spend the weekend at the ocean; *consequently,* they had to gather equipment and supplies.

1. *(Coordinating conjunction)* The orchestra played several concerts last season. _____ For the first time in years they made money.

2. *(Conjunctive adverb)* He plans to attend medical school next fall. _____ He has to work this summer to make money for tuition.

3. *(Punctuation only)* Molly will give a dinner party. _____ Only her best friends will come.

4. *(Coordinating conjunction)* Ed and Wes traveled two hundred miles on their motorcycles. _____ They found the trip too hard to try again.

5. *(Conjunctive adverb)* Michael considered taking a postgraduate engineering course. _____ It seemed wise to take the position offered to him first.

6. *(Coordinate conjunction)* Tim likes to walk through the forest. _____ He always watches for rattlesnakes.

7. *(Coordinate conjunction)* Carol acknowledged him as her brother. _____ She would not allow him to reveal the fact to anyone.

8. *(Punctuation alone)* The housewife needed diversion from her daily work. _____ She volunteered her services to the hospital two days a week.

9. *(Conjunctive adverb)* Warren likes to fish, hunt, and hike. _____ He likes to read novels and science books.

10. *(Punctuation alone)* Sarah was devoted to her horse. _____ She decided to move her bed to the stable to be near him.

EXERCISE 26E

Punctuate the following sentences.

1. The men moreover wanted no part of Tom's plan.

2. They discussed every aspect however they could see no merit in the plan.

3. Finally Bob called Tom in for a conference.

4. Tom refused consequently the men cancelled further negotiations.

5. Tom as a result lost the contract.

WORDS OR WORD GROUPS IN A SERIES

COMMAS separate three or more words or word groups in a series, including the last word before *and:*

Tom bought a *hammer,*
            nails, and
            wood.

The three friends *grew up in the same town,*
                    went to school together, and
                    graduated from the same college.

COMMAS, or sometimes semicolons, separate THREE or more independent clauses within a sentence:

The ambulance took the patient to the hospital,
the nurses prepared him for surgery, and
the doctors operated immediately.

He went home the next week; he
relaxed a month; then he returned
to his job.

SEMICOLONS AND COMMAS are used with words in a series to separate the words and their modifiers or appositives (Lesson 28):

NS   Vt   Ndo   Ndo
Delegates chose *Bill Davies, president;*
                  Tom Nichols, treasurer;
                  Dwight Oaks, secretary.

Each fashion model had distinctive characteristics:
Karen Lang, tall and slender; Joan Field, short and
plump; Martie Wallace, average and curvaceous.

COMMAS are used after introductory words like *first, next, finally,* because they do not function as a part of the independent clause:

First, the newly elected president named an organizing committee; *second,* he set a meeting time; *third,* he sent out notices.

COLONS (:) are used after an INDEPENDENT CLAUSE to introduce a series:

NS   Vt   Ndo   Ndo   Ndo   Ndo
Mrs. Winter listed the supplies: *blankets, pillows, sheets.*

They may also be used after the phrases *the following* or *as follows:*

NS Vt   Ndo   Ndo   Ndo   Ndo
She ordered the following: *cots, chairs, and tables.*

A COLON may be used after an independent clause to introduce an explanation:

The new college graduate celebrated all night: she had just been accepted as a doctoral candidate.

DO NOT use a colon between the verb and its subject completer (Nsc) or direct object (Ndo):

       NS   Adj   LV   Nsc---------------------
NOT: *Those named *were: Bob, Terry, John.*

BUT: Those named *were Bob, Terry, John.*

EXERCISE 26F

Insert commas (,), semicolons (;), and colons (:) wherever they are needed in the following sentences. Begin by writing NS above each subject and V above each verb. Determine how many independent clauses the sentence contains. Identify words in a series and introductory words.

1. Bill cut the wood Tom carried the groceries Martha prepared to cook the meal.

2. The doctor ordered the following bandages splints antiseptic and adhesive tape.

3. Those chosen for the three roles were Susan Adams the older sister Thomas James the father Bernard Owens the uncle.

4. The alumni plan a yearly banquet a spring picnic and a fall theater party.

5. She needed thread needles fabric and a pattern.

6. First the author gathered ideas for a story.

7. Mrs. Jameson purchased furnishings for her husband's new office first she selected the carpeting and draperies next she ordered a large walnut desk and several chairs finally she hired an efficient gray-haired secretary.

8. The attic was filled with trunks clothes and furniture the basement could hold no more wood tools or canned food the house seemed ready to collapse under the weight of its furnishings.

9. The boy climbed on the chair opened the cupboard door and took the cookies.

lesson 27   **Sentence Errors**

When we misuse commas or omit punctuation between independent clauses in our college composi-tions and formal essays, we mislead our readers, who respond automatically to marks of punctuation much as they do to road signs. They know that they have come to the end of one idea when they see a period or semicolon, and they expect to begin a new idea following these marks. They know that single commas separate words or numbers, and commas used in pairs enclose word groups which give additional information to the main idea. In other kinds of writing—fiction, for example—they might find a comma between two independent clauses acceptable, particularly if the writer wants to give them the impression that the second thought follows quickly after the first, much as one thought might intrude on another. But until we become skillful and comfortable as writers, we probably should follow the accepted punc-tuation patterns or conventions.

Here are two kinds of problems we may have. Using Sentence Keys (Lesson 24), determine whether the word group contains one or two independent clauses and then use appropriate punctuation to elim-inate these kinds of problems:

RUN-ON

Two independent clauses written together with no connector or punctuation between them form a RUN-ON. The proper punctuation or a connector should be used.

NOT: *Nell packed the *suitcases Bill* washed the car.

BUT: Nell packed the *suitcases*   *, and*
          Bill washed the car.

OR: Nell packed the *suitcases;*
          Bill washed the car.

COMMA FAULT (CF) OR COMMA SPLICE (CS) OR RUN-ON

COMMA FAULT or COMMA SPLICE are names for this problem: two independent clauses written together with only a comma between them. (The term RUN-ON may be used for this problem as well as for the one in which no punctuation is used between two independent clauses.) To clarify the meaning and to eliminate the problem, add a conjunction after the comma, or use a semicolon instead of the comma.

NOT: *The painter finished the *mural,*   *he* cleaned the paint brushes with turpentine.

BUT: The painter finished the *mural*   *, and*
          he cleaned the brushes with turpentine.

OR: The painter finished the *mural   ;*
he cleaned the brushes with turpentine.

EXERCISE 27

If the punctuation in these sentences is acceptable,
write A in each blank. If punctuation should be
added or changed, write the mark of punctuation
and the word following it in the blank. Begin by
labeling each NS-V combination.

Example:

             NS   Vt
The young girl's fingers hit the typewriter keys in rapid *succession,*

  NS   Vi
her boyfriend smiled contentedly.   _____ ; her _____

   NS Vi
The kite danced in the *wind and then* suddenly plunged to the ground.   _____ A _____

1. The cross-country runners practiced every day for a month.   _____

2. The boys climbed the mountain, and the girls stayed in camp.   _____

3. The vacation soon ended consequently, the college group returned
   home.   _____

4. The artist painted portraits and made silver jewelry.   _____

5. The walls were white the room had no character.   _____

6. Time seemed to stand still until the start of her European trip.   _____

7. The trees stood black and bare, and the snow covered the ground.   _____

8. Without a doubt Owen Black had given his best performance in many
   years, as a result, the audience applauded wildly.   _____

9. The steel mills belched acrid smoke into the gray sky.   _____

10. Murray pruned all the fruit trees, and then he plowed the wheat field.   _____

IF YOU MISSED MORE THAN TWO sentences in
the first part, review Lesson 27, and then complete
the second part.

11. The bird found a worm, he ate it hungrily.   _____

12. The flowers were red, blue, and yellow, Marie picked a bouquet.   _____

13. The detective questioned the suspect for an hour then he released the man.   _____

14. The students chose five contestants; these were outstanding speakers.   _____

15. Trees on the side of the mountain were bent by the wind; those in the valley stood erect.   _____

16. Television offers entertainment in addition, it sometimes features educational programs.   _____

17. The statue was crusted with corrosion, it was over three hundred years old.   _____

18. The concrete hardened in twenty-four hours consequently, the patio was ready to use for the party.   _____

19. Yellow chrysanthemums were banked on the speaker's table small bouquets dotted the other table.   _____

20. Ivy covered the stone walls, millions of insects lived among the leaves.   _____

lesson 28   Coordination—Appositives

APPOSITIVES

APPOSITIVES are single nouns or noun phrases (a noun and its modifiers) placed beside another noun in the same sentence to explain it or rename it:

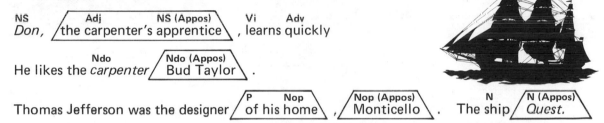

NS   Adj   NS (Appos)   Vi   Adv
Don, /the carpenter's apprentice\ , learns quickly

Ndo   Ndo (Appos)
He likes the *carpenter* / Bud Taylor \ .

               P   Nop   Nop (Appos)   N   N (Appos)
Thomas Jefferson was the designer / of his home \ , / Monticello \ .   The ship / *Quest.*

The appositive and the object complement (Noc) are not the same for this reason: an object complement (Noc) can rename only the direct object (Ndo) and appears after verbs like those listed in Lesson 22; the appositive, on the other hand, can rename the subject (NS), direct object (Ndo), indirect object (Nio), subject complement (Nsc), and the object of the preposition, as the examples above illustrate.

To determine whether a noun following a direct object (Ndo) is an object complement (Noc), use this test: Make the direct object the subject and change the verb form by using a form of the verb *to be* as an auxiliary. The object complement should follow the verb logically:

NS   Vt   Ndo   Noc
Steven Hill appointed Ralph Jennings supervisor.

NS   Noc
Ralph Jennings *was appointed* supervisor.

The following sentence with the appositive cannot be rewritten in the same way:

NS   Vt   Ndo   Ndo (Appos)
Steven Hill punched Ralph Jennings, the supervisor.

NOT: *Ralph Jennings was punched the supervisor.

Notice that the appositive has the same function as the noun with which it is in apposition. The two nouns are parallel (the same grammatical) constructions. The appositive can be a pronoun with the pronoun showing the correct form—NS, Ndo, Nio, or Nop.

           NS   NS   NS
The two *riveters,* / *Eric and he* \ , reported for duty today.

The supervisor hired the two *riveters,* /Ndo Ndo\ *Eric and him* \ .

Both /Nop\ *of them* \ , /Nop Nop\ *him and her* \ , like to drive sports cars.

FUNCTION OF APPOSITIVES

The appositive provides a way (or method) of combining two sentences if the subject (NS), direct object (Ndo), indirect object (Nio), or object of the preposition (Nop) in both sentences represent the same person or thing. Notice also that the verb in one of the sentences is a linking verb (LV), a form of the verb *be:*

NS
The artist was educated at Gibson Art Institute.

LV NS
His name is *Ben Caldwell.*

The sentences may be combined either way:

Punctuation needed: NS *Ben Caldwell,* /NS *the artist* \ , was educated at Gibson Art Institute.

No punctuation needed: NS *The artist* /NS *Ben Caldwell* \ was educated at Gibson Art
(See explanation   Institute.
below.)

PUNCTUATION WITH APPOSITIVES

Usually appositives are set off by commas. The exceptions are called restrictive appositives: appositives which are necessary to explain the noun named, as in the example above:

Ben Caldwell, the artist, . . .   (The appositive *the artist* adds extra
                                          information.)

The artist Ben Caldwell . . .   (The appositive *Ben Caldwell* provides
                                          required information.)

Hemingway's novel *A Farewell to Arms*   (The appositive *A Farewell to Arms*
was made into a movie.   provides required information.)

Hemingway's first war novel, *A Farewell* (The appositive *A Farewell to Arms* in
to Arms, was made into a movie.   this sentence provides additional
                                          information.)

The best way for determining punctuation of appositives is, therefore, to test whether or not the appositive must be given to identify the noun it follows. If so, it does not need punctuation. If the appositive merely adds extra information, it is set off with commas.

In the following sentences, because the Ndo's are general and require use of an appositive, no punctuation is needed.

Ndo   Ndo
Dickson telephoned the treasurer *Ted Hamilton.*

Ndo   Ndo
The professor discussed the word *chaos.*

EXERCISE 28

First, identify the noun in each sentence that represents the same person or thing. Second, make the noun and its modifiers in one sentence the appositive of the noun in the other sentence. (Remember, an appositive is a noun that renames another noun.) Third, use punctuation only if the appositive adds extra information.

Example: Rex is a *dog. Rex* does tricks.

Rex, a *dog,* does tricks.

OR

The *dog Rex* does tricks.

REMEMBER PUNCTUATION

1. Mrs. Martin teaches sculpturing.
   She is our next door neighbor.

2. Margaret has a boyfriend named Bob.
   He is the winner of several golf trophies.

3. Stanley Black is concertmaster of the orchestra. He plays a violin.
   .(Change *violin* to *violinist* and use in apposition with Stanley Black.)

4. Deep in the mountain is a huge cave.
   It had been a hiding place for rustlers.

5. The plane flew for several hours through a raging storm.
   It is a new supersonic jet.

6. The Blakes' house burned down last night.
   It was a Victorian mansion.

7. Ted's books lay on the desk.
   There were textbooks and novels.

8. The knight charged wildly through the castle.
   He was one of King Arthur's men.

9. The report was lively and informative.
   The speaker outlined ten ways to prevent water pollution.
   (Make *speaker* a possessive modifier of *report* (Lesson 14). Make one of the predicates the appositive of *report.*)

10. The high fence concealed the old house.
    The house had been the residence of an eccentric millionaire.

Now that you have completed the last exercise in this unit, YOU ARE READY FOR THE UNIT FOUR REVIEW.

If you need additional practice, complete the X-TRAS which follow.

UNIT FOUR

UNIT FOUR REVIEW will consist of exercises like the ones in Lessons 25 through 28. To prepare for the REVIEW, read the lessons and go back over the exercises. Note any corrections you have made; if you do not understand any part of the exercises thoroughly, ask your instructor for help. Make sure that you understand the directions for each exercise because those on the REVIEW will be very similar.

Complete these exercises only if you want additional practice before you attempt the UNIT FOUR REVIEW, Form A or Form B. Answers for these are in the Answer Key.

I. Complete the following by writing the kinds of sentences asked for and by answering the questions.

   1. Write a simple sentence. Label NS and V.

   2. Explain why it is a simple sentence.

   3. Write a compound sentence. Label NS and V.

   4. Explain why it is a compound sentence.

   5. Write a simple sentence with a compound subject. Underline the compound subject.

   6. Write a simple sentence with a compound predicate. Underline the compound predicate.

7. What mark of punctuation is used between two independent clauses when no connectors are used?

8. What words and punctuation can be used together between two independent clauses?

II. Insert necessary punctuation in these sentences. First, write V over each verb and NS over each subject. Second, identify each independent clause. Third, insert a conjunction and punctuation, or punctuation alone, between independent clauses. Fourth, use appropriate punctuation for coordinate adjectives and words in a series.

1. The San Francisco skyline looked golden in the setting sun soon darkness would settle over the city.

2. There are at least three activities one can take part in at Sky Ranch horseback riding hunting and fishing.

3. Boys usually like to learn to build kites paddle canoes dive for fish and collect rocks.

4. Rocky cliffs beautiful meadows filled with flowers tree-covered ridges and sandy beaches make up the area called Halley's Haven.

5. The flavor of bacon and ham comes from slow smoking over fragrant hickory fires the curing process takes a long time.

6. Convertible sofas are fascinating to open and close by day they provide comfortable seats and at night they become luxurious beds.

7. The enthusiastic crowd boarded the train with suitcases and skis ten hours later they faced bare brown soil at the top of the ski slope.

8. Gift packages of cheese cookies canned meats and cakes filled the postman's bag he shrugged his shoulders and lifted the bag slowly.

9. Cycle-shop owners have noticed a gradual increase in sales of all kinds of bicycles people use them for weekend touring for afternoon spins in the park and for daily exercising.

10. Bicycles seem to offer a way to control pollution for several reasons first they emit no gasses second they make no noise third they do not clog streets like automobiles fourth they require less parking space than automobiles.

unit FIVE

Pronouns and
Subject-Verb Agreement

lesson 29   Pronouns—Noun Substitutes

Pronouns, words that stand in place of nouns, are different from other words in the language because some of them, like the personal pronouns, undergo a complete spelling change for each of their forms. Personal pronouns have both singular and plural forms. Like some nouns, some of the personal pronouns show gender: *he, him, his,* masculine; *she, her, hers,* feminine; *it, its,* neuter. In addition, they represent three persons:

First Person is the person speaking.
Second Person is the person spoken to.
Third Person is the person spoken about.

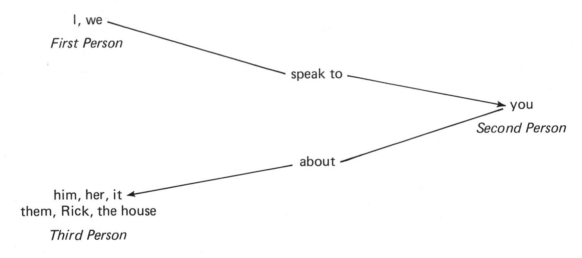

ALL NOUNS except words of direct address as in "John, come in" are *Third Person*, the person or thing spoken about.

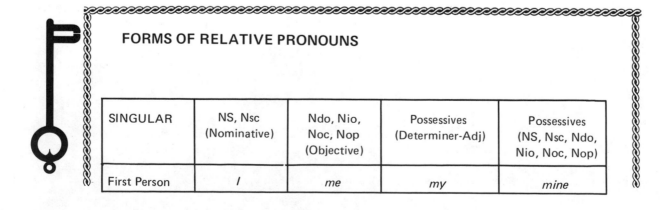

FORMS OF RELATIVE PRONOUNS

SINGULAR	NS, Nsc (Nominative)	Ndo, Nio, Noc, Nop (Objective)	Possessives (Determiner-Adj)	Possessives (NS, Nsc, Ndo, Nio, Noc, Nop)
First Person	*I*	*me*	*my*	*mine*

Second Person	you	you	your	yours
Third Person (M)	he	him	his	his
(F)	she	her	her	hers
(N)	it	it	its	its

PLURAL				
First Person	we	us	our	ours
Second Person	you	you	your	yours
Third Person	they	them	their	theirs

RELATIVE PRONOUNS				
First, second, or third persons M, F, or N	who	whom	whose	whose
	which	which		
	that	that		

FUNCTION AND POSITION

Pronouns serve as substitutes in sentence patterns for subject (NS), subject completer (Nsc), direct object (Ndo), indirect object (Nio), object complement (Noc), and object of the preposition (Nop):

<pre>
NS   Vt   Ndo   NS   Vt   Nio   Adj   Ndo
Barbara polished the silverware.   Terry gave Leslie theater tickets.
  ↑   ↑   ↑   ↑   ↑
She   polished   it.   He (she) gave him (her) them.
</pre>

(*Terry* and *Leslie* can be either masculine or feminine names.)

Some of us have trouble trying to decide whether to use *I* or *me* with the forms of the third person pronouns—*he/him, she/her, they/them.* As children we might have said, "Me and Bob won the race!" But instead of the adult listener sharing our excitement, he or she said firmly, "Don't put yourself before the other person. Say '*Bob and I.*'" Trying to please the adult, we attempted to eliminate a pattern that had probably developed when we learned to speak—when we learned to identify ourselves as *me*—"Me want a drink." Because we remember being told to use *I* so frequently, it may sound better to us even in sentences where the pronoun is used as the direct object or object of the preposition and should be *me*. The acceptable forms follow:

NOT: *Mr. Walker bought *Dan and I* ice skates.

             NS   Vt   Nio C Nio   Ndo
BUT: Mr. Walker bought *Dan and me* ice skates.

NOT: *All the class members *except Dale and I* attended the prom.

              NS   P   Nop C Nop
BUT: All the class members *except Dale and me* attended the prom.

NOT: *Dick and him* hitched a ride to town.

       NS   C NS Vt   Ndo Adv-------
BUT: *Dick and he* hitched a ride to town.

NOT: *Us sailors* crowded into the dance hall.

       NS NS
BUT: *We sailors* crowded into the dance hall.

As we label the sentence parts, we can determine which form of the pronoun belongs in each position. Another way to check is to read the sentence with the pronoun alone. It then becomes obvious which form should appear:

~~Dick and~~ *him* hitched a ride to town.   . . . *he* hitched a ride to town.

Mr. Walker bought ~~Dan and~~ *I* ice skates.   . . . bought . . . *me* ice skates.

The possessive forms listed in the third column of the chart function as determiners (Adj), and those listed in the fourth column function as noun substitutes:

NS   LV Adj Nsc
This is *my* book.

Adj NS Vi------------
My cap is missing.

Adj NS   LV Nsc
This book is *mine*.

NS   Vi---------- Adv
Mine is missing also.

RELATIVE PRONOUNS

The forms of the RELATIVE PRONOUN *(who, whom, whose)* are used to refer to human beings; they can refer to all three persons; they do not change to indicate sex of the antecedent.

I, who am your representative, cast your vote.

You whom we recognize may enter.

He who speaks is a friend.

The *woman whose* address we have will also help.

INTERROGATIVE PRONOUNS

If the words *who, that,* and *which,* or the word *what,* are used to ask questions, they are called INTERROGATIVE PRONOUNS. In such questions the interrogative pronoun substitutes as a noun:

NS LV   NS
Who is the winner?

Ndo   Vt NS Vt
What did he lose?

Ndo   Vt   NS   Vt
Whom did the people elect?

NS   LV Adj Nsc
Which is her home?

If the interrogative pronoun is immediately followed by a noun, however, it functions as a noun-determiner (Adj):

Adj   Ndo Vt NS Vt
What book did he lose?

Adj   NS   LV Adj Nsc
Which house is her home?

EXERCISE 29A

Underline the pronouns in the following sentences and label them NS, Nsc or Ndo, Nio, Nop, Adj, according to their function in the sentence. Begin by finding the verb first and labeling it with a V.

NS Vi---------   LV Adj NS
Example: Ken and I are engaged. Here is my ring.

1. Myron bought her a ticket for the play.

2. Carol gave them their keys.

3. Who attended your meeting?

4. They told us the details of the accident.

5. Are you the chairman of the dance committee?

6. Mary and she received their awards.

7. She sent him a part of mine.

8. A part of his belongs to them.

9. Mary likes his cooking.

10. I am I.

EXERCISE 29B

Underline the pronoun in each sentence. If the form is acceptable, write A in the blank. If it should be changed, write the revision in the blank.

Example: Wynn and me applied for the job.   _____I_____

1. Christine and him found a small snake on the sidewalk.   _____

2. The store manager gave John and I new work assignments.   _____

3. We organizers recruited new team members.   _____

4. Dale told that lie to Tim and I several times.   _____

5. Mary sent an announcement to every one but Karen and I.   _____

lesson 30   Third Person in Essays

College essays and research papers, many newspaper editorials, and many reports in professional journals use third-person point of view. In other words, the author does not address his audience as *you;* he does not refer directly to himself. There are, of course, exceptions, particularly in informal essays or specialized news columns. Acquire skill in using the third person for writing in which it is appropriate: essays, abstracts, and reports. Restrict use of first and second person to personal letters or informal, creative work.

Compare the difference in style of the following paragraphs. The first one is not acceptable for written college reports. The second one, somewhat informal, uses the advertising approach by addressing the reader. The third one, written entirely in third person, is appropriate for written reports.

1. Hitting the road is the best way to learn. You can read travel books, or you can listen to a teacher talk about other countries. Then you find out he never went anywhere. You can see right away that you know more than him because you traveled.

2. Traveling, seeing people as they are, is the best way to become educated. Compare this on-the-spot experience with reading travel books or sitting in a classroom listening to someone drone on and on about distant places he has read about, and you can see immediately that traveling is the best way to learn.

3. Traveling, seeing people as they are, is the best way to become educated. Students who have traveled in the United States and abroad know that this kind of learning is far superior to reading travel books or sitting in a classroom listening to someone drone on and on about distant places which he has never actually seen. The conclusion is obvious: traveling provides the best way to become educated, to know the world.

Even though it may be hard at first to use third person consistently, we can acquire the skill by continuing writing practice. It is best to set ideas down on paper and then to go back, strike out all the *you*'s, and substitute appropriate third person pronouns like *he* or *she*.

EXERCISE 30

Change the pronouns and nouns to the person and number indicated in parentheses. The numbers 1, 2, 3 represent first, second, and third person. *Sing.* is singular; *pl.* is plural. Rewrite the entire sentence. Use the list of personal pronouns in this lesson if you need help.

Example: *I* (3 pl.) called *John* (3 sing.) last night.

They called *him* last night.

1. I *(3 sing.)* bought myself *(3 sing.)* a pet python. *(3 sing.)*

2. You *(3 pl.)* liked yours *(1 pl.)* better than theirs. *(3 sing.)*

3. Jackson *(3 pl.)* called you *(1 sing.),* not us. *(2 sing.)*

4. They *(1 pl.)* scoured the hills for the girl. *(3 sing.)*

5. John *(3 sing.)* ordered steak for Michael and Mary. *(3 pl.)*

lesson 31 Indefinite Pronouns and Demonstrative Pronouns

INDEFINITE PRONOUNS

INDEFINITE PRONOUNS, as their name suggests, refer to a general group of people or things rather than to specific persons or things as do *you, it, they,* or *this* and *that.*

Singular			Plural	
all[†]	*everybody*	*nothing*	*all*[†]	*none*[†]
another	*everyone*	*one*	*any*[†]	*others*
any[†]	*everything*	*oneself*	*both*	*several*
anybody	*much*	*other*	*few*	*some*
anything	*neither*	*somebody*	*many*	
each	*nobody*	*some one*		
each one	*no one*	*something*		
either	*none*[†]	*such*		

FUNCTION AND POSITION

Indefinite pronouns function as the subject (NS), subject completer (Nsc), direct object (Ndo), indirect object (Nio), and object of the preposition (Nop):

NS
Everybody enjoyed the slides.

Nio
Dick gave *everyone* a sample.

Ndo
Martha had taken *some.*

Nop
Mark showed the slides /to *many*\ .

Some of the indefinite pronouns, like *another, anybody,* and *everyone,* form their possessives by adding *-'s:*

[†]Used with both singular and plural verbs, depending on context.

everyone's house   *anybody's* choice

Other pronouns can be substituted for most of the indefinite pronouns or can be used to refer back to them. We use forms of *he, she* and *it* as substitutes for the singular forms. In spoken language, especially, some people use plural forms, but for expository writing the singular forms are preferable:

NOT: **Each one* has *their* equipment.

BUT: *Each one* has *his* equipment.

For the plural forms of the indefinite pronoun we substitute forms of *they*:

Many have *their* equipment.

Many of the indefinite pronouns—like *all, neither, one*—may also function as determiners. (See Lesson 13.)

DEMONSTRATIVE PRONOUNS

Unlike the indefinite pronouns, the demonstrative pronouns refer to specific persons or things:

Singular	Plural
this	*these*
that[†]	*those*

FUNCTION AND POSITION

Demonstrative pronouns single out or point to someone or something. They can serve as subject (NS), subject completer (Nsc), direct object (Ndo), indirect object (Nio), or object of the preposition (Nop). When they precede a noun, they can function as a determiner (Adj) (Lesson 13):

Adj
These draperies will hang in the house.

NS
Those will be hung in the office.

Before the word *kind*, which is singular, use *this* or *that*, not *these* or *those*, which should be used only with plural nouns:

NOT: **Those kind* of clothes is durable.

BUT: *That kind* of clothes . . .

OR: *Those kinds* of clothes . . .

[†]*That* may also be a relative pronoun.

EXERCISE 31

Underline the indefinite pronouns. Determine
whether they are singular or plural. Sometimes
examining the verb and possessive in the sentence
or substituting *he* or *they* gives a clue. Then write
S for *singular* or P for *plural* in the blank at the
right.

Example: All of the actors received praise.   P

1. Each one will choose his partner. _____

2. Few take the time to write letters. _____

3. Several have given their help eagerly. _____

4. Anything is good enough for Jim. _____

5. One must make his own decision. _____

6. Joe told both of them the good news. _____

7. Mabel talks to anybody she meets. _____

8. Neither is really capable. _____

9. Sarah selected others. _____

10. Many have taken the cruise. _____

lesson 32 Pronoun Reference— Antecedents

PRONOUN ANTECEDENTS

Because pronouns are substitutes for nouns, they function in a sentence as nouns. But because pronouns, as substitutes, are general rather than specific in their meaning, each one must refer to the particular noun, called its ANTECEDENT, which PRECEDES the pronoun. The word ANTECEDENT means *going before*. Examine these sentences:

The *tiger* growled ferociously.
↑
ANTECEDENT

PRONOUN

The trainee brought *him* raw meat.

What the pronoun *him* represents is clear because it refers to the word *tiger* in the preceding sentence.

Suppose we substitute pronouns for all the nouns in the sentences:

ANTECEDENT?	ANTECEDENT?	ANTECEDENT?	ANTECEDENT?
↑	↑	↑	↑
PRONOUN	PRONOUN	PRONOUN	PRONOUN
↓	↓	↓	↓
He growled ferociously.	*He* brought	*him*	*it.*

Obviously we have created confusion. We create further problems for the reader if we use a pronoun to refer vaguely to a noun implied or understood but not stated:

NOT: *In the hospital *they* wear uniforms.

BUT: In the hospital *doctors and nurses* wear uniforms.

NOT: *Three cars were parked outside the building. *They* had come to settle the estate.

BUT: Three cars were parked outside the building. *The passengers* had come to settle the estate.

OR: Three cars were parked outside the building. They belonged to the people who had come to settle the estate.

When a pronoun can refer to more than one noun, no one but the writer can interpret the meaning:

NOT: *John Hawkins told his son *he* could not drive the family car until *he* repaired the flat tire.

BUT: John Hawkins told his son, "*You* will not be able to drive the family car until *you (or I)* repair the tire."

OR: John Hawkins' son could not drive the family car until *he (or his father)* repaired the tire.

NOT: *The students gave three instructors a list of classes *they* wanted. *They* spent hours deciding which ones *they* should suggest for the new schedule.

BUT: The students gave three instructors a list of classes *the students* wanted. *The students (or the instructors)* spent hours deciding which ones *the instructors (or the students)* should suggest for the new schedule.

-SELF, -SELVES

The following pronouns, often called reflexive pronouns since they "reflect" action back, should be used only when they have an antecedent in the *same* sentence:

	Singular	**Plural**
First Person	*myself*	*ourselves*
Second Person	*yourself*	*yourselves*
Third Person	*himself* NOT *hisself*	*themselves* NOT *theirselves*
	herself	
	itself	

The reflexive pronouns can be used to emphasize the person named, as well as refer back to the person named earlier in the sentence:

Emphasis: *Gordon himself* rescued the girl.

Reference: The *girl* had hurt *herself.*

DO NOT use these pronouns instead of personal pronouns in sentences like these:

NOT: *Ruth and *myself* went shopping. (*Myself* went shopping?)

BUT: Ruth and *I* went shopping. (*I* went shopping.)

NOT: *George invited Tom and *myself.* (*Myself* has no antecedent.)

BUT: George invited Tom and *me.*

WHOM, WHICH (QUESTIONS)

When *who* and *which* are used to ask questions, they probably will not have antecedents because the writer or speaker is seeking information.

Who made the arrangements?

Which is the better choice?

IT, THIS, WHICH

If we check to see whether each pronoun we use has an antecedent as we revise our papers, we will be able to strengthen the relationship of ideas and achieve coherence in paragraphs. Words like *it*, *this*, and *which* (when it introduces a dependent clause) need nouns to refer to.

Here is an example of faulty pronoun reference:

The girl had appendicitis.

ANTECEDENT?   ANTECEDENT?
↑   ↑
PRONOUN   PRONOUN
↓   ↓
It burst before the doctor removed *it.*

To what does *it* refer? It cannot refer to *appendicitis* which means *inflammation of the appendix.* It does not refer to *girl.* Therefore, *it* does not have an antecedent, a noun to which it can refer. One way to revise the second sentence is to substitute *appendix* for the first *it:*

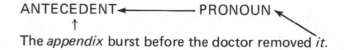

ANTECEDENT ◄──────── PRONOUN
↑
The *appendix* burst before the doctor removed *it.*

The words *this* and *which* should be used with care. Either can refer to a single noun antecedent or to a preceding idea expressed. However, unless the idea is clear and explicit, the sentence beginning with *this* or the clause beginning with *which* is vague. People who do not know how to summarize their ideas or how to choose a single word to summarize what they want to say often use *this* several times in a paragraph. The reader is at a loss to know exactly what the writer means.

NOT: *Susan collected clothing for the refugees. *This* made them appreciative.

NOT: *Susan collected clothing for the refugees, *which* made them appreciative.

BUT: Susan collected clothing for the refugees. *The donation* made them appreciative.

OR: Susan collected clothing for the refugees. *Her concern for them* made them appreciative.

NOT: *She liked helping people, *which* made everyone admire her.

BUT: She liked helping people; *as a result,* everyone admired her.

OR: She liked helping people; *her efforts and understanding* made everyone admire her.

EXERCISE 32A

Find the pronouns or possessives and their antecedents. Write the antecedent in the first blank and the pronoun or possessive in the second blank. If you have difficulty, first underline the pronoun. Then examine the nouns in the sentence. You should be able to substitute the noun for the pronoun.

	Antecedent	Pronoun
Example: *Bill* tore *his* coat sleeve. *Bill* tore *(Bill's)* coat sleeve.	Bill	his
1. Each bird has a spot of orange on its throat.		
2. Tom has to bring his own chair.		
3. The plants wilted, but they did not die.		
4. The yellow convertible had its tires slashed.		
5. Owen has his guitar here.		
6. Mary saw the play, and she liked it.		
7. The jury voted, and it reached a verdict.		
8. Cora and Bob bought themselves clothes.		
9. The team won its fifth trophy.		
10. The children want radios, but they will have to earn money first.		

EXERCISE 32B

Find the pronoun and its antecedent in each sentence or sentences. Write the antecedent in the
first blank and the pronoun in the second blank.
If you find a pronoun but not a definite antecedent, place an X in the first blank and think about
a possible revision.

	Antecedent	Pronoun
1. Steve called Virginia at home. She did not answer the telephone.	_____	_____
2. Who will drive Jim to the airport?	_____	_____
3. Mabel told him a story.	_____	_____
4. Dick had a hard life while he was in Africa.	_____	_____
5. I myself bought all the supplies.	_____	_____
0. Don collects antiques. Those are prize winners.	_____	_____
7. Harvey was very angry. This bothered Jane.	_____	_____
8. Joy and myself enjoy cotton candy.	_____	_____
9. They snatched Myrna's watch.	_____	_____
10. Bob studies engineering in order to become one.	_____	_____

IF YOU MISSED MORE THAN TWO SEN-
TENCES in the first part, review the information
on pronouns. Then complete sentences 11-20.

	Antecedent	Pronoun
11. Bill and Joe like to fish, but they need equipment.	_____	_____
12. They say the house is haunted.	_____	_____
13. When the committee completed business, it voted for adjournment.	_____	_____
14. Mark worked himself hard.	_____	_____
15. When Sue and Sandy shop, they spend all their money.	_____	_____

16. The hoodlums race cars on city streets. This cannot be permitted.
_____   _____

17. Meg is learning to speak French in order to visit it.
_____   _____

18. Bob gave Jon and myself souvenirs.
_____   _____

19. Barbara and Phil still date. It goes on and on.
_____   _____

20. Judy hates school. She sees no reason for going.
_____   _____

EXERCISE 32C

Rewrite these sentences by giving each pronoun an antecedent, a specific noun to which it can refer. Either insert nouns in place of vague pronouns, or rewrite the sentences completely.

Example: Martin's plane arrived in San Francisco at noon.
His next flight left fifteen minutes later. *This did not give him time to call Susan.*

REVISION: He did not have time to call Susan between planes.
OR: The brief stopover did not give him time to call Susan.

1. Donna told her mother that she needed new bed sheets.

2. When Bruce saw his brother, he knew they would fight and he would get hurt.

3. The salesmen discussed several selling techniques; they covered the advantages of the product they sold.

4. Nancy cleaned off the desk and covered the typewriter each night, which is what every secretary should do.

5. Louis decided to study German for two years because he plans to visit it after graduation.

6. Importers bought pottery in several countries, which made it necessary for them to rent more display space.

7. Two safety specialists were hired by the large car manufacturer to examine car design. They have a maximum speed of 150 miles per hour.

8. The map of the United States shows all the state capitals, which is good, but they did not include the main highways.

lesson 33 Pronoun-Antecedent Agreement

Every pronoun must have an antecedent, a noun to which the pronoun refers. In addition, the pronoun must also agree with its antecedent in person, number, and gender.

SINGULAR ANTECEDENTS	PLURAL ANTECEDENTS
Singular antecedents (noun or pronoun) are followed by singular pronouns and possessives of the appropriate gender:	Plural antecedents are followed by plural pronouns and possessives:
1. Singular noun and pronoun antecedents. ANTECEDENT ANTECEDENT *Mabel* is proud of her new *dress.* ↑ *She* made *it herself.* *Her, she, herself,* third person singular feminine pronouns, refer to *Mabel,* third person singular feminine noun. *It,* third person singular neuter pronoun, refers to *dress,* third person singular neuter pronoun.	1. Plural noun and pronoun antecedents. The *men* packed *their* cars for the trip. *They* planned to reach *their* camp by nightfall.
2. Indefinite pronoun antecedents. *Everyone* has *his* own face mask. NS P Nop Vt Adj *Each* of the divers brought *his* Adj Ndo *own gear.* NOTE: Even though *divers* is plural, the pronoun reference is singular because the subject of the sentence is *each,* a singular	2. Compound antecedents. *Michael and Robin* watch *their* weights constantly. *He and she* count *their* calories carefully.

pronoun. Notice that the prepositional phrase *of the divers* could be omitted in an article or paragraph on diving.

3. Collective nouns require singular pronouns for agreement if the noun designates the group working or acting as a unit:

The *committee* has announced *its* decision.

The *team* won *its* fifth game.

3. Collective nouns require plural pronouns for agreement if the noun designates a group working or acting as a number of individuals:

Why did the *committee* hesitate to discuss *their* problems?

The *team* ordered *their* meals before the game.

NOUN ANTECEDENTS

Pronouns which replace nouns should always be third person, either singular or plural, because all nouns, except nouns of direct address, are third person:

NOT: **Sarah* prefers making her clothes. *You* can design them for *yourself.*

BUT: Sarah prefers making her clothes. *She* can design them for *herself.*

NOT: **Americans* are world travelers; *we* have visited most of the globe.

BUT: *Americans* are world travelers; *they* have visited most of the globe.

EXERCISE 33

In the following sentences find the pronoun and its antecedent. Write the pronoun (or possessive) and its antecedent in the blanks at the right. If the pronoun does not agree with the antecedent, write the corrected form of the pronoun in the second blank.

	Antecedent	Pronoun
Example: *Everyone* has *their* luggage.	Everyone	his
1. One must guard their possessions.		
2. Each of the men has their own uniform.		
3. The children washed theirselves carefully.		

4. Everyone chose their partner.

5. Each piece of equipment has their own place in the tool room.

   _____   _____

6. When someone whistles, I do not look at them.

   _____   _____

7. Everyone who wants a sample of the material should send their name to Joe.

   _____   _____

8. Each nail in houses is needed to keep it from falling apart.

   _____   _____

9. Does Dick really manage the business hisself?

   _____   _____

10. The mothers of the boys agreed to take her turns providing refreshments.

    _____   _____

IF YOU HAVE MISSED TWO OR MORE
SENTENCES in the first part, review pronoun
antecedent information and then complete the
second part.

11. When a customer replies to the letter, send them a postcard.

    _____   _____

12. Dogs and cats like to have their ears stroked.

    _____   _____

13. The lonely man believes all his friends have left town.

    _____   _____

14. Everyone thinks they can have good roads without paying taxes.

    _____   _____

15. Nobody wants to rent their mountain cabin for the vacation.

    _____   _____

16. Neither boy wanted the manager to blame them for fighting.

    _____   _____

17. Why has everybody left their football equipment in the field?

    _____   _____

18. No one feels it is their fault.

    _____   _____

19. The good actor spends many hours rehearsing their part.   _____   _____

20. News reporters seem to enjoy their jobs.

    _____   _____

lesson 34 **Subject-Verb Agreement**

If a subject (NS) is singular, its verb should also be singular. If the subject is plural, its verb should be plural. When we talk about the present, we use Part 2 of the verb with singular nouns (Lesson 7). With plural nouns we use Part 1 (Lessons 4-10):

Singular noun and Part 2:
The *ship weighs* anchor.

Plural noun and Part 1:
The *ships weigh* anchor.

We use the auxiliary *has* with singular nouns and *have* with plural nouns:

Singular noun:
The ship *has* weighed anchor.

Plural noun:
The *ships have* weighed anchor.

With past tense verb forms we do not have to make a decision because the form is the same for both the singular and plural.

The *ship* sailed.
He ran.

The *ships* sailed.
They ran.

To decide whether a noun is singular or plural, substitute *he* (or *it*) or *they* for the noun and observe whether the verb is singular or plural:

Singular:
The *forest (it)* is dense.
Mathematics (it) is a challenging subject.
The *news (it)* sounds encouraging.

Plural:
The *deer (they)* are eating all the grass.
Suds (they) fill the washer.
Her new *clothes (they)* are attractive.

SOME OBSERVATIONS ABOUT SUBJECT-VERB AGREEMENT

SINGULAR VERBS

1. When a singular subject is followed by a modifying phrase containing a plural noun, the verb is singular:

NS   Adj————   Vi   Adv————
Neither / of the archaeology students \ *is digging* / for Indian pottery \ .

NS   Adj——   Vt   Ndo
Yet *one* / of the men \ *has found* a vase.

2. When qualifying phrases—*together with*, *along with*, *as well as*, *besides*, *in addition to*—follow the subject to introduce an addition, the verb remains singular if the subject is singular:

      NS   Vi

The *cat* together with its kittens *is looking* for food.

           NS   Vi

The *leading man* as well as the director and his assistant *lives* in the trailer.

3. When the subject is a singular indefinite pronoun like *everyone*, *each*, *somebody*, the verb is singular:

      NS   Vt   Ndo

Everyone likes praise.

4. When two or more singular subjects are joined by *or* or *nor*, the subject is singular because we consider each noun separately:

             NS   NS   LV Adj-c

Neither the sound *nor* the color *is* good.

           NS   NS   Vi Adv Vi

Either the pump *or* the motor *is* not functioning.

5. When the subject is a plural number used to indicate a unit, the verb is singular:

      NS--------------------------- LV   Adj   Nsc

Two hundred dollars is the rental fee.

PLURAL VERBS

When two or more singular subjects are connected by *and*, the verb is plural:

      NS--------------------------------------- Vt   Ndo

Soil, water, air, and sunshine promote plant growth.

SINGULAR OR PLURAL VERBS

1. When a sentence begins with the words *there* or *here*, the verb agrees with the subject which follows:

         LV Adj   NS   Adj-----------

There *are* several *snapshots* of Miranda. (snapshots are . . .)

         LV   Adj   NS

Here *is* my favorite *one.* (one is . . .)

The pronouns *any* and *none* may take singular or plural verbs:

      NS   Adj---------------------- LV Adj-c

Any of the contestants *are* eligible.

Any of the contestants *is* eligible.

      NS   LV   Nsc   Adv

None is the winner yet.

None are winners yet.

2. When two subjects, one singular and one plural, are joined by *either . . . or* or *neither . . . nor*, the verb agrees in number with the noun nearer to it:

> Neither Mrs. Holt nor her *sisters believe* the absurd story.

> Either the sisters or *Mrs. Holt intends* to talk with the neighborhood gossip.

3. When a collective noun representing a group, like *staff, congregation, band, team, tribe, jury, faculty, family, choir*, is considered to be acting as a unit, the verb is singular:

> **NS   Vt** --------------- **Ndo**
> The *band is practicing* today.

4. When members of the group are considered to be acting individually, the verb is plural:

> **NS   Vt** ----------------- **Ndo**
> The *band have forgotten* their instruments.

EXERCISE 34

In the following sentences find the subject and verb. Write the subject (NS) in the first blank and the verb in the second blank. If the form of the verb has to be changed to make it agree with the subject, write the preferred form in the second blank.

1. Each of the boys have his own bicycle.   _____   _____

2. Meg and Tom are to call the dean.   _____   _____

3. Bill or John is coming to sell tickets.   _____   _____

4. The group of students intend to travel by bus.   _____   _____

5. There is three people waiting for you.   _____   _____

6. Peggy and Anne conduct craft classes.   _____   _____

7. Neither the man nor his son has a job.   _____   _____

8. The surgeon as well as the interns attend staff meetings. _____   _____

9. *The Skyfighters* is a thrilling novel.   _____   _____

10. The team go to their homes after practice.   _____   _____

11. One of the representatives have not registered today. _____   _____

12. Ten dollars seems like a high price to pay.   _____   _____

13. None is present for roll call.   _____ _____

14. Old guns are his most valuable possession.   _____ _____

15. Is the boys ready for the trip?   _____ _____

16. Mathematics is a difficult subject for Steve.   _____ _____

17. Where is the treasures from the ocean?   _____ _____

18. Every one of the children need new shoes.   _____ _____

19. Here is Dick, Bob, and Joe.   _____ _____

20. There is many cars on the highway.   _____ _____

**IF YOU HAVE MISSED THREE OR MORE
SENTENCES** in the first part, review subject-verb
agreement and then continue with the second part.

21. The corners of the picture is bent.   _____ _____

22. You and John are my friends.   _____ _____

23. Either Robin or Jane is to choose the gift.   _____ _____

24. Each one of the men has a team shirt.   _____ _____

25. Any of these boys is ready for work.   _____ _____

26. The collection contains rare books from European
    libraries.   _____ _____

27. The jury announces its verdict today.   _____ _____

28. Each man has certain responsibilities.   _____ _____

29. The dog as well as the cats make noise all night.   _____ _____

30. Your news is the best this week.   _____ _____

31. Is twenty-five dollars enough for two tickets?   _____ _____

32. Is this the tape recorder from the biology lab?   _____ _____

33. Joe and Mike is always together.   _____ _____

34. None of the participants is here.   _____ _____

35. Here is art objects from his gallery.   _____ _____

36. There is the houses for rent.   _____   _____

37. The stars at night seem like jewels.   _____   _____

38. Neither Joe nor Ted nor Bill intends to help.   _____   _____

39. Nobody likes to be the last one in line.   _____   _____

40. The rooms of the house needs painting.   _____   _____

Now that you have completed the last exercise in this unit, YOU ARE READY FOR THE UNIT FIVE REVIEW.

If you need additional practice, complete the X-TRAS which follow.

UNIT FIVE

UNIT FIVE REVIEW will consist of exercises like the ones in Lessons 29 through 33. To prepare for the REVIEW, read the lessons and go back over the exercises. Note any corrections you have made; if you do not understand any part of the exercises thoroughly, ask your instructor for help. Make sure that you understand the directions for each exercise because those on the REVIEW will be very similar.

Complete these exercises only if you want additional practice before you attempt the UNIT FIVE REVIEW, Form A or Form B. Answers for these are in the Answer Key.

I.   Make the following sentences third person by using nouns or third person pronouns in place of first and second person pronouns. Make verbs agree with subject.

Most people like some form of entertainment. Some really enjoys musical performances like

concerts, opera, marching bands, or rock groups. You might choose plays or movies for an evening

out. Or we prefer to stay home to watch television. Still others want to take part in their entertainment. You participate in sports like golf, tennis, or swimming, or they may join discussion

groups or enroll in college classes. You can also enjoy hobbies as entertainment. Imaginative people

usually can find entertainment they enjoy to fill leisure hours.

II. Write the subject in the first blank and the
     verb in the second blank. If the verb does not
     agree with the subject, write the appropriate
     form of the verb in the second blank.

1. The boxes of cards is lying on the desk.   _____   _____

2. Ice, snow, and wind makes traveling dangerous.   _____   _____

3. The alumni is planning a summer picnic.   _____   _____

4. Neither the chair nor the desk are suitable.   _____   _____

5. Each of the pilots have flown five hundred hours.   _____   _____

6. There is five bids for the construction work.   _____   _____

7. Here is the shipping carton for the phonograph.   _____   _____

8. None of the equipment is usable.   _____   _____

9. The alumni plans a dinner-dance today.   _____   _____

10. Twenty dollars is too much for that wig.   _____   _____

III. Rewrite these sentences by giving each pro-
     noun an antecedent, a specific noun to which
     it can refer. Either insert nouns in place of
     vague pronouns, or rewrite the sentence
     completely.

1. Brian told Richard that he would get the new job.

2. Nancy told her sister about a new dress she would like.

3. Bill offered to lend Tom some money. This made Tom happy.

4. Everyone bet Barbara would marry Tom, not Ben, which made Tom nervous.

5. Mr. Hopkins had a toothache all night. The dentist pulled it the next day.

unit SIX

Subordination

lesson 35   Subordination— Adverbial Clauses

REVIEW OF SIMPLE AND COMPOUND SENTENCES

We have been writing SIMPLE SENTENCES and COMPOUND SENTENCES. We have identified the simple sentence as one INDEPENDENT CLAUSE that can stand alone as a sentence and the compound sentence as TWO INDEPENDENT CLAUSES joined by a comma (,) and conjunction (C) or only a semicolon (;). Two long clauses may be joined by a semicolon plus a conjunction.

Simple Sentence: Joe and Jane Hudson celebrated their fiftieth wedding anniversary this week.

Compound Sentence: Their daughter entertained them at dinner, and their son gave them a television set.

SUMMARY—PHRASES AND CLAUSES

PHRASE—a meaningful word group WITHOUT a subject and predicate

1. **Verb phrase**—auxiliary verbs + main verbs—functions as the verb in the sentence:

   Ted *should be coming* soon. He *will have arrived* before dinner.

2. **Prepositional phrase**—preposition (P) + object of preposition (Nop)—functions as adjective or adverb:

   NS Adj----------- Vi   Adv------------
   The top *of the tree* swayed *in the wind.*

3. **Appositive**—a noun and its modifiers—renames the subject (NS) or subject complement (Nsc) or direct object (Ndo) or object of the preposition (Nop):

   NS   NS   Vt   Ndo   P   Nop   Adj   Nop
   Malcolm, *a shepherd,* built a cabin on the island, *a desolate place.*

CLAUSE—a meaningful word group WITH a subject and predicate

1. **Independent clause**—subject and predicate—can stand alone as a sentence if the first word is capitalized and it ends with terminal punctuation (period, question mark, exclamation point):

   Adj   NS   Vt   Adj   Ndo
   The college sophomore wrote a book review.

2. **Dependent clause**—We will examine dependent clauses in detail below.

DEPENDENT CLAUSES

To show close relationship or dependency of one part of a sentence on the idea expressed in the independent clause, we can write it as a DEPENDENT CLAUSE, also called a SUBORDINATE CLAUSE.

Subordinate means "subject to" or "dependent upon"; coordinate means of equal rank.

FORM

Dependent clauses have a definite structure: THEY BEGIN WITH AN INTRODUCTORY WORD, CALLED A SUBORDINATOR (Sr), AND THEY HAVE A SUBJECT (S) AND PREDICATE (P):

Subordinator   S   P

Either the subject or predicate may be omitted in elliptical constructions. (See Elliptical Clauses in this lesson.)

USE IN THE COMPLEX SENTENCE

When clauses are dependent, they cannot stand alone; they are like dependent children that cling to their parents. They must be connected to an independent clause. This combination of an independent and a dependent clause makes a COMPLEX SENTENCE:

Independent clause

S   P

Dependent clause

Subordinator (Sr)   S   P

Dependent clause

Subordinator (Sr)   S   P

Compare this with the COMPOUND SENTENCE which consists of two independent clauses joined by a comma and conjunction or only a semicolon:

Independent clause   Independent clause

S   P   , C   S   P

COMPOUND-COMPLEX SENTENCE

A COMPOUND-COMPLEX SENTENCE consists of two independent clauses joined by a comma and conjunction or semicolon alone and at least one dependent clause. The following sentence contains two independent clauses, labeled *A* and *B*. The first independent clause is followed by one dependent clause, numbered 1. The second independent clause is followed by three dependent clauses, numbered 2, 3, and 4.

A
Adj   NS   Vt   Adj Ndo   P Nop   Adj
Some students find the study of history dull

1.
Sr   NS   Vt   Ndo----------------------   C   *B* NS   Vt Adv Vt
because they dislike remembering dates   , but   they do not realize

2.
Sr   NS   LV------ Adv   Adj-c
that history can be more fascinating

3.
Sr   Adj   NS
than a good novel (is)

4.
Sr   NS LV Adv-c-----------------
because it is about real people   .

ADVERBIAL CLAUSES

One kind of dependent clause is the ADVERBIAL CLAUSE, which can show the relationship of a series of events, such as time relationship in the sentence below. We can begin with three independent clauses:

| The party was over | ; | the guests had left | . | The hostess carried the dirty dishes |

to the kitchen   .

If we place the word *after* before *The party was over* and the word *and* following it, we can add *The guests had left* and create a compound adverbial dependent clause:

/After the party was over and the guests had left/ ,

Because a dependent clause can NOT stand alone, we can connect it to the third independent clause. This combination makes a COMPLEX SENTENCE:

/After the party was over and the guests had left/ ,   the hostess carried the dirty

dishes to the kitchen   .

An adverbial clause functions much like a single-word adverb. For instance, *afterwards* could be substituted for the clause "after the party was over."

INTRODUCTORY WORDS: SUBORDINATORS

Adverbial clauses, which can appear at the beginning, in the middle, or at the end of a sentence, begin with SUBORDINATORS (Sr) which usually have no other grammatical function within the clauses they introduce. They merely serve as a link between the dependent clause and independent clause. Here is a partial list:

after[†]	because	provided	though	where
although	before[†]	provided that	until[†]	wherever
as[†]	how	since[†]	whatever	whether
as if	if	so that	when	while
as long as	in order that	than	whenever	why
as . . . as	even though			unless

He came *because he wanted the mechanical engineer's assistance.*

When the bell rang, the store closed.

She tried, *although she lacked the physical strength,* to carry the television set.

[†]SUBORDINATOR OR PREPOSITION?

The following words can function as SUBORDINATORS (Sr), but they can also function as PREPOSITIONS (P):

as   before   after   since   until

To determine whether they are introducing a phrase or a clause, begin by labeling sentence parts. Write V above each verb, NS above each subject, and identify the subordinator or preposition:

1. Bret has not been happy *since he returned home.*   /CLAUSE/
   (NS V   V   Sr   NS V)

2. Bret has not been happy *since his accident.*   /PHRASE\
   (NS V   V   P   Nop)

In the first sentence a subject and verb—*he returned*—follow *since;* therefore, the word group is a dependent clause and *since* functions as a subordinator. In the second sentence, only a noun—*accident*—follows *since;* therefore, the word group is a phrase, and *since* functions as a preposition.

IDENTIFYING SUBORDINATORS, PREPOSITIONS, and CONJUNCTIONS

Perhaps the easiest way to identify SUBORDINATORS (Sr), PREPOSITIONS (P), and CONJUNCTIONS (C) is to learn them as individual items, even memorize them. Another way is to identify them by their function in sentences; they act as connectors between words and word groups. A third way is to look them up in the dictionary. Still another way is to be aware that these words are STRUCTURE WORDS which ALWAYS HAVE THE SAME FORM AND SPELLING. They do NOT take prefixes or suffixes or undergo spelling changes like nouns, pronouns, verbs, adjectives, and adverbs.

FUNCTION OF ADVERBIAL CLAUSES

Adverbial clauses function as adverbs and modify sentences, adjectives, verbs, and other adverbs. They answer questions *when*, *where*, *why*, and *how* in sentence patterns:

When: /*When he arrived*/ , the others left.

Why: He came /*because he was needed*/ .

How: He worked /*as if he could go on forever*/ .

Where: He continued /*where the others had left off*/ .

PUNCTUATION WITH ADVERBIAL CLAUSES

Adverbial clauses at the beginning of the sentence are followed by a comma:

When you talk with him, explain your responsibilities.
Because he is your friend, he should be able to understand.

Adverbial clauses within an independent clause are enclosed in commas:

He understood, *because he had studied it several hours,* the significance of the report.

Adverbial clauses at the end of the sentence usually are not preceded by a comma:

He agreed with the report *although it suggested many changes.*

ELLIPTICAL CLAUSES

When words are omitted from a clause, even though they are understood, the clause is INCOMPLETE or ELLIPTICAL. We use these constructions to avoid unnecessary repetition:

Complete	Elliptical
NS LV Adj Adv---------------- He is taller *than I am tall.*	He is taller *than I.*
NS LV Sr Adj Adv-------------- He is as tall *as I am tall.*	He is as tall *as I.*
NS Vt Ndo Adj Adv--------------------- He knows her better *than he knows me.*	He knows her better *than me.*
Sr NS Vi------------- NS Vi *When I am traveling,* I drive.	*When traveling,* I drive.
Sr NS LV Adv Vt Ndo *While you are there,* buy a hat.	*While there,* buy a hat.

EXERCISE 35A

Underline each adverbial clause in these sentences.
If there is no adverbial clause, place an X in the
blank. Begin by writing V above each verb and NS
above each subject. Determine whether the NS-V
combination is an adverbial clause by finding a
subordinator before it.

        P   **Nop NS Vi**

Example: Since his European trip Bob thinks only about traveling.   __X__

        Sr   NS Vi   NS Vt   Ndo

<u>After Bob returned home</u>, he planned another European trip.   _____

1. After their arrival they found a house to rent.   _____

2. Although Bob was engaged to Nan, he really loved her sister.   _____

3. The free-form statue in the park arouses a lot of comment.   _____

4. While waiting for the test results, he paced back and forth nervously.   _____

5. On the way back to town he had a flat tire.   _____

6. The plaintive wail of the flute haunted him for several months.   _____

7. The toolbox stayed where he had placed it two years before.   _____

8. The town's one taxi gave service only in the daytime.   _____

9. Because he likes his job, he goes to the office early.   _____

10. The swimmer floated on his back while he enjoyed the gentle rocking motion
    of the waves.   _____

IF YOU HAVE MISSED TWO OR MORE OF THE
SENTENCES in the first part, review the lesson on
adverbial clauses and complete the second part.

11. Until he agrees to cooperate, I cannot help him.   _____

12. When the truck had a flat tire, the hijackers abandoned their loot.   _____

13. As the plane descended, he saw the city below.   _____

14. The helicopter frightened the horses when it landed on the racetrack.   _____

15. The detective arrested the shoplifter when he tried to leave the store.   _____

16. After the evening meeting the faculty greeted the new president.   _____

17. Will you please call me when the shipment arrives?   _____

18. After he had talked for five hours, he had laryngitis.   _____

19. He took the reading class because he wanted to improve his comprehension.   _____

20. Her dark brown eyes opened wide as she watched the horror movie.   _____

EXERCISE 35B

In the following sentences the italicized group of
words may be a phrase, a dependent clause, or an
independent clause. In the blank write P for phrase,
D for dependent clause, and I for independent
clause. Begin by writing V above each verb. Then
write NS above each subject. Next, determine
whether the italicized word groups are phrases
or clauses.

1. *After Jody gets his degree,* he will travel around the world.   _____

2. *Since his arrival home,* he has done nothing but sleep.   _____

3. *Call me* when your father comes home.   _____

4. *Has he offered his assistance?*   _____

5. Why do you torment yourself *with such thoughts?*   _____

6. The dog looked *under the rock* for the lizard.   _____

7. Ask George to stop *at Mike's house.*   _____

8. *After he had been late once,* he reset his watch.   _____

9. Why does he buy the paper *when it is a day old?*   _____

10. Surely you *will be given* an opportunity to try your plan.   _____

IF YOU HAVE MISSED TWO OR MORE
SENTENCES, review lessons on phrases and
clauses, and then complete the second part.

11. Open the windows wide, and *let fresh air in.*   _____

12. *Before he accepted the challenge,* he trained for two weeks.   _____

13. *Even though he was prepared,* he did not win.   _____

14. *In times like these,* one must watch his step.   _____

15. I did not sleep last night *because of all the noise.*   _____

16. Wait here *until I can help you.*   _____

17. *He is excited about his new job,* and he is ready to work.   _____

18. *As he closed the car door,* he caught his jacket.   _____

19. The man thanked his rescuers *for their help.*   _____

20. Will you please send Meg *to Europe* next summer?   _____

EXERCISE 35C

Combine the following sentences by making one
an independent clause and the other an adverbial
clause. Place a subordinator before one of the sentences to make it a dependent clause. Make the
other sentence an independent clause.

> **Example:** I go to an art museum. I enjoy looking at medieval armor.
>
> REVISION: *When* I go to an art museum, I enjoy looking at medieval armor.
>
> I go to an art museum *because* I enjoy looking at medieval armor.

1. Max Thompson donated five hundred dollars. He could have used the money himself.

2. He stayed here for the convention. He should be in Boston now.

3. They had driven all night. They finally found a motel with a vacancy.

4. He enjoys writing stories. He has never sold one.

5. Jack has chosen medicine for his profession. He faces many years of arduous study and work.

6. The sun rose over the horizon. John felt he could hardly face the day.

7. He decided to buy the new car. He talked with several friends.

8. The prom was over. Everyone went to the drive-in.

9. Bill waited for Cora outside the school. He saw two cars collide.

10. The wind slammed the door closed. The shivering girl could not get back into the house without her key.

lesson 36   Subordination—Comparison

One way to make an *unknown* understandable is to compare it with a *known*. The person making the comparison must choose objects or ideas that are similar in order to make the comparison logical and understandable and parallel. Comparison is accomplished by using appropriate forms of adjectives and adverbs.

COMPARISON OF ADJECTIVES AND ADVERBS

For most adjectives and adverbs, there are three forms, or degrees, for comparison:

	Positive	**Comparative**	**Superlative**
Adjective	*smooth*	*smoother*	*smoothest*
Adverb	*smoothly*	*more smoothly*	*most smoothly*

SOME IRREGULAR ADJECTIVES AND ADVERBS

	Positive	**Comparative**	**Superlative**
Adjective	*good*	*better*	*best*
	bad	*worse*	*worst*
	(equal)	*less*	*least*
Adverb	*well*	*better*	*best*
	badly	*worse*	*worst*
	(equally)	*less*	*least*
	far	*farther*	*farthest*
	far	*further*	*furthest*

NOTE: *Farther* and *farthest* refer to measurable distances.
      Further and *furthest* refer to degree, time, or quantity.

He traveled *farther* than I did.

Think *further* about the problem.

Use *as far as* or *the farthest* instead of *all the farther*.

New York is *the farthest* (or *as far as*) the musicians can travel for five hundred dollars.

Most ADJECTIVES of one or two syllables, like the ones given, form the comparative and superlative degrees by adding *-er* and *-est* to the first form. However, adjectives of more than two syllables usually show comparison by using the words *more* and *most: more fortunate, most fortunate.* Some adjectives may be compared either way: *handsomer* and *handsomest,* or *more handsome* and *most handsome.* Most ADVERBS use the words *more* or *most* to form the comparative and superlative degrees.

USE OF COMPARISON

POSITIVE DEGREE

POSITIVE DEGREE of the adjective may be used with the subordinator (Sr) *as . . . as* before an adverbial clause which modifies the adjective and also completes the comparison (See Elliptical Clauses, Lesson 35):

```
     Adj------------------ NS  LV Sr Adj   Sr  Adj NS      LV Adj
The twelve-year-old boy is AS TALL AS his father (is tall).
```

```
 Adv            NS     LV Adv    Sr  Adj       Sr   NS    LV Adj
Today the ocean is almost AS SMOOTH AS a lake (is smooth).
```

COMPARATIVE DEGREE

COMPARATIVE DEGREE of the adjective or adverb shows comparison of TWO persons or things. The comparative adjective may precede a noun and modify it:

```
  Adj     Adj       NS  LV Adj-c-----------
John's YOUNGER son is ten years old. (John has two sons.)
```

The comparative adjective may follow a linking verb (LV); it is modified by an adverbial clause beginning with *than* which completes the comparison:

```
 NS   LV Adj-c      Sr    Adj NS      LV Adj-c
Bob is TALLER than his father (is tall).
```

The comparative adverb may modify a verb, and it may be modified by an adverbial clause beginning with *than:*

```
 NS  Vi       Adv     Adv              Adv  Sr   NS Vi        Adv
Dale worked MORE ENERGETICALLY today than (he worked) yesterday.
```

The PRONOUN FOLLOWING *THAN* may be the SUBJECT or the DIRECT OBJECT in the elliptical clause, depending on the meaning the writer wishes to convey:

<pre>
     NS   Vt   Ndo Adv   Sr   Ndo   Sr   NS Vt   Ndo
</pre>
The poodle likes Jim *BETTER than me. (. . . than he likes me.)*

<pre>
    NS   LV Adv   Adj-c   Sr NS   Sr   NS LV Adj-c
</pre>
Susan is *MORE CONSIDERATE than she. (. . . than she is considerate.)*

SUPERLATIVE DEGREE

SUPERLATIVE DEGREE of the adjective and adverb shows comparison among THREE or more persons or things:

<pre>
          Adj   NS LV   Adj   Nsc
</pre>
The ocean liner is the *LARGEST* (ship) of the ships in the harbor.

<pre>
    NS Vi   Adv   Adv
</pre>
She dances the *MOST GRACEFULLY* of the whole troupe.

John's *YOUNGEST* son is ten years old. (John has three or more sons.)

COMPLETE COMPARISONS

Comparison made with comparative and superlative degrees must show completion of the comparison made by naming the person or thing to which the first item is being compared:

NOT: *Who could be *more wonderful?*

BUT: Who could be *more wonderful than my father?*

NOT: *This bread is *so good.*

BUT: This bread is *so good that I want more.*

ABSOLUTES

Certain adjectives and adverbs are absolute and cannot be compared. If, for example, something is *empty*, it cannot be *emptier* or *less empty* than something else. Here are other absolutes:

Adjectives: perfect, circular, straight, unique, dead, empty

Adverbs: uniquely, perfectly

If compared, the accepted form is *more nearly (perfect), most nearly (perfect).*

PARALLEL STRUCTURE IN COMPARISONS

In making a comparison, one should choose objects, ideas, or qualities which are similar to make the comparison valid. In addition, the comparison should be made in a balanced or parallel construction:

NOT: *The pink rose is more attractive *than red.*

(*Rose* is a noun and *red* is an adjective. The comparison must be made between two roses or two colors.)

BUT: The pink *rose* is more attractive *than the red one.*

NOT: *Mary's purse is much larger *than Jane.*

(Comparison here is between *purse* and *Jane.)*

BUT: Mary's purse is much larger *than Jane's* (or *Jane's purse*).

NOT: *Mary is a better accountant than *any employee in the office.*

(Mary is also *an employee in the office.* She cannot be compared with herself and should be excluded from the comparison.)

BUT: Mary is a better accountant than *any other employee in the office.*

Comparison among three persons or items must be made clear by completing the comparison:

NOT: *Mary liked Ruth better *than Molly.*

(This can be interpreted two ways.)

BUT: Mary liked Ruth better *than she liked Molly.*

OR: Mary liked Ruth better *than Molly did.*

EXERCISE 36

Rewrite the following sentences to make comparisons logical. Correct any errors in usage. Add, omit, or change words wherever necessary.

1. Dick is the tallest of my two sons.

2. Mrs. Smith hates weddings more than her husband.

3. A light blue dress is more becoming than yellow.

4. Martha says that her frog can jump farther.

5. Jim is a more powerful weight lifter than any man in the neighborhood.

6. Jerry already weighs more than him.

7. Brad's camping equipment is more complete than Tom.

8. Mr. Hollis says that Meg is the better typist of the four girls in the office.

9. I do believe that this new arm chair is comfortable than the old one.

10. Jim likes Paul better than Bob.

11. Students in large classes often get lower grades.

12. An intern's monthly salary is usually lower than an unskilled worker.

13. Riding comfort in a modern car is far superior to a stagecoach.

14. Sacramento is closer to Auburn than San Francisco.

15. The loyalty of a dog to his master is unlike any animal.

16. The physical endurance of a mountain climber is probably greater than an executive sitting at his desk all day.

17. Does a pound of potatoes weigh more than feathers?

18. Storms in Florida seem more violent than Ohio or Indiana.

19. The Empire State Building is so tall.

20. This restaurant serves delicious food but it is much less expensive.

lesson 37 Subordination— Adjective Clauses

The ADJECTIVE CLAUSE, a dependent word group with subject and predicate, is another means of combining two sentences by making one idea dependent upon another:

Sentence: George constantly watches *Emily* .

Sentence: *Emily* lives next door .

Independent Clause: George constantly watches *Emily*

Dependent Clause: /who lives next door/ .

The word *who*, a relative pronoun, is substituted in the second sentence for *Emily*.

USING ADJECTIVE CLAUSES IN SENTENCES

Adjective clauses begin with subordinators (Sr) which may be RELATIVE PRONOUNS. These function as subject (NS), direct object (Ndo), object of the preposition (Nop), or Adj in the clauses:

	NS	Ndo, Nop	Adj
Refer to persons:	who	whom	whose
Refer to animals, objects, things:	which	which	
Refer to persons, animals, objects, things:	that	that	

```
       NS    Vt            Ndo  ┌─Adj─┐
                               / Ndo NS    Vt----------------
Susan enjoyed the salad / that Joyce had prepared/ .
```

The word *that* refers to *salad*. The word *salad* can be used in place of *that* in writing an independent clause:

```
NS    Vt---------------    Ndo
```
Joyce had prepared a salad.

In the sentence above *which* could be used rather than *that*. The choice is left to the writer, although some people feel the word *that* is preferable.

If the word *that* serves in the dependent clause as the direct object (Ndo) or the object of the preposition (Nop), it is sometimes omitted, but the word group is still an adjective clause and the word *that* understood refers to the noun preceding it:

Susan enjoyed the salad *Joyce had prepared.*

The house /(that) Joyce bought near the river/ is one hundred years old.

The word *whom* may also be omitted, but it is understood and refers to the noun preceding it:

```
NS                    NS     Nop    NS    Vt      Ndo   P        LV   Adj   Nsc
```
Blake Thomas, the realtor /(whom) Susan bought the house from,/ was a close friend.

In the next example the word *who* refers to *Susan.*

```
NS        NS   Vi   Adv       Vt        Adj    Ndo
```
Susan, /who lives alone/, appreciated Joyce's invitation.

The name *Susan* can be used in place of *who* in writing an independent clause:

```
NS    Vi   Adv
```
Susan lives alone.

The following subordinators (Sr) function only as introductory words. They do not refer to a preceding noun, but the whole clause modifies the noun before it:

where   *wherever*   *after*   *when*

```
NS    Vt    Ndo          NS  Vi
```
Susan likes the apartment /where she lives/ .

EXERCISE 37A

If the pronouns *who, which,* and *that* are wrongly used in the following sentences, underline the pronoun to be replaced and write the preferred form in the blank. If no change is necessary, write C in the blank.

Example: The man *which told the story* is an auto mechanic.   ___who (that)___

1. The sailor which arrived last night is at the front door.   _____

2. The dog who barks at us every day is now wearing a muzzle.   _____

3. Max told me about the horse that won the race.   _____

4. The woman that owns the dress shop will go to Europe next month.   _____

5. During the night the flowers that grow near my bedroom window were trampled.   _____

6. The man which made that statement is wrong.   _____

7. Knights who wore armor must have been a great burden to their horses.   _____

8. The logs that burned brightly in the fireplace filled the air with pine fragrance.   _____

9. The young girl which fell off the bicycle broke her arm.   _____

10. Do you know why the woman which lives across the street watches this house?   _____

FUNCTION AND POSITION IN THE SENTENCE

Because the adjective clause is a modifier, it should be as close as possible to the noun it modifies for clarity:

NOT: *Mr. Brian listened closely to the young men *who wears a hearing aid.*

BUT: Mr. Brian, *who wears a hearing aid,* listened closely to the young men.

PRONOUN-ANTECEDENT AGREEMENT

Because the pronouns *who, which,* and *that* serve as substitutes for nouns, the noun they could replace —and that they refer to—should be stated:

Darlene drove her mother's car, *which* is painted light pink. (*Which* replaces the word *car.*)

NOT: *Darlene did not come home last night, *which* made her parents worry. (There is no noun that *which* can replace.)

BUT: Darlene worried her parents *because she did not come home last night.* (The adverbial clause shows the reason why.)

EXERCISE 37B

Underline the adjective clause in each sentence,
and write the word it modifies in the blank. If
there is no adjective clause, place an X in the blank.
Begin by writing V above each verb and NS above
each subject. Identify the adjective clause by locat-
ing the relative pronoun, a word like *who, which,*
and *that.* Remember, if the relative pronoun serves
as direct object in the dependent clause, it may be
omitted.

                   NS   NS Vi Vt   Ndo
Example: The knight *who won* received a prize.   ___knight___

1. The radio that he bought two months ago will not operate.   _____

2. The little girl who was lost in the department store cried hysterically.   _____

3. He waited for the letter that would bring the contract.   _____

4. He directed his attack against those whom he despised.   _____

5. The puppy Sue showed at school was her birthday present.   _____

6. After the manager ordered the new furniture, he had the office painted
    and carpeted.   _____

7. The small brown dog chased the car which turned the corner.   _____

8. After the heavy rains the fields that had been brown turned green.   _____

9. The unusual jewel collection intrigued those who viewed it.   _____

10. The young man could not understand his fiancée because she cried at their
    engagement party.   _____

EXERCISE 37C

These sentences contain dependent clauses that
may be misplaced adjective clauses or that may

not have antecedents (nouns preceding them) to
which they can refer. Begin by underlining the
dependent clause. Then draw a line to the word
that should be its antecedent, or insert a noun
which can be an antecedent, or rewrite the sentence completely.

1. Many men dislike mowing lawns, which irritates their wives.

2. The promotion came after many years which he had earned.

3. The trip to Australia cost much more than Marie had, which disappointed her.

4. The *No Smoking* signs were fluorescent red that had been placed on the classroom walls.

5. The news magazine lay on the living room table that contained depressing reports.

PUNCTUATION WITH ADJECTIVE CLAUSES

Adjective clauses that give additional information about the nouns or pronouns they modify are called
nonrestrictive modifiers. They are set off by commas:

Margaret owns a mink stole, *which she wears frequently.*

Margaret's mink stole is a specific part of her wardrobe. *Which she wears frequently* gives additional
information. It could be omitted, and the sentence would still be meaningful. Or it could be added as a
separate sentence since it is not needed to identify the stole being discussed.

In the next example, *Hugh Barton* is the name of a particular person. The adjective clause *who services
x-ray machines in three counties,* gives additional information about him. It is nonrestrictive.

Hugh Barton, *who services x-ray machines in three counties,* received his pilot's license
last week.

In the following sentence the same clause *who services x-ray machines in three counties* helps to
identify Hugh Barton if there happen to be two men with the same name.

The Hugh Barton *who services x-ray machines in three counties* will land at the airport in an hour.

DO NOT set off with commas adjective clauses that identify the noun or pronoun they modify. These clauses are needed to identify a particular one (or ones) among a group; they are restrictive modifiers.

```
        NS      Vt      Ndo    Adj----------------------------------
The Walkers own the cabin *that stands near the stream.*

     NS   Vt       Ndo   Adj-------------------------------
They know the place *where the fishing is good.*

        NS        Vt   Ndo    Adv--------- Adj-------------------------------------------
The policemen gave tickets to all cars *that were parked on Lincoln Street.*
```

If either of the adjective clauses were omitted, the remaining sentences would not give adequate information about *the cabin, the place,* or *the ticketed cars.* Compare these modifiers and their relationships to these sentences:

```
        NS      Adj---------------------       Vt       Ndo
The math teacher, *who lives near us,* really knows his subject.

        NS      Adj---------------------       Vt       Ndo
The math teacher *who lives near us* really knows his subject (but the one
Adj-------------------------------------
*who commutes from Dixon* does not).
```

EXERCISE 37D

Some of the following adjective clauses are needed to identify the noun they modify. Others merely give additional information about the noun. Enclose in commas ONLY THOSE MODIFIERS WHICH GIVE ADDITIONAL INFORMATION.

Example: Ted Wilson, who wrote *Tides,* autographed his book.

1. Jeff Brown who owns the big yacht is the new bank president.

2. The dog that has brown spots caught a mouse.

3. Tod bought the car that Mr. Hansen had owned.

4. The teacher read stories that his students had written.

5. Janet Oakes who has acted here before will appear in a new play.

6. The course which he feared most was psychology.

7. Warren Hill who owns the bakery is a candidate for city councilman.

8. The weatherman who forecast sunshine for today got his shoes very muddy at the picnic.

9. The guest of honor who was Bennett Evans fell asleep while the chairman read the hour-long tribute.

10. Blake fell off the roof which covers the patio.

COMPARISON OF ADVERBIAL AND ADJECTIVE CLAUSES

Both adverbial clauses and adjective clauses are ADDITIONS to basic sentence patterns; they serve to restrict or qualify or else to modify by giving additional information. As a result, the word group remaining, if the dependent clauses are omitted, is an independent clause that can stand alone. Notice, however, that some dependent clauses are needed (they are restrictive) and others give additional information (they are nonrestrictive):

Needed: The compartment / *that contains the oxygen mask* / is / *above the seat* .

Additional: The oxygen mask, / *which all commercial airplanes must have,*

drops automatically / *in an emergency* .

Additional: The stewardess demonstrates the use / *of the mask*

/ *before the plane takes off* / .

The ADVERBIAL CLAUSE begins with an introductory word—a subordinator (Sr)—which connects the dependent clause to the independent clause, but it does not function within the clause:

　　Sr　　　NS　Vi　Adv
. . . *before* the plane takes off.

If the subordinator is omitted, the remaining word group is an independent clause which can function as a simple sentence:

　　NS　Vi　Adv
The plane takes off.

The ADJECTIVE CLAUSE begins with a relative pronoun like *who, which,* and *that,* which functions as subject (NS), direct object (Ndo), or object of the preposition (Nop) in a dependent clause:

　　NS　Vt　　　　Ndo
. . . *that* contains the oxygen mask.

If the relative pronoun substitutes for the direct object (Ndo) or object of the preposition (Nop), it may be omitted.

The stewardess always replaces the mask

Ndo   NS Vi   Adv------------------------------
(that) she uses for the demonstration.

The only way to change the adjective clause into an independent clause is to replace the relative pronoun with its antecedent:

                    NS   **Vt**
The *compartment* contains the oxygen

Ndo
mask.

EXERCISE 37E

Combine the following sentences by making one an independent clause and the other an adjective clause. Begin by changing a noun or pronoun to a relative pronoun—*who, which,* or *that.* Then place the adjective clause after the word it modifies. Remember punctuation.

Example: Jerry finally earned enough money. He bought his bicycle Saturday.

REVISION: Jerry, *who finally earned enough money,* bought his bicycle Saturday.

Jerry finally earned enough money, *which he used to buy a bicycle Saturday.*

1. The magician is appearing at the Rialto. He has performed in many cities.

2. The menu consisted of beef, fish, and pork. It did not appeal to the vegetarians.

3. The red sports car was her graduation gift last June. It has dents in all the fenders and a smashed headlight.

4. We consulted Jeff Williams before we bought this carpeting. He recently opened his interior decorating shop.

5. My sister has always enjoyed operas. She will attend the opening night with me.

6. Daisy lives next door. She will finally get married tomorrow after a seven-year engagement.

7. The cat is wearing a jeweled collar. It is sitting high in the oak tree.

8. The rain is the heaviest in years. It flooded all the downtown streets.

9. She threw an empty hair-spray can into the incinerator. It exploded with a bang.

10. Willoughby owns a German Shepherd. He nipped the leg of an intruder last night.

lesson 38   Subordination— Noun Clauses

Noun clauses are dependent clauses which, like adjective and adverbial clauses, can be used to combine two sentences:

Bob owns a sailboat. The club members know this.

   NS   **Vt**   **Ndo**

The club members know /that Bob owns a sailboat/ .

Noun clauses can begin with the same subordinators (Sr) that introduce adjective clauses: *who, which, that,* and also with *where, why, after, before, when, what, how.* The word *that,* used as an introductory word, can sometimes be omitted:

            Ndo

Bob realizes /*(that) he has a valuable piece of property*/ .

FUNCTION AND POSITION

Noun clauses—the whole word group—function as subject (NS) or subject complement (Nsc), direct object (Ndo), indirect object (Nio), or object of the preposition (Nop) within sentences. They also can function as appositives.

     — **NS** —

NS   **Vt**----------   **Ndo**   **LV Adj**

Who will build the sailboat is uncertain.

They function in one of the noun positions in basic sentence patterns. They are a PART OF THE INDEPENDENT CLAUSE. If the noun clause is omitted, the sentence no longer exists:

NS------------------------------------- **LV Adj**

~~Who will build the sailboat~~ is uncertain.

In the following examples the enclosed word groups are noun clauses; they function as each symbol indicates:

Subject: **NS**--------------------------------   **LV**------ **Adj**   **Nsc**

                  What each member will do will be Bob's decision.

Direct Object: **NS**   **Vt**   **Ndo**------------------

                  David asked   how he can help .

Indirect Object:

NS Vt----------   Nio-------------------------------   Adj Adj   Ndo
Bob will give   *whoever does the work*   free sailing lessons.

Object of Preposition:

NS Vi   Adv   P   Nop--------------------------
He talks enthusiastically *with* *whoever is interested* .

Appositive:

Adj NS   NS--
His suggestion,   *that everyone participate in the building* ,

Vt   Adj Ndo
pleased the club members.

EXERCISE 38A

Underline the noun clauses in the following sentences, and indicate in the blank whether the
clause is NS, Nsc, Ndo, Nio, or Nop. If there is no
noun clause, write X in the blank. Begin by writing
V above each verb and NS above each subject.
Label subordinators (Sr).

                NS   Sr-Ndo NS   Vt   V
Example: The watch that Marilyn selected had a luminous dial.   _____X_____

         Sr   NS V   LV   Adj-c
What she chose was very attractive.   _____NS_____

Then determine whether the NS-V combination is
an independent or dependent clause.

   Independent Clause: The watch had a luminous dial.

   Dependent Clause: that Marilyn selected

   Independent Clause: (Noun) was very attractive.

   Dependent Clause: *What she chose*

Finally, decide whether the dependent clause is a
noun clause by its function in the sentence:

   Adjective Clause: *that Marilyn selected*—modifies *watch*

   Noun Clause: *What she chose*—subject of the verb *was*

Remember that introductory words may be
omitted in certain sentences.

   1. The old lady had a son whom she loved dearly.   _____

2. He said he would operate the mill next year.   _____

3. Why the accident happened cannot be explained easily.   _____

4. Jackson, who owned the livery stable, had a stroke yesterday.   _____

5. The order was written by whoever signed it.   _____

6. The picture you admired was sold yesterday.   _____

7. He complains that he has no time for sleep.   _____

8. His excuse is that unexpected guests arrived last night.   _____

9. Tell whoever calls the title of the movie.   _____

10. The reason for his failure is that he cannot dissect frogs.   _____

THE REASON IS BECAUSE . . .

Although *The reason is because . . .* is used in speaking and informal writing, it is preferable to use *The reason is that . . .* in formal writing. Following the linking verb *is*, we expect to find a noun clause which usually begins with *that:*

NOT: *The reason he is depressed *is because* he lost his job.

BUT: The reason he is depressed *is that* he lost his job.

OR: He is depressed because he lost his job.

(Sometimes *The reason is . . .* adds unnecessary words to a sentence. Write a sentence both ways to decide which is the better version.)

. . . IS WHEN . . .

The expression *is when* in definitions is awkward. Actually the term being explained should be defined by a term of similar construction. A noun should be used to define a noun:

NOT: *Treason is *when a person betrays his country.*

BUT:
     NS   LV   Nsc
    Treason is a person's *betrayal* of his country.

     NS   LV   Nsc
    A *macrocyte* is a very large red blood corpuscle.

     NS   LV Nsc
    Anger is a *feeling* of rage or hostility.

     NS   LV Nsc
    A *robin* is a *bird* with a red breast.

EXERCISE 38B

Rewrite the following sentences to eliminate
expressions such as *is when,* and *is because.* You
may also choose to eliminate the word *reason.* In
rewriting, you will need to make other minor
changes.

1. The reason you do not trust me is because I told your mother about your accident.

2. Imagination is when one forms pictures in the mind of objects or people not present.

3. Mark's disappearance from home last night is because he thinks his parents are unreasonable.

4. The reason the college team won the football trophy is because every player worked to win.

5. Homework is when you have assignments from every class to do at home.

6. His failure in school was because he never took time to study.

7. Remuneration is when a person receives money for work he has done.

8. An art collection is when paintings are on display for examination or sale.

9. The reason he did not earn much money picking apples is because he slept under the tree most of
   the time.

10. Baptism under fire is when new troops go into battle the first time.

lesson 39 Clauses within Clauses

EMBEDDED CLAUSES

As we have seen in the preceding lessons in this unit, dependent clauses, because they cannot stand alone, are embedded in independent clauses as modifiers or as noun substitutes. In addition, dependent clauses can be embedded in other dependent clauses, and these also function as modifiers or as noun substitutes:

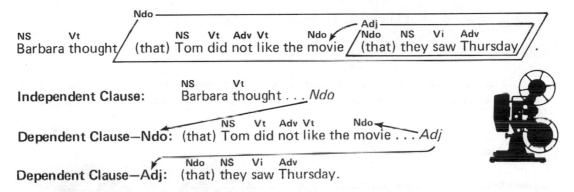

In the preceding example the incomplete verb (Vt) *thought* is followed by a direct object (Ndo) that is a noun clause: *(that) Tom did not like the movie.* The direct object (Ndo) *movie* is modified by an adjective clause: *(that they saw Thursday)*.

In the next example the incomplete verb (Vt) *told* is followed by an indirect object (Nio) *employees* and a direct object (Ndo) which is a noun clause: *that he believed . . . .* Because the verb *believed* is incomplete (Vt), it also is followed by a direct object (Ndo), another noun clause: *they did not know the techniques for plant operation.* The last dependent clause, *as he (did know the techniques for plant operation)*, is an adverbial modifier of the adjective *well.* It is an elliptical clause (Lesson 35) (the words in parentheses are understood) which completes a comparison (Lesson 36). Notice the relationship of the clauses within clauses:

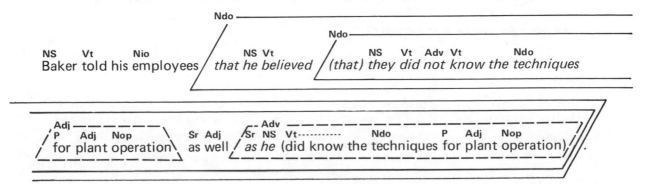

Independent Clause:
NS   Vt   Nio
Baker told his employees . . . *Ndo*

Dependent Clause—Ndo:
NS Vt
that he believed . . . *Ndo*

Dependent Clause—Ndo:
NS   Vt   Adv   Vt   Ndo   Nop
(that) they did not know the techniques for plant operation

Sr Adj
as well . . . *Adv*

Dependent Clause—Adv:
Sr NS Vt-----------   Ndo   P   Adj   Nop
as he (did know the techniques for plant operation).

Each of the dependent clauses could be written as independent clauses:

Baker told his employees his opinion.

Baker believed his opinion.

The employees did not know the techniques for plant operation.

Baker knew how to run the plant very well.

It is obvious that the single sentence with several dependent clauses relates each of the ideas logically to the others and is more effective because unnecessary, repeated, and vague words are eliminated.

EXERCISE 39

Put parentheses around each dependent clause in these sentences, and label it N, Adj, or Adv. Begin by writing V above each verb and NS above each subject. Identify subordinators (Sr), words that begin dependent clauses.

Example:

NS-------------- V------------- Sr   NS   V----------
Bob and Irene had planned that they would go out for dinner on Saturday evening with Dick and

NS   V---------------- Sr   NS   NS-Sr V   V
Judy; but they were surprised when several friends, who brought food and presents, arrived at their

new home for a house-warming party.

Then determine whether the clause is independent or dependent.

Independent Clause------------- Dependent Clause--
Bob and Irene had planned *that* they would go out for dinner on Saturday evening with Dick and

------- C   Independent Clause   Dependent Clause----- Dependent Clause-------------------- -----------------
Judy, but they were surprised when several friends, *who* brought food and presents, arrived at their

----
new home for a house-warming party.

Finally, determine how the dependent clauses
function in the sentence by examining their
relationship to the rest of the sentence.

Ndo--
Bob and Irene had planned (*that* they would go out for dinner on Saturday evening with Dick and

-------   **Adv**--------------------- **Adj**------------------------------------- ------------------
Judy,) but they were surprised (when several friends, (*who* brought food and presents,) arrived at their

----
new home for a house-warming party.)

1. Dennis, who attends a private school, informed his parents that he will not go back when the fall
   semester begins.

2. After Cleo had finished her father's portrait, she decided she would paint a picture of a mountain
   cabin she remembered.

3. The moon, which was full that night, cast bright light on the mirror-smooth lake that lay at the
   edge of town.

4. Marianne wished she had visited Switzerland while she was in Europe last year.

5. Soft music, fragrant flowers, a candlelit dinner table were the setting which greeted Dawson's guests
   when he opened the dining-room doors.

lesson 40 Fragments— Nonsentences

If a word group written as a sentence does not contain any of the basic sentence patterns, or if it has a subject and a predicate but is preceded by a subordinator, it is called a fragment, a construction usually unacceptable in expository writing. Fragments can either be attached to a sentence or revised into a full sentence.

We can add words:

Fragment: *Being alert and ready for action*

Sentence: *Being alert and ready for action,* Tod avoided many problems.

(V-ing used alone functions as an adjective or noun. See Verb Parts 4 and 5, Lesson 8. In the sentence above the entire phrase "Being alert and ready for action" functions as a modifier of the subject (NS) *Tod.*)

We can change words:

Fragment: *Being* a happy person.

Sentence: Mark *was* a happy person.

We can attach the fragment to a preceding sentence:

NOT: *The performance continued. *Even though the pianist did not feel well.*

BUT: The performance continued *even though the pianist did not feel well.*

Fragments often appear in certain kinds of writing like fiction and advertising; however, these are special kinds of fragments.

Soft . . . gentle . . . pure.

A starlit night. Waves breaking on the beach. The two of them oblivious to everything except this moment.

Until we acquire skill writing essays, we probably should eliminate all fragments by rewriting the word groups. As experienced writers, we will know how to write effective fragments and when to use them.

EXERCISE 40A

Capitalize first word and use terminal punctuation
for each group of words that is a sentence.

1. the heart is a hollow, muscular organ

2. divided into four chambers

3. the heart is a double pump

4. the first pump receives blood containing carbon dioxide

5. pumping the blood to the lungs

6. oxygen enters the bloodstream in the lungs.

7. the blood returns to the heart

8. the second pump receiving the oxygenated blood

9. which is pumped through the aorta

10. the heart pumps the blood to all parts of the body

IF YOU HAVE MISSED MORE THAN TWO SENTENCES, complete Exercise 40B.

EXERCISE 40B

1. the duckbill platypus is a strange mammal

2. the young hatching from eggs

3. the platypus has a ducklike bill

4. which is used for finding worms in the mud

5. and broadly webbed feet used for swimming

6. the male platypus has a poisonous spur on his hind foot

7. used for self-defense

8. the platypus is an expert swimmer

9. feeding on worms, tadpoles, and small fish

10. the platypus dwells in Australia and Tasmania

EXERCISE 40C

The following word groups are fragments. Make them sentences by adding words or by changing words and using punctuation needed.

1. At the time of his departure for the Orient.

2. Which resulted in his being dismissed.

3. Being the last man to leave the meeting.

4. While he could not manage his own affairs.

5. The scientific experiment being conducted in the laboratory.

6. History reports reviewed at the end of the semester.

7. Hoping to find at least one friend in Europe.

8. Magnificient view from every room in the house.

9. Unlike any other play he had ever seen.

10. Not wanting to appear overly inquisitive.

Now that you have completed the last exercise in this unit, YOU ARE READY FOR THE UNIT SIX REVIEW. If you need additional practice, complete the X-TRAS which follow.

UNIT SIX

UNIT SIX REVIEW will consist of exercises like the ones in Lessons 35 through 40. To prepare for the REVIEW, read the lessons and go back over the exercises. Note any corrections you have made; if you do not understand every part of the exercises thoroughly, ask your instructor for help. Make sure that you understand the directions for each exercise because those on the REVIEW will be similar.

Complete these exercises only if you want additional practice before you attempt the UNIT SIX REVIEW, Form A or Form B. Answers for these are in the Answer Key.

I. Underline each dependent clause and draw a line above each phrase. Because a phrase may be a part of a dependent clause, you may have lines below and above the same words. Begin by writing V above each verb and NS above each subject.

1. After most of the boys had delivered their papers, they met at the corner soda fountain.

2. Mrs. Gardner placed her order for rose bushes with Mr. Hall, who manages a small nursery.

3. The coffee pot bubbled and steamed as heat pushed water up the stem and over the coffee in the basket.

4. The pedestal where the stuffed owl perched was ornately decorated with flowers and leaves.

5. The chair Neil valued most was the threadbare recliner in the den.

6. The sandals Gretchen wore had flat soles and thin leather straps that crisscrossed up her legs to her knees.

7. Her pale pink gown, which hung loosely from her shoulders, cascaded in soft folds to her feet.

8. The committee of scientists applauded vigorously after the young bacteriologist concluded his report about his research project.

9. Although Michael and Sandra Holmes were both experienced race-car drivers, they chose less hazardous jobs after they were married.

10. Mr. Hill knew that the man he had trusted many years was now incompetent.

II.   Revise faulty comparisons to make them
       logical. If the comparison is satisfactory,
       place an X in the blank.

       1. Our mountain property is the most perfect place for a vacation cabin.   _____

       2. Bob's car rides more comfortably than Tom.   _____

       3. Which is the highest of the two mountains—Mt. Whitney or Mt. Ranier?   _____

       4. Harold Walker appears to be more conscientious than Ted Brownell.   _____

       5. The town furthest south in the United States is located in Hawaii.   _____

III.   Revise the following sentences by eliminating
       is when or *is because* expressions. Either sub-
       stitute another subordinator for *when* or
       because, or rewrite the sentence.

       1. The reason Greg hesitates to fly the plane alone is because he fears getting lost.

       2. Sympathy is when a person understands, even shares, another's sorrow or pain or happiness.

       3. The reason Sally likes Jeremy is because he makes decisions for her.

IV. Write sentences which contain at least one dependent clause. Underline the dependent clauses.

1.

2.

3.

V. Combine the following sentences by making one a dependent clause and the other an independent clause. Begin by placing a sub-ordinator before one of the sentences to make it a dependent clause. Then place the independent clause before or after the dependent clause. Remember to use punctuation if it is required.

1. Miguel waited in a long line in front of the theater. He watched the girls pass by.

2. The house was unbearably hot. The airconditioner had stopped working.

3. The Sacramento Valley was cooled by ocean breezes. The temperature dropped forty degrees in an hour.

4. Some students study night and day. They prepare for final exams.

5. Mr. Hughes' secretary typed the mailing list. It represented all the customers in two cities.

VI. Put parentheses around each dependent
clause and label it N, Adj, or Adv.

1. Sarah felt a cold chill as Ben told her abruptly that he was too busy to talk with her.

2. As the temperature climbed to 100 degrees, people traveled to the beaches where they hoped they would get cool while swimming in the lakes and rivers which skirted the large city.

3. After Dan had purchased the plans for the sailboat, he bought a table saw which he needed; and then he cleaned the garage and organized the tools before he began construction.

VII. The following word groups are fragments
(parts of sentences). Make them sentences by
adding words or changing words and using
punctuation needed.

1. As the white-capped waves broke on the sandy beach.

2. Having very little time for working on the car engine.

3. In planning for the arrival of several hundred foreign visitors.

unit SEVEN

Sentence Inversion, Passive Verbs, Verbals

lesson 41 Sentence Inversion

Almost all English sentences have the Subject-Verb-Object (or Subject-Verb-Completer) pattern. However, to give variety to writing or to change emphasis, we can change word order in a sentence. The predicate—or a part of it—can precede the subject, but the relationship of the words to one another stays the same.

When we use a complete verb (Vi), for example, NS is subject whether it is at the beginning or at the end of the sentence:

NS   Vi   Adv   Adv   Vi   NS
The moon shines brightly.   Brightly shines the moon.

When we invert a sentence containing a direct object (Ndo), we place Ndo first, then the subject (NS) followed by the verb (Vt):

```
NS Vt        Ndo                              Ndo         NS Vt
I appreciate his consideration.      His consideration I appreciate.
```

Notice that the emphasis of the sentence changes. The writer emphasizes *consideration* in the inverted sentence by placing it first. This inversion is not used unless this emphasis is desired.

Inversion of a sentence containing an indirect object (Nio) is not used often. Once again, notice the change in emphasis. In speaking, the emphasis is strengthened by the louder pronunciation used for *books*.

```
NS  Vt     Nio     Ndo
He showed Dale the books.
```

```
   Ndo    NS Vt    Nio
The books he showed Dale. (. . . but not the sketches or paintings.)
```

Inverting a sentence containing a linking verb (LV) does not show much change because the subject (NS) and subject completer (Nsc) name the same person or thing. Reversing their order may produce an awkward sentence, and it may give emphasis not intended.

```
   NS        LV Nsc                    NS         LV   Nsc
The chairman is Dan Thomas.      Dan Thomas is the chairman.
```

```
            NS                LV     NS        LV          Nsc
The ten-story dormitory on campus is   Davies Hall is the ten-story dormitory
Nsc                                    on campus.
Davies Hall.
```

```
NS  LV  Nsc                            NS      LV Nsc
Bob is a wrestler.                   A wrestler is Bob. (Awkward)
```

However, when we place an adjective or adverb before a linking verb and the subject after it, we can produce effective sentences. But we must make sure that they are readable sentences and that they say what we intend.

```
NS    LV Adv                   Adv   LV NS
Dave is here.                  Here is Dave.      (Used frequently,
                                                  especially in
                                                  conversation.)
```

```
   NS    LV Adj               Adj      LV    NS
The bride is happy.           Happy is the bride.
                                                  (Used infrequently,
The roses smell sweet.        Sweet smell the roses.  usually in poetry.)
```

THERE IS . . . , HERE IS . . . , IT IS . . .

By beginning a sentence with *there, here,* or *it,* using them as introductory words, we can place the subject after the verb (Lesson 23). For some expressions, such as "It is raining," the introductory *it is* constitutes an idiomatic pattern in English.

    LV NS Adv----------------   **Vi----------**
There is an island across the bay.   *It* is raining.

Remember that when the subject is plural, the verb following *there* must also be plural (Lesson 34):

    LV NS   Adv----------
There *are* five *ostriches* in the zoo.

This pattern and subject-verb agreement also apply when we use verbs like *seem, exist, remain, come* and others:

    LV   Adv Adj NS Adj------- Adj
There *remains* not one *bit* of work undone.

QUESTIONS

Another kind of inversion—the question—is not used as often in expository writing as it is in conversation, in fiction, and in informal writing, but it does offer variety to a writing style. To write a question we change word order; and, in addition, we may use certain words like *what, who, when, how,* to introduce the question:

First, make a statement:

  NS Vi Adv----------------
My plane leaves at 10 o'clock.

Change it to a question:

 Adv----------- Vi   NS Vi
What time does my plane leave?

Notice that the question begins with *what* and that the verb needs an auxiliary or helping verb; in this sentence we add a form of the verb *do*. Questions may begin with an auxiliary verb like *are* or *will* (Lesson 5):

Vi NS Vi Adv   **Vt NS Vt Ndo**
Are you going home?   Will Tom call Jeff?

Here is one sentence—*Several people reported the accident.*—written as a question several ways:

Are several people reporting the accident?

Did several people report the accident?

How many people reported the accident?

Why did several people report the accident?

EXERCISE 41

Below are sentences and their patterns. Rewrite each sentence using the pattern given before the

blank. Notice that some may be questions. Begin
by labeling sentence parts. Then change their order
to match the pattern given.

1. (NS Vi Adv) Travelers come from all over the world.

    (Adv Vi NS) _____

2. (NS Vt Ndo) Most people enjoy San Francisco.

    (Ndo Vt Vt?) What city _____

3. (NS Vt Ndo) The house-covered hills please sightseers.

    (Vt NS Vt Ndo?) _____

4. (NS Vi Adv) Cable cars roll suddenly down steep hills.

    (Adv Adv Vi NS) _____

5. (NS Vt Ndo) The earthquake threat does not frighten residents.

    (Vt NS Vt Ndo?) _____

6. (NS LV Nsc) A serious threat to San Francisco is water pollution.

    (NS LV Nsc?) What _____

7. (NS LV Nsc) A serious threat to San Francisco is water pollution.

    (LV Nsc NS?) _____

8. (NS Vt Ndo) The new subway system relieves traffic congestion.

    (Vt NS Vt Ndo?) _____

9. (NS Vi Adv) Millions of people live in the Bay Area.

    (Adv Vi NS) _____

10. (NS Vt Ndo) Several bridges link the Bay Area lands.

    (Vt NS Vt Ndo?) _____

lesson 42   The Passive Transformation

Sentences consisting of a subject (NS), incomplete verb (Vt), and direct object (Ndo) represent a common—probably the most common—sentence pattern in English. Such sentences state that the action completed by the subject is done to the direct object. The verb is ACTIVE:

NS   Vt   Ndo
Jack repaired the car.

VERBS—ACTIVE AND PASSIVE

We can transform this kind of sentence by changing the relationship of the words and by changing the verb from ACTIVE to PASSIVE.

1. Place the direct object (Ndo) in the NS position. For the sentence above, *the car* becomes NS.

2. Use the correct form of the verb *be* plus Part 4 of the verb. For the sentence above, place *was* before *repaired* to make the verb passive (PV).

3. Write the preposition (P) *by* before NS. Thus, *Jack* becomes the object of the preposition (Nop). Place the prepositional phrase after the verb.

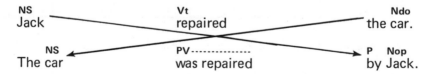

When the doer of the action—*Jack*—is the subject (NS), the VERB IS ACTIVE:

Jack repaired . . .

But when the receiver of the action—*the car*—becomes the subject, the VERB IS PASSIVE:

The car was repaired . . .

The verb is made passive by placing *am, is, are, was, were, will be, has been, have been,* and other forms of *to be* before the V-ed form (Part 4) of the verb. The passive verb phrase can also include auxiliaries like *can, may,* and *shall* (Lesson 5).

Here are sentences with ACTIVE VERBS:

Doer (NS)	Active verb (Vt)	Receiver (Ndo)
The plane	*transported*	the jewel collection.
The pilot	*completed*	his assignment.
The museum director	*complimented*	the pilot.

Here are the transformed sentences with PASSIVE VERBS:

Receiver (NS)	Passive Verb (PV)	Doer (by Nop)
The jewel collection	*was transported (may have been transported)*	by the plane.
The assignment	*was completed*	by the pilot.
The pilot	*was complimented (has been complimented)*	by the museum director.

In each sentence (by Nop) can be omitted.

Some sentences with the intransitive verb (Vi) can also be made passive:

Active	Passive
NS Vi Adv	NS PV----------- Adv
The story *began* slowly.	The story *was begun* slowly.
NS Vi-----------------	NS PV---------------------
The dinner *was cooking.*	The dinner *was being cooked.*

Sentences with an objective complement (Noc) can be changed from active to passive:

NS Vt Ndo Noc
Martin *called* Jim a liar.

NS Vt Ndo Adj
Martin *made* Jim unhappy.

NS PV----------- Ndo (by Nop)
Jim *was called* a liar by Martin.

NS PV----------- Adj   (by Nop)
Jim *was made* unhappy by Martin.

Sentences that have verbs like *cost, have, weigh*—frequently called *mid-verbs* or *middle verbs*—cannot be transformed to passive voice:

YES: The vase *cost* five thousand dollars.

NOT: *Five thousand dollars was cost by the vase.

YES: The clock *weighs* five pounds.

NOT: *Five pounds was weighed by the clock.

USE OF PASSIVE VERB SENTENCES

Passive verb sentences are appropriate if the receiver of the action is more important than the doer or if the doer of the action is unknown or better not mentioned. Overuse of passive voice often makes writing seem wordy and boring. Avoid constructions like "The play was enjoyed by us." Use the passive voice to emphasize the receiver of the action, or use it when it is necessary or better to avoid naming the doer of the action.

Ben *was appointed* administrator.

(*Ben* is emphasized. The doer of the action may be unknown, or the doer may seem unimportant to the speaker.)

The election news *will be televised.*

(The doer is unimportant.)

EXERCISE 42A

Find the verbs in these sentences. Indicate whether each one is an active verb or passive verb. Write A for active, and P for passive in the blanks.

1. Diving deep into the ocean gives a person a thrilling experience.   _____

2. A competent diver must be trained mentally as well as physically.   _____

3. Diving schools all over the world offer varying qualities of instruction.   _____

4. Some schools sell a poorly trained diver a ticket to suicide.   _____

5. Others provide a full thirty-hour course and, eventually, certification.   _____

6. For a long time diving was taught by the fear technique.   _____

7. Nowadays good diving techniques are emphasized.   _____

8. A diver must have reliable equipment.   _____

9. The well-equipped, well-trained diver plunges into the water eagerly.   _____

10. For safety, the diver never travels alone.   _____

EXERCISE 42B

Rewrite the following sentences making the verb passive. Use the verb form given in parentheses following each sentence.

1. Edmund Hillary and Tensing Norgay conquered Mount Everest in 1953. (was conquered)

2. Towers of ice surrounded the climbers. (were surrounded)

3. The men wore goggles, padded clothes, and oxygen masks. (were worn)

4. On the way up the mountain the climbers set up camps. (were set up)

5. Hillary, Norgay, and other men erected the last camp at 25,850 feet. (was erected)

6. Hillary and Norgay spent a stormy night in a tent 1,200 feet from the peak. (was spent)

7. They climbed the steep slopes in the morning. (were climbed)

8. At one point a ridge of ice stopped them completely. (were stopped)

9. Fortunately they found a passage to the top. (was found)

10. They finally reached the top just before noon. (was reached)

Read the ten sentences once again as a story. Next read the sentences you have written. Notice that the passive verbs change the tone of the story. For which sentences are passives effective? Contrast the use of the passive for Sentence 1 and for Sentence 4. Or Sentence 10 and Sentence 6. Remember: use the passive when there is reason to emphasize the receiver of the action or reason to omit or deemphasize the doer of the action. Otherwise use the active verb.

EXERCISE 42C

Rewrite the following sentences, making the verb active.

1. Houses are being constructed of nonwood products by builders.

2. Urethane foam can be molded into beams and columns by manufacturers.

3. Easily assembled door frames are among other urethane products manufactured by them.

4. The future uses of urethane have hardly been scratched by manufacturers.

5. More insulation is achieved by two inches of foam than by six inches of traditional insulation.

6. The insulating foam can be sprayed on surfaces by the workman.

7. Dusty air and moisture are blocked out by the foam insulation.

8. The sprayed foams are being used by some builders in place of shingles.

9. All kinds of freedom in design are offered by foam plastics.

10. An exciting new concept in building is presented by urethane building materials.

Once again read all the sentences as an article. Then read your rewritten sentences. Which version do you prefer?

lesson 43   **Verbals**

In studying verb forms, we find that words like *torn* and *faded* (V-ed, Part 4) and *talking* and *listening* (V-ing, Part 5) always follow auxiliary verbs when they are a part of a verb phrase, and they are always the last word in a verb phrase (Lesson 5):

NS   Vi------------------ Adv-----------
Martin *was swimming* in the pool.

NS PV--------- Adv ─────────
             P   Nop
He *was tired* / by the prolonged exercise \ .

These same forms, used without the auxiliary verbs, can function as NOUNS and ADJECTIVES, but they retain some of the characteristics of a verb.

NS   Vt   Ndo
Martin likes *swimming*.

NS   Adj   Adv----------- Vt   Ndo
Martin, *swimming* in the pool, enjoyed himself.

Adj NS Vi   Adv------------
Tired, he rested for an hour.

In addition, the infinitive—*to* + the verb—can function as a NOUN, an ADJECTIVE, or an ADVERB.

V-ED WORDS

Part 4 of the verb can function as a NOUN or ADJECTIVE:

             N
Noun: The wounded . . .

             N
            The employed . . .

             Adj N
Adjective: The *torn* coat . . .

             Adj   N
            The *damaged* car . . .

             Adj   N   Adj   Adj
            The football player, *beaten* and *bloodied* . . .

These three examples represent a way of revising by eliminating a form of the verb *to be:*

The coat I̶s̶ *torn.*

The car w̶a̶s̶ *damaged.*

The football player w̶a̶s̶ *beaten* and *bloodied.*

By making Part 4 an adjective, we can include a second idea in a simple sentence:

The coat ìš torn.

Thé ¢ǿát gave evidence of a struggle.

The torn coat gave evidence of a struggle.

MODIFIERS OF V-ED WORDS

Modifiers of V-ed words are adverbs:

Adv
The *badly* wounded . . .

Adv
The *newly* employed . . .

Notice the flexibility and the variety of functions of the V-ed words:

              NS   Vt----------------   Ndo
Active Verb: Nicholas *has cancelled* his dental appointment.

              Adj   NS   PV---------------- Adv-------------
Passive Verb: The dental appointment *was cancelled* by Nicholas.

By omitting *was*, the word *cancelled* can become an adjective modifier. Examine the next sentence.

              Adj   NS   Adj   Adv-------------   PV----------
Adjective: The dental appointment, *cancelled* by Nicholas, was given

Adv----------------------
to another patient.

              Adj   Adj   NS   Vt   Nio   Adj   Ndo
Adjective: The *cancelled* dental appointment cost Nicholas a night's sleep

Adv--
when his tooth tormented him.

V-ING WORDS

Part 5 of the verb can function as a NOUN or ADJECTIVE.

V-ING WORDS AS NOUNS

Noun: *Working* can be tiresome.

            Everyone enjoys *relaxing.*

Modifiers of noun verbals can be:

Adjectives: *Careful sewing* produces attractive clothes. [Adj = Careful, NS = sewing]

Skillful driving prevents accidents. [Adj = Skillful, NS = driving]

Adverbs: *Sewing carefully* produces attractive clothes. [NS = Sewing, Adv = carefully]

Driving skillfully prevents accidents. [NS = Driving, Adv = skillfully]

DETERMINERS WITH NOUN VERBALS

Use determiners like *his, our, her,* and possessive forms of nouns and possessives like *Mary's* with V-ing when it functions as a noun:

His trying to win the prize encouraged the others.

Everyone admired *his trying* to win the prize. (Everyone admired his attempt.)

Compare: Everyone admired *him trying* to win the prize. (Everyone admired him *while* he was trying . . .)

V-ING WORDS AS ADJECTIVES

Adjective: The *running* water . . . [Adj = running]

The *falling* star . . . [Adj = falling]

The old woman, *smiling* and *nodding* . . . [Adj = smiling, Adj = nodding]

Modifiers of the adjective verbals are adverbs:

The *swiftly* running water . . . [Adv = swiftly]

The old woman, *barely* smiling . . . [Adv = barely]

TO + VERB (INFINITIVE)

Infinitives consist of *to* + Part I (Lesson 7) of the verb or *to* + auxiliaries and Part 4 or Part 5 (Lesson 8):

to communicate   to have been chosen
to have accomplished   to be winning

INFINITIVES can function as NOUNS, ADJECTIVES, or ADVERBS:

Noun: NS------------

To succeed is fulfilling. He chose *to volunteer.*   Ndo------------

Adjective: Ndo   Adj----

They have food *to eat.*

Adverb: Vi   Adv-----

He worked *to win.*

Adv Adv----------

He tries hard *to succeed.*

Adj   Adv-------

He is eager *to learn.*

With verbs like *help* the *to* sign of infinitives may be omitted:

NS   Vt   Ndo Inf   Ndo

They helped him load the car.

EXERCISE 43

The following sentences contain verbals used as
nouns, adjectives, and adverbs. In the first blank
write the verbal, and in the second blank indicate
its function by writing N, Adj, or Adv. Begin by
writing V over each verb and NS over each subject.
Use SENTENCE KEYS (Lesson 24) to analyze
sentences.

1. The barking dog scared the baby.   _____   _____

2. The injured were taken to the hospital.   _____   _____

3. Eating is necessary for survival.   _____   _____

4. Exercising usually develops a strong body.   _____   _____

5. Jerry is reluctant to resign.   _____   _____

6. The boiling water scalded his hands.   _____   _____

7. He will try to cooperate.   _____   _____

8. The pilot enjoys flying.   _____   _____

9. The forgotten message lay on the desk.   _____   _____

10. Writing can be a challenge.   _____   _____

IF YOU HAVE MISSED TWO OR MORE OF THE

PRECEDING SENTENCES, read again about verbals and continue with the second part.

11. He offered to help.   _____   _____

12. The fire was caused by faulty wiring.   _____   _____

13. The boating accident could not be avoided. _____   _____

14. Try fishing in the river.   _____   _____

15. The airplane builder will attempt to fly.   _____   _____

16. Swinging on a trapeze can be dangerous.   _____   _____

17. The torn envelope lay in the wastebasket.   _____   _____

18. Thinking is sometimes a painful process.   _____   _____

19. David gave his winnings to charity.   _____   _____

20. Walt is happy to cooperate.   _____   _____

lesson 44 **Verbal Phrases**

A very effective way to put several ideas together into one sentence is to express them in verbal phrases. By linking these sentence parts in sequence, we can develop highly concentrated, very informative sentences because we are able to leave out unnecessary words. If well written, they are readable and rhythmic.

FORM

The verbal phrase contains a verbal and words that modify or complete it. Because a verbal retains verb characteristics, it can be modified by an adverb, it can have a subject, or it can be completed by a direct object and indirect object, and the noun verbal can be modified by an adjective. Here are examples of some verbal phrases:

V-ing:

    V-ing   Ndo   V-ing   Adj   Ndo
    managing the office   *lacking* the necessary experience

    Adj   V-ing   Vt
    careless *driving* causes
    Ndo
    accidents

V-ed:

    V-ed   Adv----------------   Adv V-ed   Adv   V-ed
    exhausted by the ordeal   *well qualified* and highly *trained*

Infinitive:

    Inf------------- Adj   Ndo   Inf---------   Adj   Ndo
    to examine office procedure   *to make* a detailed study

FUNCTION

The verbal phrase itself functions as a unit in the sentence. The entire phrase can be subject (NS), subject completer (Nsc), direct object (Ndo), object of the preposition (Nop), adjective (Adj), or adverb (Adv). To see how these phrases function, we can compare sentences containing phrases with the basic sentences giving the same information.

Basic Sentences	Revision
The president *manages the office.*	Subject: NS V-ing Ndo *Managing the office*
It is a full-time job.	LV Adj ------- Nsc is a full-time job.

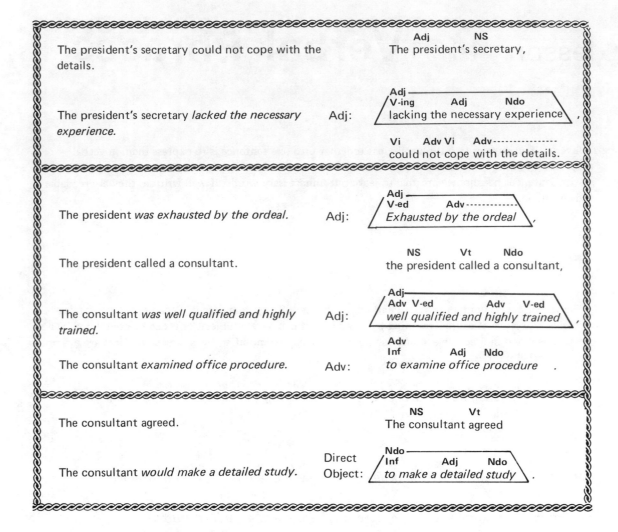

An example of the complex relationships of verbal phrases is illustrated in these sentences; however, the number of possible relationships is many times greater than what we show here. Notice how one verbal phrase may complete another one or how prepositional phrases modify verbals and how dependent clauses either modify or complete verbals. The symbols immediately above the words identify each word's function. The symbols given within the boxes identify the function of the enclosed word group:

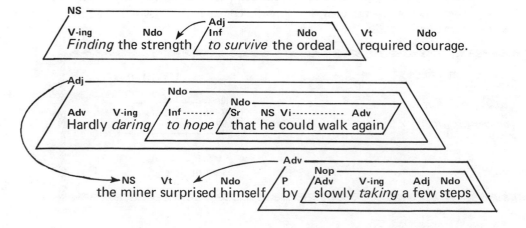

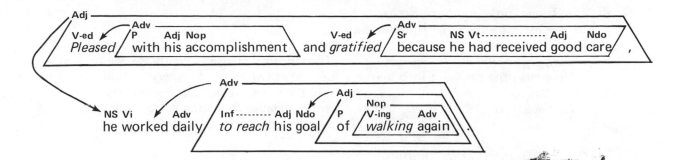

PUNCTUATION WITH VERBAL PHRASES

NO PUNCTUATION is used if the verbal phrase functions as NS or Ndo:

NS------------------------
Walking a tightrope requires great skill.

NO PUNCTUATION is used if the verbal phrase functions as an adverbial modifier:

　　　　　　　　　　Adv　Adv----------------------
The artist struggled long *to win recognition.*

COMMAS ENCLOSE adjective verbal phrases that give additional information about the nouns they modify. If the modifier begins the sentence, only the comma following it is written. If the modifier appears within the sentence, two commas enclose it. If it appears at the end, a comma precedes it:

Wrecked beyond repair, Brian's car became rusted and corroded.

Brian's car, *wrecked beyond repair,* became rusted and corroded.

Brian, nevertheless, traveled everywhere, *riding a new motorcycle.*

NO PUNCTUATION is used if the verbal phrase functions as an adjective modifier that is needed to explain or identify the noun it modifies:

　　　　　　　　Adj---
The cabin *situated near Rattlesnake Bar* does not belong to Gordon.

USE OF ADJECTIVE MODIFIERS

Be certain that the V-ing or V-ed adjective modifier has a clearly stated subject; otherwise the modifier seems to be "dangling," unrelated to the rest of the sentence.

NOT: *Having looked at our watches,* no　　(Use of the passive verb deleted the
　　　　time was lost in getting started.　　required subject.)

BUT: *Having looked at our watches,*
        we lost no time in getting started.

NOT: **While looking at the unusual
        scenery,* the car went into the
        ditch.

(The elliptical clause [Lesson 35] *while
looking at the unusual scenery* should
have the same subject *(car)* as the independent clause following it; however, the
car obviously cannot "look.")

BUT: *While looking at the unusual
        scenery,* Tom drove the car into
        the ditch.

NOT: **Confused by the vague directions,*
        the party ended before we
        arrived.

(The phrase should modify *we,* but the
sentence has to be rewritten so that *we*
becomes the subject.)

BUT: *Confused by the vague direc-
        tions,* we did not arrive before
        the party ended.

EXERCISE 44A

Find the verb phrases and the verbal phrases in
each of these sentences. Underline the verb phrases
(Lesson 5), and draw a line above the verbal
phrases.

1. Opening the door, Dela greeted her friends.

2. Willie had torn the sheets to shreds.

3. The red sports car, streaking along the highway, gulped gasoline eagerly.

4. John's first goal was to win the track meet.

5. The chance to earn recognition never came.

6. The enormous stadium was filled to the
   brim.

7. Norris considered buying a new car.

8. He finally asked several friends to accompany him.

9. Mrs. Jasper enjoyed arranging artificial
   flowers.

10. Bert has been considering the company's
    offer.

EXERCISE 44B

Underline the verb and verbal phrases. Indicate
the function of each phrase by writing NS, Nsc,
or Ndo for noun, V for verb, Adj for adjective,
and Adv for adverb. Begin by writing V above the
verbs and NS above the subjects.

1. He hurried to help his father.

2. Washing dishes is a boring job.

3. Finding a treasure is an exhilarating experience.

4. Sitting very still, Bill watched the fawns.

5. Nan was painting his portrait.

6. Playing the piano was his weekend job.

7. He has been making a butterfly collection.

8. The cowboys, laughing and yelling at the townspeople, rode their horses through mud puddles deliberately.

9. He had the opportunity to buy more land.

10. The colonial-style house built by my grandfather is for sale.

lesson 45   **Absolute Phrases**

The ABSOLUTE PHRASE is a means of attaching a related secondary idea to the main sentence. Though the phrase is related semantically to the independent clause, the phrase has no grammatical connection with the clause: there is no connecting word like a conjunction or preposition between them; only a comma is used to separate them. The ABSOLUTE PHRASE consists of a NOUN which functions as its subject and a VERBAL, followed by words to complete the verbal or modify it.

We can convert a sentence to an absolute phrase in this way:

1. Keep the subject (NS) of the sentence. It is a person or thing different from the subject of the independent clause.

2. Change the verb to a verbal, either V-ed or V-ing.

3. Add the words to complete or modify the verbal.

4. Attach the absolute phrase to an independent clause, and use a COMMA between them.

Original Sentences	Sentence with Absolute Phrase
NS Vi The steering pin *broke*.	NS V-ed-------------- The steering pin *having broken* ,
NS Vi Adv-------------------- The car plunged off the mountain ------- Adv------------- road into a chasm.	NS Vi Adv-------------------- the car plunged off the mountain ------- Adv------------- road into a chasm.
Margot entered the room like a queen.	Margot entered the room like a queen,
NS PV----------- Adv Adv------------ Her hair *was piled* high on her head.	NS V-ed Adv Adv------------ her hair *piled* high on her head ,
NS LV Adj-c Her rhinestone necklace was *glittering*.	NS V-ing her rhinestone necklace *glittering* .

EXERCISE 45

Combine the following sentences by making one
an absolute phrase and the other the independent
clause. Begin by changing the verb in one sentence
to a verbal.

1. The young woman prepared the dinner automatically.
   Her mind was fixed on her handsome dinner guest.

2. The mission was accomplished.
   The astronauts were able to return to earth.

3. He relaxed in his large chair.
   The fire was blazing in the fireplace.
   The wind was blasting the trees and shrubs outside.

4. The new owners moved eagerly into the old house.
   Its rooms were newly painted and carpeted.

5. The heir had been located.
   The attorney was able to settle the old man's estate.

lesson 46   Sentence Revision with Phrases

To make two sentences from one, we sometimes add words. To combine sentences, we may omit words, we may change the form of some of the words, and we may use punctuation. First, we decide which is the main idea and which are the subordinate or secondary ideas. Then we cross out unneeded words.

USING APPOSITIVES AND PREPOSITIONAL PHRASES

In the first example we omit *are*, a form of the verb *to be*, and the pronoun *they*. We use an appositive (Lesson 28) and prepositional phrases (Lesson 19). The words to be retained in the revised sentence have been italicized:

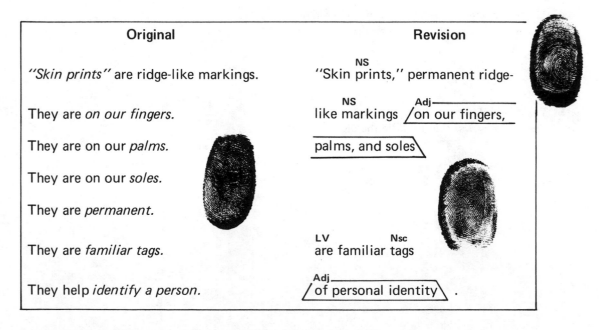

Original	Revision
"Skin prints" are ridge-like markings.	**NS** "Skin prints," permanent ridge-
They are *on our fingers*.	**NS** like markings /**Adj** on our fingers,
They are on our *palms*.	palms, and soles\
They are on our *soles*.	
They are *permanent*.	
They are *familiar tags*.	**LV** are familiar **Nsc** tags
They help *identify a person*.	/**Adj** of personal identity\ .

Notice that the word *permanent* was moved to modify *ridge-like markings*, and *ridge-like markings* became an appositive. The infinitive phrase *identify a person* (with *to* omitted after *help*) became a prepositional phrase—*of personal identity*. The prepositional phrases *on our fingers, on our palms, on our soles* were combined to make one adjective prepositional phrase modifying *markings*. In addition, commas were inserted between *fingers, palms,* and *soles,* items in a series. The end result, then, is one simple sentence containing a subject, followed by an appositive modified by an adjective prepositional phrase, a linking verb, and subject complement modified by an adjective prepositional phrase.

USING VERBAL PHRASES

We can combine two sentences into one by making one sentence a verbal phrase and the other an independent clause. This kind of combining is possible if both sentences are about the same person or thing. If one of the verbs is passive, we can omit the auxiliary verb and the V-ed form can then function as an adjective modifier. Here are two sentences about a California city:

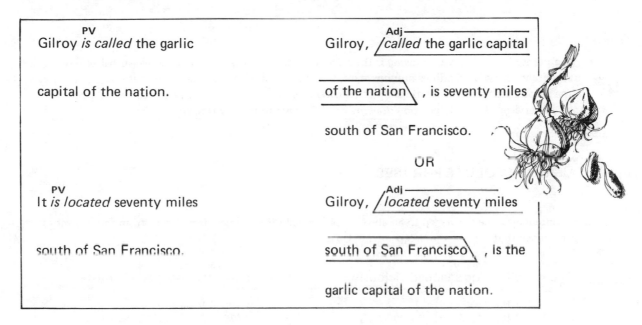

Both versions are acceptable. The writer has to determine whether the city's reputation or its location is of prime importance to him.

In revising we must always be sure to keep the same relationships by placing the verbal modifiers near the words they modify. We can anticipate problems if we note that one sentence contains two nouns, each representing something different. In the preceding example, we have *Gilroy* and *San Francisco.* An inexperienced writer might have combined the two sentences in this way:

Gilroy is located seventy miles south of *San Francisco, called* the garlic capital of the nation.

The word *called,* placed immediately after *San Francisco,* makes it a modifier of *San Francisco,* not *Gilroy,* which is at the beginning of the sentence.

When we want verbal phrases at the end of an independent clause to function as modifiers of the subject of the independent clause, we have to be sure that we do not have a second noun which the verbals might modify instead. Examine these two sentences:

NS   Vi   Adv   Adv
The hummingbird darted quickly up and

Adv   Adv   Adv   Adj————————
down, back and forth, /drawing nectar

————————————————————————
first from a large orange hibiscus blossom

and then from a red one\ .

NS   Vi   Adv
The hummingbird flew quickly

Adv————   ?
/Adv   Nop\   ?   Adj————————
to the flowers\ , /drawing nectar

————————————————————————
first from a large orange hibiscus blossom

and then from a red one\ .

The phrase beginning with *drawing* is the same in both sentences. It is an adjective verbal phrase. In the first sentence *drawing* modifies *hummingbird,* the only noun in the sentence, without question; however, in the second sentence the relationship of *drawing* to *hummingbird* is confused because the word *flowers* appears between them. By position *drawing* would appear to modify *flowers.*

USING ABSOLUTE PHRASES

A sentence can be converted to an absolute phrase only if its subject is different from the subject of the sentence that is to be the independent clause:

NS Vi
The growling dog snapped viciously.

NS   Vi
His white teeth flashed menacingly.

NS Vi
The growling dog snapped viciously,

NS   V-ing
his white teeth flashing menacingly.

Dog and *teeth* are the subjects of the two original sentences. In the revision, *dog* is subject of the independent clause, and *teeth* becomes subject of the verbal *flashing.*

USING VERBAL ADJECTIVE PHRASES

Remember that an adjective verbal (Lesson 44) must have a noun to modify. Unlike sentences with an absolute phrase, sentences with adjective verbal modifiers must have only one subject, clearly indicated:

NOT: *Having finished our lunch,* the steamship sailed down the river.

BUT: *Having finished our lunch,* we sailed down the river on the steamship.

EXERCISE 46

Combine the following sentences by making one
the independent clause and the other a phrase—
verbal phrase, appositive, prepositional phrase,
absolute phrase.

Example: *He looked out the window.*
He saw a moving van next door.

REVISION: *Looking out the window,* he saw a moving van next door.

1. Omaha has thousands of residents subject to transfer. Omaha needs furnished apartments.

2. Scholarships have helped many college students. They have been donated by businessmen in the community.

3. Marcia typed the letter rapidly. Her fingers scarcely touched the keys.

4. The little old lady puffed nervously on the cigarette. She tried hard to look sophisticated.

5. The airplane was overloaded with cargo. It barely missed the tree tops at the end of the runway.

6. He wanted to appear well-informed. He used words he could scarcely pronounce.

7. The girl is Dave's friend. She is the one combing her hair.

8. Barbara paid no attention to the strolling musicians. She was sobbing uncontrollably. They were singing beneath her window.

9. Sportsmen came from all over the world. They gathered in a small mountain town. They intended to spend a week celebrating.

10. A statue of Jacob Lester was donated by his admirers. It stands in the museum. It is near the main entrance.

Now that you have completed the last exercise in this unit, YOU ARE READY FOR THE UNIT SEVEN REVIEW. If you need additional practice, complete the X-TRAS which follow.

UNIT SEVEN

UNIT SEVEN REVIEW will consist of exercises like the ones in Lessons 41 through 46. To prepare for the REVIEW, read the lessons and go back over the exercises. Note any corrections you have made; if you do not understand any part of the exercises thoroughly, ask your instructor for help. Make sure that you understand directions for each exercise because those on the REVIEW will be very similar.

Complete these exercises only if you want additional practice before you attempt UNIT SEVEN REVIEW, Form A or Form B. Answers for these are in the Answer Key.

I.   Underline the verbal phrase and list its func-
     tion—NS, Ndo, Nop, Adj, or Adv—in the blank
     at the right.

1. Operating a laundromat kept Mr. Hutchins busy seven days a week.   _____

2. Greg preferred to do his lessons alone.   _____

3. Margaret stopped sending letters every day.   _____

4. The vase filled with spring flowers brightened the drab room.   _____

5. Donna, informed about her appointment as a representative, smiled broadly and whirled about happily.   _____

6. The two runaway girls nervously waited to speak with the probation officer.   _____

7. He earned his living by guarding visiting diplomats.   _____

8. Chopping the vegetables carefully, the young bachelor prepared an appetizing stew.   _____

9. Nora greeted the tall, gray-haired man, labeled an outstanding chemist.   _____

10. By carrying three cartons, Brian proved he was stronger than Lee.   _____

11. Appalled by the sight, Marcia covered her eyes and screamed loudly.   _____

12. The television network offered to present the recently completed wildlife film.   _____

13. Not knowing anything about San Francisco, the visiting newlyweds lost their way.   _____

14. Craig Hudson was eager to show everyone his first published novel.   _____

15. Coming together from all parts of the country, the delegates discussed their regional problems.   _____

II. Combine the following sentences by making one the independent clause and the other a *phrase*. Underline the phrase you have written.

1. The new rotary mower was engineered to protect its users. It has a blade guard and rear protector shield.

2. Now available is a torch lamp. It is designed to project 800 degrees of heat for a wide variety of uses.

3. The volunteer fire fighters will meet for four days next week. They plan to examine new equipment. They will discuss fire-fighting techniques.

4. Michael awoke suddenly and saw five men in the hotel room. They were all peering out the door and down the hall.

5. The young veteran has been studying lip reading at the hospital. He hopes to teach deaf children some day.

III. Rewrite these sentences and make the verbs active.

1. The bouquet of yellow roses was delivered to Nora by her husband.

2. Transportation problems have been blamed for the spoilage of frozen fish.

3. Judson and Tomkins have been encouraged by the treasurer's report.

IV. Write sentences to match these patterns.

1. PV NS PV (by Nop)?

2. Vt NS Vt Ndo?

3. NS PV (by Nop).

4. NS PV (by Nop).

unit EIGHT

Punctuation
and Capitalization

lesson 47 Punctuation— Periods, Question Marks, Exclamation Points

Marks of punctuation are signals along our reading route that tell us when to stop and prepare to begin the reading of another idea and when to slow down for additional bits of information. They may also represent certain writing habits that we accept as conventions of written language. They are attempts to indicate in written English some of the signals of spoken language, like a stress, a falling pitch, and a pause. The most frequently used marks of punctuation are the period, comma, and semicolon. The other marks include the question mark, exclamation point, colon, quotation marks, dash, hyphen, parentheses, brackets, and ellipses.

As readers, we usually have no trouble responding to the marks of punctuation as they appear in printed books and papers. In fact, we probably do not think about them at all. But, as writers, we have a hard time placing them unless we know when to use them. This understanding develops as we recognize sentences and units within sentences that need to be separated from other parts of the sentence, joined together, or enclosed within the sentence. What follows is a summary of punctuation usage and conventions. For detailed explanations of the grammatical constructions named, refer ahead to the Index or back to the unit(s) noted in parentheses following the name of the grammatical construction.

● PERIOD

The PERIOD (.) is placed at the end of a sentence and separates it from the next one:

The newlyweds made plans for a European trip.
They read travel books and studied maps.

It is used conventionally after initials:

T. E. Mason   R. E. M.   H. S. Milton

It is also used after abbreviations:

Dr.   Mrs.   Jan.   Wed.   N.Y.   p.m.

QUESTION MARK

The QUESTION MARK (?) indicates the end of a direct question:

Did they really want to travel? What kinds of clothing should they take?

It is not used after an indirect question, a sentence in which the question is a part of a declarative statement:

They asked themselves why they wanted to see Europe.
They wondered how much money they would need.

EXCLAMATION POINT

The EXCLAMATION POINT (!) appears after words, phrases, or clauses expressing shock or excitement:

For fun!   The opportunity of a lifetime!

EXERCISE 47

Add periods, question marks, or exclamation
points to the following sentences.

1. What a shocking experience

2. Very narrow, winding stairways connect the floors of the White Tower, built by William the Conqueror

3. Anne Boleyn asked Henry VIII to send for a swordsman from Calais for her execution

4. How could he deny her request

5. Dr and Mrs Henderson drove Tod and Ellen to the airport at 7 a m

6. Ellen wondered how high the plane would travel

7. Tod had his initials T E M stamped on his luggage

8. She pushed me How dare she do that

lesson 48   **Commas**

The comma is used to help provide sentence clarity by marking off words and word groups, and it also has certain conventional uses—the listing of dates, addresses, numbers, and other items.

❜ COMMAS WITH CLAUSES

1. A COMMA is generally used in COMPOUND SENTENCES (UNIT FOUR) before the coordinators *and, but, for, yet, or, nor* which link two INDEPENDENT CLAUSES (UNIT FOUR):

   The newlyweds talked about their European trip for several weeks, but they could not decide how long to stay.

   a. If each independent clause is short, NO COMMA is needed:

   They talked and they thought.

   b. NO COMMA is used before *and* if it is only joining a COMPOUND SUBJECT or COMPOUND PREDICATE (UNIT ONE):

   Compound subject: *Tod and Ellen* visited travel agencies.
   Compound predicate: They *talked with airline representatives and discussed plans with friends.*

2. A COMMA follows a connector like *however* or *moreover* when it joins two independent clauses to form a compound sentence. Notice that the connector is preceded by a semicolon (Lessons 26 and 49):

   They decided to visit London first; *in addition,* they planned to visit Stratford-on-Avon.

3. A COMMA follows INTRODUCTORY ADVERBIAL CLAUSES (UNIT SIX), dependent clauses which begin with words like *because, although, if, as,* and separates them from the independent clause which follows:

   Before they made further plans, they both had vaccinations.

   a. However, NO COMMA is used before an adverbial clause at the end of the sentence:

   They had their pictures taken *because they needed passport photographs.*

4. A COMMA follows a PREPOSITIONAL PHRASE (UNIT TWO) at the beginning of the sentence if it is long, or if it acts as a connective with the preceding sentence:

During the weeks of making plans for the trip, Ellen began counting the days they had to wait.

    a. However, A COMMA usually does not follow a short prepositional phrase:

In twenty-six days she and Tod would be on the plane.

5. A COMMA may be used after a short prepositional phrase to prevent misreading:

For Ellen, June could not come soon enough.

6. A COMMA separates a noun from a VERBAL PHRASE MODIFIER (UNIT SEVEN) at the beginning or end of the sentence:

Having listed all the clothes they needed, Ellen then piled them on the cedar chest. She spent hours, *sorting the clothes and moving them from one suitcase to another.*

    a. When a VERBAL is a subject or a complement, not a modifier, NO COMMA should separate it from the rest of the sentence:

Packing the suitcases was not easy.
Tod also tried *arranging the clothes.*

COMMAS USED WITH SINGLE WORDS

7. A COMMA follows transitional words like *moreover,* *as a result,* and *finally* when these words begin a sentence:

Finally, Ellen had assembled everything they needed.

8. A COMMA is used after items in a series (UNIT FOUR)—words, phrases, or clauses—including the word before *and:*

She took *dresses, shoes, sweaters, and skirts.* Tod had *sports coats with coordinated shirts and trousers, three pairs of shoes, and five bottles of aspirin.*

9. A COMMA is used between COORDINATE ADJECTIVES (UNIT FOUR). These are adjectives that each modify the noun separately. Their order may be reversed. The comma is used between them instead of the word *and:*

an attractive, soft-spoken hostess	a soft-spoken, attractive hostess
a tall, dark, well-built pilot	a tall and dark and well-built pilot

    a. NO COMMA is used between consecutive adjectives. Usually the adjective preceding the noun is a noun derivative:

airline terminal	leather suitcase

Both *airline* and *leather* may function as nouns in other word relationships:

cooperative airline   damaged leather

An adjective placed before *airline terminals* or *leather suitcase* modifies the two words which make a unit. The word *and* cannot be used between the two words; therefore, no comma is needed:

crowded airline terminal   brown leather suitcase

EXERCISE 48A

Add commas wherever necessary to the following sentences. Some sentences may not need commas. In the blanks at the right, write the numbers of the explanations which tell why you did or did not add commas. There may be more than one explanation for a sentence.

1. Notre Dame Cathedral was built on an island in the Seine River but it is easily accessible because of bridges from both banks.   _____

2. The Cathedral is old and it is beautiful.   _____

3. Projecting out on all parts of the outside walls of the Cathedral are gargoyles.   _____

4. The gargoyles look like all the horrible demons one has seen in bad dreams—winged creatures with claw feet grotesque satanic faces with bulging eyes and sharp pointed teeth and unreal combinations of different kinds of animals.   _____

5. However the gargoyles serve a practical purpose; troughs in their backs carry rain water away from the ornate building walls to prevent erosion.   _____

6. The water trickles through their open mouths and falls to the street below.   _____

7. Another attraction most visitors to Paris see is the Eiffel Tower built for the 1903 World Exposition.   _____

8. When people stand beneath the Eiffel Tower they feel very insignificant.   _____

9. Towering high above them the massive network of metal rises almost four hundred feet into the air.   _____

10. Slow-moving elevators carry hundreds of people to the four levels; consequently the lines of people waiting often become very long.   _____

11. From the top one can see Paris spread below.   _____

COMMAS TO ENCLOSE

10. COMMAS are used before and after an APPOSITIVE (UNIT FOUR) if it gives extra information about the noun it renames:

    The giant 747, *the plane Ellen and Tod boarded,* carried more than 300 passengers and twenty crew members.

    a. However, if the appositive is needed to identify the noun it follows, no punctuation is used:

    The Shakespearean actor *Dudley Hanes* came aboard.

11. COMMAS are used before and after an ADJECTIVE CLAUSE (UNIT SIX) if it gives additional information about the noun it modifies:

    The head stewardess, *who spoke French, German, and Spanish in addition to English,* explained safety precautions.

    a. However, if the adjective clause is needed to identify the noun, no punctuation is used:

    A stewardess *who had large blue eyes and attractively styled lemon-blonde hair* handed passengers pillows and blankets.

    A way to test whether the adjective clause is a necessary part of the sentence is to read the sentence without it and to see whether the remaining part is meaningful:

    The head stewardess explained safety precautions.

    Since there is only one head stewardess, the modifier is not necessary to identify which member of the crew was speaking.

    A stewardess handed the passengers pillows and blankets.

    The modifier is needed to tell which of the several stewardesses was making the passengers comfortable.

    Another way is to substitute the word *that* for *who* or *which.* If it can be substituted, then the adjective clause is a necessary part of the sentence and should not be enclosed in commas:

    A stewardess that had large blue eyes . . .

12. COMMAS enclose modifiers following nouns:

    The blue-eyed, blonde stewardess, *gracious and helpful,* made the passengers comfortable.

13. COMMAS are used before and after sentence connectors (UNIT FOUR) and phrases, words, or word groups like *however, consequently, I believe, it seems, on the other hand, of course, by the way:*

    Tod, *it seems,* found the blonde stewardess very attractive.

14. If sentence connectors appear at the beginning of the sentence, they are followed by a comma (See Commas Used with Single Words):

However, Ellen made certain that Tod did not need help from the stewardess.

EXERCISE 48B

Add commas wherever necessary to the following sentences. Some sentences may not need commas. In the blank at the right, write the numbers of the explanations in the preceding lesson which tell why you did or did not add commas.

1. Tod and Ellen enjoyed Budapest the capital of Hungary situated on both sides of the Danube River.   _____

2. The city Buda is on one side of the river; on the other side is Pest.   _____

3. The white stone castle that looks like something out of a fairytale kingdom was built by the Fishermen's Guild on one side of the river.   _____

4. The lacy Gothic-style Parliament building which still bears the World War II scars of bullets and bomb fragments lends its magnificence to the other side of the river.   _____

5. The fairy-like atmosphere is heightened moreover when these and other decorative buildings are bathed in soft yellow lights at night.   _____

COMMAS USED CONVENTIONALLY

15. A COMMA follows a noun of direct address at the beginning of the sentence:

"*Tod,* look at the sky."

16. A COMMA is used to separate the main part of the sentence from the direct quotation enclosed in quotation marks:

"It's night on one side and morning on the other," *said Ellen* as she looked through the cabin window in wonder at the horizontal layers of yellow, orange, and red in the eastern sky.

17. A COMMA is used to separate a broken quotation, enclosed in quotation marks, from the main part of the sentence:

"Tod, how in the world," *Ellen asked,* "can you sleep now?"

18. COMMAS are used in dates to separate the day of the month from the year, and after the year when the date appears in a sentence:

    June *24, 1972,* was their travel date.

    a. If only the month and year are given, the separating comma between them is optional:

    They planned to travel during June(,) 1972.

19. COMMAS separate parts of addresses—town or city, county, state, and country:

    Tod and Ellen live in *Sacramento, California, United States.*

20. COMMAS are used between proper names and degrees and titles that follow the name:

    George Talbot Hunt, PhD, Professor of History, Western Reserve University

21. A COMMA is used after the close in a letter:

    Sincerely,   Fondly,

22. A COMMA is used after the salutation in a personal letter:

    Dear Bob,   Dear Mother and Dad,

EXERCISE 48C

Add commas wherever necessary to the following
sentences. Some sentences may not need commas.
In the blank at the right, write the numbers of the
explanations in the preceding lesson which tell
why you did or did not add commas.

1. "Tod the Colosseum must be down there where the bright lights are shining," Ellen said, as she and Tod walked hesitatingly on cobblestone pavement down a curved, narrow, dark street in Rome.   _____

2. As they walked into the floodlighted area, Tod explained "It's a movie set. We're on a movie set. The cameraman is over there."   _____

3. Tod and Ellen joined the watching crowd at the other end of the narrow street and marveled that they were in Rome Italy on a movie set on a warm July night.   _____

4. "I'll have to write Mother and Dad" Ellen said excitedly "and tell them all about this."   _____

5. Dear Mother and Dad
   You'll never guess what Tod and I saw tonight . . .   _____

6. . . . The trip is fabulous. Why don't you plan a second honeymoon?
   Love from both of us
   Ellen   _____

lesson 49 Semicolons and Colons

● SEMICOLON

, THE SEMICOLON AS A CONNECTOR

The SEMICOLON (;) may be used as a CONNECTOR between sentence parts:

1. The SEMICOLON joins two INDEPENDENT CLAUSES (UNIT FOUR) with closely related ideas to form a COMPOUND SENTENCE (UNIT FOUR):

   Ellen and Tod planned to visit *Italy;* Rome, Florence, and Venice captured their interest.

2. The SEMICOLON is used before a coordinating conjunction *(and, but, or, nor, for)* if commas appear in either independent clause. It helps the reader identify the second independent clause which could be hidden because of the other commas in the sentence:

   They wanted to see Michelangelo's *David* in Florence, his *Pieta* in Rome, and his *Pieta* in *Milan; but* they could visit only three cities, not four.

3. The SEMICOLON is used before long connectors like *however, nevertheless, consequently* (UNIT FOUR), and short connectors like *still* and *then* to join two independent clauses. The long connectors are usually followed by a comma, but the short connectors are not.

   Tod wanted to travel Venice's Grand Canal in a gondola; *however,* Ellen was afraid she would become seasick.
   Tod assured Ellen that the Grand Canal was calm; *still* she hesitated to say yes.

THE SEMICOLON AS A SEPARATOR

The SEMICOLON may be used as a SEPARATOR.

4. The SEMICOLON may be used between words or word groups in a series if items in the series contain one or more commas:

   Other points of interest they listed were San Marco's Basilica, Venice; Castel Angelo, St. Peter's Basilica, and the Colosseum, Rome; and Michelangelo's tomb in Santa Croce Church, Florence.

● COLON

The COLON (:) is used conventionally in these ways:

1. The COLON appears at the end of an INDEPENDENT CLAUSE (UNIT FOUR) to introduce a list, a series of appositives (UNIT FOUR), or an explanation:

> Tod and Ellen wanted to visit two other countries: *Czechoslovakia and Hungary.*

> Ellen had a good reason for visiting Czechoslovakia: *she wanted to see the small towns where her grandparents had lived.*

2. The COLON often is preceded by words like the *following* or *as follows:*

In Prague they would travel with the following guides: the escort from Vienna, the guide representing the country of Czechoslovakia, and the guide for the city of Prague.

3. However, NO COLON is used between a verb and the noun following it (UNIT FOUR):

> NOT: Their bus would *carry: the* passengers, the guides, and the luggage.
> BUT: Their bus would *carry the* passengers, the guides, and the luggage.

> NOT: Other countries included in their itinerary *were: Austria,* Czechoslovakia, and Hungary.
> BUT: Other countries included in their itinerary *were Austria,* Czechoslovakia, and Hungary.

4. The COLON is used after the salutation in a business letter:

> Dear Mr. Mason:
> All your reservations have been confirmed . . .

5. The COLON separates hours and minutes in writing time:

> Departure time is *12:30* p.m., and arrival in London is *6:15* a.m.

EXERCISE 49

These sentences contain semicolons, colons, and commas where they should be. In the blanks at the right, write C for semicolon and D for colon and the number of the explanation which tells why the semicolon or colon has been used.

1. Tod and Ellen began to feel a link with the ancient world as they walked among Roman ruins; in addition, they saw the beginnings of the Christian era.   _____

2. The ravaged Colosseum, its metal and marble taken to build Christian churches, was a quiet ruin overrun by hundreds of cats at night; it was a grim reminder of some of the vicious Roman games.   _____

3. The catacombs, burrowing hundreds of miles on three and four levels below the earth's surface, give evidence of small, short-lived people; then the life span was about thirty years.   _____

4. The catacombs contain hundreds of "graves": openings about five feet long had been carved into the earth on both sides of long, low, narrow passages and had housed the cloth-wrapped corpses.   _____

5. The Catholic Brother who served as a guide in the catacombs gave the following explanation: "Because there are no air passages to the lower levels and no evidence of household articles, it is very unlikely that the Christians lived here to escape the Romans."   _____

6. Other links between the Roman and Christian eras are Castel S. Angelo, originally Hadrian's mausoleum; the Pantheon, a Roman temple, now a Catholic church; and the Vatican Museum, filled with Roman relics and statuary.   _____

lesson 50   Hyphens and Dashes

■ **HYPHEN (-)**

THE HYPHEN AS A SEPARATOR

1. The HYPHEN may be used as a separator between syllables. When a word of more than one syllable at the end of a line has to be divided and carried to the next line, the hyphen appears after a syllable and the remainder of the word is carried to the next line. Only words of more than one syllable can be hyphenated and *only between the syllables.* Check your dictionary for syllables in a word.

> The court questioned his *judg-
> ment* in releasing the prisoner.

THE HYPHEN AS A CONNECTOR

The HYPHEN may be used to connect two or more words used as a unit; however, some of these compound words may be written as separate words, or they may be spelled as single words. Current usage, detailed in dictionaries, determines how each word appears.

Separated word form	Hyphenated form	Solid form
all right	heart-to-heart	milkweed
head wind	teen-ager	juryman

2. Two words may be combined to form a new noun:

   cover-up
   run-down
   run-in

3. Two words may be combined to function as an adjective:

   heavy-duty   stout-hearted
   sharp-eyed   red-headed

4. Verbs may be combined to function as an adjective:

   divide-and-conquer tactic   wait-and-see attitude

5. Numerals and fractions may be used as compound adjectives:

three-fourths   ninety-five   thirty-third

6. Numeral and noun may be used in combination as adjectives:

thirty-cent   five-year

7. The word *self* may be combined with another word:

self-esteem   self-control   self-evident

8. Two adjectives may be combined to name nationalities:

Anglo-Saxon   Franco-Prussian   German-American

DASH (—)

The DASH, approximately twice as long as the hyphen, is used in these ways.

1. A single DASH can indicate a break in thought:

I volunteered to explain—but why bother now?

2. Two DASHES can set off an explanatory series:

She tries all the new cosmetics—pale lipsticks, frosted eye shadows, and white nail enamels—but she looks more like a circus clown than a beauty queen.

3. A single DASH may be used to set off an appositive (UNIT FOUR) at the end of a sentence:

Richard Bach wrote an imaginative story about a sea gull—*Jonathan Livingston Seagull.*

4. Two DASHES may be used to set off an appositive (UNIT FOUR) within the sentence:

The story about a seagull—*Jonathan Livingston Seagull*—won the hearts of millions of readers.

EXERCISE 50A

Divide the following words into syllables by writing them in the blank at the right with a hyphen between each syllable. Use your dictionary if you need help.

1. organize _____   4. creativity _____

2. syllabication _____   5. lightning _____

3. absolute _____   6. mathematics _____

EXERCISE 50B

Insert hyphens and dashes wherever they are
needed in the following sentences.

1. The fifty year old lighthouse the one on Bard's point is no longer used.

2. The black haired villain but why talk about him now?

3. The Anglo American treaty is still in effect.

4. Ted had his newest suits dry cleaned.

5. The sad faced clown Tom and Sue saw him yesterday delighted the children.

lesson 51   Quotation Marks, Italics, Ellipsis, Parentheses, Brackets

QUOTATION MARKS

1. DOUBLE QUOTATION MARKS (" . . . ") enclose the actual words of a speaker or passages quoted from a publication:

   The historian wrote, "In the early days travel was difficult because of poor roads."

2. DOUBLE QUOTATION MARKS enclose titles of short stories, poems, songs, articles, and other short works:

   "The End of Something"   "A Very Precious Love"   "Decorative Stitchery"

   Sometimes they enclose the title of a movie, play, or a television program. (See also ITALICS, No. 1, p. 000):

   "The Poseidon Adventure"
   "One Flew over the Cuckoo's Nest"
   "Maude"

3. DOUBLE QUOTATION MARKS enclose words being discussed (See also ITALICS, No. 3, p. 250):

   Some people confuse the word "formerly" with "formally."

4. DOUBLE QUOTATION MARKS are used to indicate a shift in usage or to suggest irony:

   The young executive tried to be a "cool cat."

   His friend, on the other hand, always used "correct" English.

5. SINGLE QUOTATION MARKS (' . . . ') enclose a second quotation or title within a first quotation:

   "Tell him to begin his story with 'Once upon a time . . .' to catch their attention," he suggested.

   "Have you read 'Neighbour Rosicky' by Willa Cather?"

6. PUNCTUATION WITH QUOTATION MARKS

Although the practice is not completely uniform, the following punctuation is usually acceptable:

a. Place all periods and commas within the quotation marks.

b. Place question marks and exclamation points within the quotation marks if they are a part of the quotation, or place them outside the quotation marks if they terminate the sentence in which the quotation appears.

c. Semicolons and colons, which almost never appear as part of quoted material, are placed outside quotation marks.

d. A dash within a quotation is placed within the quotation marks and is not followed by a period unless the quotation ends the sentence.

ITALICS

ITALICS are shown in both handwritten and typewritten manuscripts by underlining. They are used in these ways:

1. Italicize titles of books, magazines, newspapers, operas, motion pictures, and other long works:
   Aida, Newsweek, The New York Times, Midnight Cowboy, Slaughterhouse Five.

Use quotation marks for chapters, short stories . . .		Use italics for books, magazines . . .
"Carbon and Its Oxides"	in	*General Chemistry*
"The Prophet"	in	*Moby Dick*
"Thrill Seekers"	in	*Hot Rod*

2. Italicize foreign words or phrases not regarded as English words:

   persona non grata   *coup d'etat*

3. Italicize words that are being discussed: (See also Double Quotation Marks, No. 3, p. 249):

   The word *maximum* comes from the Latin words *magnus* and *maximus.*

4. Italicize words for emphasis.

   He *did* agree with me.

● ● ●   **ELLIPSIS (. . .)**

1. The ELLIPSIS is used to indicate something omitted, either a single word or whole sentences. It is used especially in quoted material:

   Let me give you some indication of what he said: "I stand firm in my belief that this country cannot survive . . . unless everyone sets himself the task of making it the strongest country in the world."

2. If the omitted material comes at the end of the author's sentence, a fourth period is added to terminate the sentence:

   I believe that he substantiates what I have felt when he says in part that we can "win only by full cooperation . . . . Everyone must be willing to do his part."

 PARENTHESES ( ) AND BRACKETS [ ] (ALWAYS USED IN PAIRS)

1. PARENTHESES enclose additions which may be illustrations, definitions, or added information. It is preferable to use parentheses sparingly. If the material is really pertinent to the paper, it should be included in the general content.

   The old car (Bob was the fifth owner) rattled and wheezed.

2. PARENTHESES are used to enclose numerals or letters in a series of items:

   Roger had three choices: (1) he could cooperate with his co-workers; (2) he could work alone; (3) he could urge his co-workers to follow his plan.

3. BRACKETS are used to insert information into a quoted passage, like the name of a book as explanation, the writer's personal comment about a quotation, or words inserted by an editor:

   "Micah made a flying machine in the late 1800's [1872]."

 4. BRACKETS may be used within parentheses:

   The doctors will need several assistants (secretaries, nurses [*both RN's and LVN's*], bookkeepers, and laboratory technicians) when the new clinic opens next month.

PUNCTUATION WITH PARENTHESES AND BRACKETS

5. Do not use punctuation within parentheses unless the sentence is set completely apart from other sentences. Otherwise, if the punctuation, such as commas or the end mark, are part of the main sentence, they are placed outside the parentheses and brackets.

   Charles Hamilton invented a dust mop. (He also invented a carpet cleaner.)

   Brian Parker (he had lived in the Bay Area) now has his office in Los Angeles.

EXERCISE 51

Insert quotation marks, italics, ellipsis, parentheses,
or brackets wherever they are needed in the following sentences. Circle your marks of punctuation.

1. The Times-Herald is published daily.

2. The columnist wrote in part, The new television situation comedies offer this season little that is
   new.

3. When the telephone rang it seemed to ring constantly the fat little man scowled, then answered it.

4. He thought the word libel was the same as liable.

5. Mark Hudson wrote sentimentally about his boyhood: I grew up in a small town Editor's note:
   Medina, Ohio where everyone knew every one else.

6. "Hamlet's soliloquy To be, or not to be is still my favorite," said the stooped, gray-haired actor.

7. The song Happy Days Are Here Again seemed to give us hope when we had very little, Tom's
   grandmother recalled.

8. Have you heard I really should not say this that Jane had another argument with Dick?

9. When will the tenth volume of History of the World be published? the book reviewer asked the
   editor.

10. The origin of the Greek word biblos meaning book is from the Egyptian word for papyrus.

lesson 52   **Capitalization**

To show that a word represents a particular person or thing, we capitalize the first letter of the word. We also use capital letters in titles, at the beginning of a sentence, and in some abbreviations. Here is a summary of capitalization in expository writing.

1. The first word of the following is capitalized:

   a. Sentence:

   The college's track star broke his leg.

   b. Lines of poetry:

   "For thy sweet love remembered, such wealth brings
   That then I scorn to change my state with kings."

   Exception: Some poets disregard this usage in order to create special effects. E. E. Cummings often omits all capitalization as part of his poetic devices.

   Haiku poetry from the 18th century provides one example:

   In the city fields
   contemplating cherry trees . . .
   strangers are like friends.
   —Issa

   c. A direct quotation:

   He asked, "When will the plane arrive?"

   Exception: When partial quotes are given, the first word may not be capitalized:

   When he refers to the "land of the free and the home of the brave," everyone knows what nation he means.

2. Proper names and abbreviations of proper names:

   a. People: Henry Robinson, Jos. Griffin

   Names of relatives: Mother (when it is used as a substitute for her given name), Uncle John, Aunt Mary.

   Exception: Do not capitalize when the word is preceded by a possessive: my mother, his uncle.

   b. Places: New York City, N.Y., Europe

    c. Races: Caucasian, Negro

    d. Languages and their abbreviations: English, Russian, German, Spanish, (Span.)

    e. Days of the week and their abbreviations: Sunday, Monday, (Mon.)

       Exception: The word *tomorrow* refers to any day of the week.

    f. Months of the year and their abbreviations: January, February, (Feb.)

    g. Points of compass to denote a region: North, West, Pacific Northwest

       Exception: Do not capitalize when they indicate direction.

         She turned west at the corner.

    h. Armed forces when they refer to forces of a particular country: United States Air Force, British Navy

    i. Reference to deity: God, Jesus, Zeus, Jehovah

       Exception: The word *god* is not capitalized when it refers to a nonspecific deity.

    j. Derivatives formed from proper nouns:
Shakespeare—Shakespearean drama; Victoria—a Victorian lamp; England—English literature.

       Exceptions occur for commonly used derivatives: Pasteur—pasteurized milk; China—chinaware.

3. The first and last word in all titles; all major words in titles, including verbs like *is* and *be*, except articles (*a, an, the*), conjunctions, and prepositions less than five letters in length.

    a. Books, articles, songs, etc.:

       The Old Man and the Sea
       Fate Is the Hunter

    b. Organizations and historical events:

       Boy Scouts of America

       The Battle of Bunker Hill

    c. Positions of importance (whether they are used as the name or following the name):

       President of the United States
       the Chief Justice of the Supreme Court

4. Specific courses but not areas of study. Names of languages are capitalized:

       He has enjoyed History 17A better than any other history course he had previously taken.

He also studied French and Spanish.

5. Nouns which are part of names made up of two or three words when they are used as a substitute for the complete name:

Lake for Lake Tahoe
University for Kent State University

6. Abstract nouns when they are personified or refer to ideals or institutions:

the Church
the State
the North Wind

7. *Street, River, Park,* etc., when they follow a proper name:

Sacramento River
Market Street

Exception: In informal writing many magazines and most newspapers do not capitalize these words.

EXERCISE 52

Capitalize all words that should be capitalized in the following sentences.

1. juan garcia is spanish.

2. harold radcliff wrote *car repair is a challenge.*

3. last sunday bob visited his mother.

4. his uncle lives on wild oak street.

5. people from new york city visited lake tahoe.

6. last march terry moved to eugene, oregon.

7. jeff enrolled in life science 2a.

8. martha did not take english or psychology.

9. the french play pleased the mayor.

10. judge walters greeted council members.

Now that you have completed the last exercise in this unit, YOU ARE READY FOR THE UNIT EIGHT REVIEW. If you need additional practice, complete the X-TRAS which follow.

UNIT EIGHT

UNIT EIGHT REVIEW will consist of sentences like the ones given here and another exercise in which quotation marks, italics, dash, parentheses, and hyphen will be needed. In order to add the necessary punctuation and capitalization, you should read the lessons and go back over the exercises. Note any corrections you have made; if you do not understand any part of the exercises thoroughly, ask your instructor for help. Make sure that you understand the directions for this exercise because those on the REVIEW will be the same.

Complete this exercise only if you want additional practice before you attempt the UNIT EIGHT REVIEW, Form A or Form B. Answers for it are in the Answer Key.

I.   Add PUNCTUATION AND CAPITALIZATION to the following sentences by writing the capital letter ABOVE the letter to be capitalized and by writing the punctuation ABOVE the space where the punctuation is to be inserted. The marks to be used include the following: period (.), question mark (?), exclamation point (!), semicolon (;), colon (:), comma (,), hyphen (-), dash (—), quotation marks (" . . . "). In some cases there may be two choices. For example, the first sentence in the illustration may end either with a semicolon or a period.

Example: "gay paree   ellen said happily   she and tod had arrived in paris about 7 30 a m after

racing through the french countryside on a midnight train from basel switzerland (17-18)

1. let s have dinner at the french restaurant near notre dame cathedral tod suggested to ellen i ll

    find out how much french i remember (18)

2. they walked down the dark narrow shop lined street finally they found the entrance to the

    restaurant (8-9)

3. seated on benches at a rustic table in the crowded dimly lit room they waited for the waiter to

    bring the menu but he set a large basket of bread on the table without saying a word (5)

4. a short time later he brought another basket to the table this one was filled with raw unpeeled

    vegetables tomatoes peppers onions cucumbers cauliflower and celery again he said nothing

    (11-13)

5. i wonder what we ll get next ellen said as she chewed on a stalk of celery while tod cut a tomato and a pepper into pieces (8)

6. they did not have to wait long the waiter brought a third basket and it was filled with a large assortment of sausages he smiled as he watched ellen s surprised expression (7-9)

7. tod i don t believe it ellen exclaimed which one should i try first (14)

8. a short time later the waiter brought the menu when he returned to take their orders tod quickly discovered that he had to order in french because the waiter knew no english (8)

9. after tod and ellen had finished the main course the waiter brought a large basket of cheeses and then he brought the menu for dessert (6)

10. as they left the restaurant at 11 15 p m ellen asked tod plaintively do you suppose you could take me back to the hotel in a wheelbarrow i m not sure i can walk (16)

II. Insert quotation marks, italics, dash, parentheses, or hyphen wherever they are needed in the following sentences.

1. The whole class will read Hemingway's short story The End of Something and his novel For Whom the Bell Tolls.

2. The Wall Street Journal gives daily stock market reports.

3. Her gross inefficiency what else can he call it cost the company five hundred dollars.

4. Pretend that you are your father the counselor told the young man. Try to show us how you think he acts.

5. Ben tried to find the words whether and weather in the dictionary.

unit NINE

Point of View, Parallelism, Editing

lesson 53   **Point of View**

When we as writers invite the reader to share an experience through our eyes, we stand in a certain relationship to the event or ideas we discuss. We write about the event FROM THE SAME POINT OF VIEW throughout the essay by making PERSON, NUMBER, TENSE, VOICE, and TONE CONSISTENT.

PERSON

If we write about a personal experience, something we are involved in, we use the first-person pronouns *I* or *we*. If we are witness to a happening, we talk about others by using the third-person pronouns *he*, *she*, *one*, *it*, or *they*. (Lessons 29 and 30)

> In expository writing we do not normally use second person—*YOU*.

In revising essays, we cross out the pronoun *you* and substitute *he, she, one, it,* or *they*. Here is an example of the kind of revision that is necessary.

Original	Revision
The *youth* of today is fighting for *their* identity. *They* want *everyone* to know *who they* are, *what they* stand for. *You* cannot get any place in the world if *you* crawl into a shell to hide. *We* must organize and speak with one voice so that *we* can be heard.	The *youth* of today is fighting for *his* identity. *He* wants everyone to know *who he* is, *what he* stands for. He realizes *that he* cannot get any place in the world if *he* crawls into a shell to hide. *He* urges others to organize and speak with one voice so that *they* can be heard.

All pronouns are italicized in both paragraphs. The word *youth* in the first line is italicized because it is the noun to which all the subsequent pronouns refer. It is a collective noun used to designate a group acting as a unit. Therefore, it is considered to be a third-person singular noun. The pronoun to be substituted for the pronouns in the original is *he (him, his)*—third-person singular masculine—which usually refers to a group, even if women are included. By changing all the pronouns to *he*, we have a coherent paragraph with consistent point of view.

TENSE

When we write about an event, we use appropriate verb forms consistently to relate the event to the time it happened (Lesson 9). We do not shift point of view by mixing tenses. However, we may use many of the tenses in one paragraph to show a sequence of events:

Although Jon Karney *had won* many new friends while he *campaigned* for the state senator's seat, he *lost* to his opponent who *seems* to have great strength in the urban areas. Nevertheless, Karney *has said* he *will be* a candidate in the next general election.

We may at times use the present tense (called historical present) to give immediacy to an event that happened in the past:

The gladiator is entering the arena, and all eyes *are* on him as he *bows* and *pays* homage to the dignitaries present.

VOICE

Although passive verbs are useful at times, we find that we can MAINTAIN CONSISTENT POINT OF VIEW IF WE USE THE ACTIVE VOICE and show the doer acting (Lesson 42). In the paragraph about the youth fighting for his identity, all the verbs are active. Readers can see the youth in action. The passage about the climbers of Mt. Everest (Exercise 42B) is much more effective in active voice than in passive voice.

Use passive voice only when the receiver should be emphasized. Use it sparingly.

TONE

Tone in writing can be generally defined as the cumulative effect given by word choice and the types of grammatical constructions used. Tone, therefore, depends on the kind of language we select. In either written or spoken English, we all use different kinds of language, depending upon the language situation. *Nonstandard English*, used in spoken language by many people who have relatively little formal education, is never appropriate for essays, letters, or other business, social, or literary writing. *Standard English* offers us at least three varieties or styles: *Formal English*, the style used for sermons, ceremonials, public addresses, lectures to certain professional groups, and very academic writing; *Informal English*, the variety used in conversation with close friends, very casual talks, or personal letters; and *General English*, the style used in the speech and writing of educated people. It is General English that is used for most correspondence, for almost all college papers, and in newspapers, magazines, and books. Characteristics of each variety of language are listed below, followed by examples. In the examples, as in actual usage, there are similarities as well as differences between the different varieties. But there are identifying features for each variety.

Formal English	**General English**
Vocabulary contains many words seldom used in speaking, usually specialized terms from scientific and scholarly fields. Sentence structure is elaborate, and sentences are fairly long. Words like relative pronouns, prepositions, and conjunctions are expressed, and they are repeated in parallel constructions. Word order may be unusual because of placement of modifiers and use of constructions found only in writing. NO CONTRACTIONS are used.	This written form is closer to speech patterns than Formal English; but it also contains constructions not regularly used in speaking, although these are not so weighty as those of Formal English. Vocabulary is specific, concrete, and uses words in general currency, like *fatherly* rather than *paternal, weather* rather than *the elements.* Sentences are of moderate length and usually have few inversions.
Informal English	**Nonstandard English**
This form reflects daily spoken language. Vocabulary ranges through a variety of colloquial expressions, newly coined words, contractions, and terms used in certain occupations. It is used in writing when the writer wants a conversational tone. Sentences are usually short and constructions uncomplicated, although some longer, more involved sentences may be used for variety.	This is primarily spoken language, but it may appear in fiction, for example, to reflect a particular kind of spoken language. Vocabulary may reflect terms used only in a particular area, or slang expressions. Sentences are short. Spelling may not reflect accurately the pronunciation given the words in spoken English. Use of the double negative occurs. Verbs may not agree in number with their subject; nonstandard forms such as *seed (saw)* and *drinked (drank)* may be used.

Following are some examples of different varieties of English. Note the contrasts between them.

Formal English	General English
The valley itself is mainly a rich alluvial plain, penetrated by a river geologically sufficiently mature to have developed meanders, irregularly elongate, about fifteen miles in length and some four miles in width at its greatest extent. It is mainly under cultivation, devoted to botanical species suitable for short-season agriculture, since frosts can be expected as late as June and as early as September, notably to oats, potatoes, and short-season root crops like sugar beets and rutabagas, to leguminous forage, timothy and clover, and, increasingly, alfalfa. 　　—Walker Gibson 　　　"Tough Talk and How to Detect It," *An Essay on Modern American Prose Styles*	The valley is mainly a rich plain formed by silt and mud deposits of the river that runs through it. Over a period of time the river has developed a wandering, irregular path. The river is about fifteen miles long and four miles across at its widest point. Most of the valley is farmland, devoted to short-season crops like oats, potatoes, and sugar beets, and, more recently, clover and alfalfa.
Informal English	**Nonstandard English**
"No, I don't think I know him," he said at last. "There isn't anyone but me out here this evening. The rest of them are all out at that fire, most likely." If you really want to hear about it, the first thing you'll probably want to know is where I was born, and what my lousy childhood was like, and how my parents were occupied and all before they had me, and all that David Copperfield kind of crap, but I don't feel like going into it, if you want to know the truth. In the first place, that stuff bores me, and in the second place, my parents would have about two hemorrhages apiece if I told anything pretty personal about them. 　　—J. D. Salinger 　　　*The Catcher in the Rye*	"No, I don't reckon I know him," he says at last. "There ain't anybody but me out here this evening, anyway. The rest of them are all out yonder at that fire, more than like." 　　—William Faulkner 　　　*Light in August*

EXERCISE 53A

Revise the following sentences to make them consistent in tone, person, and number. Cross out
words to be changed and write revisions above
or below them.

1. The artist should clean his brushes each time he finishes painting. You will find the brushes ready
   to use the next time you decide to paint.

2. Americans must vote for the men they want to run their government. We have no one to blame
   but ourselves if we get officials whom we do not want.

3. The student usually applies himself to his school work the first month of classes. They then relax
   and neglect their assignments.

4. Many partygoers seem to enjoy a game of charades. He likes dramatizing clues for his partners.

5. The youth of the nation should be given an opportunity to prove that he can be responsible. They
   sometimes act unwisely because they are rebelling against what they believe is unreasonable
   domination.

6. When preparing to write an essay, one should select a topic which he understands thoroughly. If
   you have only general information, you cannot write a convincing paper.

7. The newspaper is sometimes considered to be the voice of the people. But when they contain news
   stories against the best interests of the people, you begin to wonder whether they speak for the
   people or their own personal interests.

8. If everyone want to do their part to help others, they should work with volunteer service organizations and not expect to get paid for every minute they spend working.

9. A person who buys this car receives a guarantee which says you are not charged for parts which have to be replaced, only the labor for replacing them.

10. When a person fills out an application for a position, they should try to fill out every blank to indicate to the interviewer that they have tried to give all the information requested.

EXERCISE 53B

Revise the following sentences to eliminate all inconsistencies in point of view. Use subordination, parallelism, and comparisons to make sentences effective, and correct faulty pronoun reference, faulty modifier usage, ineffective use of passive voice, and any other problems you may find. Before rewriting, underline the words or word groups which need revision. Finally, read your revision and decide whether it needs more changes.

1. The four-course meal was served by the waitress, and before the meal is over, everyone has spots of food on them which was spilled by her.

2. Many mistakes are made by new drivers, but the experienced driver could make just as many if they were not careful.

3. All his keys were lost by Matt. He couldn't drive his car, he couldn't get into his house, and his desk was unavailable to him. He feels like giving up and going fishing, but he can't get his gear out of the garage because it's locked too.

4. Many beautiful homes were built by the Johnson brothers, but they also erect cracker boxes which can blow down in a strong breeze.

5. The horse wearing all his trappings was ridden by the knight dressed in a two-ton suit of armor and can not hardly get out of the mud puddle he backed into.

6. Jim was dressed in a real sharp suit and he feels sick when Nan meets him at the door in dungarees and shirt to go to the senior dance.

7. The football parade was organize by Ted Owen and myself. You never realize how much work you're getting into when you get involved in a project like that.

8. The movie is super. It was produced by the old movie veteran Clyde Thornton. He sure knew what he was doing when he did that.

9. It's a good thing for a person to be an excellent marksman if they're going hunting for big game in Africa. You never know when one of the enraged beasts might attack you.

10. The wheat was raised by the farmer and he was helped to harvest it by several of his neighbors which he had also helped in times past during the harvest season.

lesson 54 The Appropriate Word

To maintain consistent tone in written language we should be aware of the current usage of words and phrases. Some are appropriate for both written and spoken language, others only for spoken language. Knowing when to use them has to be learned. Even as we learn them, we know that language changes and that we should watch for these changes. Here is a partial list of words and phrases and notes about their usage. Others are listed in dictionaries. The labels *Informal* or *Colloq.* or *Slang* suggest that they may not be suitable in essays. Not all informal expressions are entirely inappropriate, but the discerning writer usually chooses the more formal expressions in preference.

Accept and *except*—*Accept* means *to receive; except* means *to omit.*

Ad—Colloquial form for *advertisement.*

Affect and *effect*—*Affect* is a verb meaning to *influence.*
   Effect can be used as a verb meaning *to bring about* or as a noun meaning *result.*

All right—The spelling shown here is the only acceptable spelling.
   Alright is not accepted as a spelling variation.

All the farther—The preferred form in written English is *as far as.*

Alot, a lot—Although pronounced as one word, *a lot* is written as two words.

Already—*Already* and *altogether* are adverbs, and *all ready* and *all together* adjective phrases which indicate all participants are ready or together.

Amount and *number*—*Amount* refers to quantity, and *number* is used for groups the individual members of which can be counted.

And/or—A combination sometimes necessary in commercial documents but not appropriate in expository writing.

Apt, liable, prone—Frequently all three words are used to mean *likely;* however, each has its own meaning. *Apt* means *suitable, appropriate,* or it may mean *skilled* or *quick to learn; liable* suggests that a person is responsible for his actions; *prone* means that he is predisposed to something inevitable.

As—Overworked word used instead of *that, whether, who, because,* and *since.*

Awful—Overworked word used colloquially to mean *ugly* or *very bad.* It is preferable to choose specific modifiers.

Back of, behind—*Behind* is preferable to *back of* in formal writing.

Being as, being that—Nonstandard substitutes for *because* or *since.*

Between, among—*Between* shows difference between two people and *among* shows difference among three or more.

Broke—Informal expression for *bankrupt* or *without funds.*

Compare with, compare to—Compare two like objects to show what they have in common (compare one with the other). Compare two unlikes to show how one might be representative or have characteristics of the other (compare a bird to an airplane).

Considerable—Acceptable as adjective but not as adverb or noun.

Continual, continuous—*Continual* conversation (person has to pause for breath) but *continuous* running of a motor.

Could of—In written English, not a substitute for *could have.*

Credible, credulous—Stories may be believable or *credible;* people are willing to believe or are *credulous.*

Different than—*Different from* is still preferred in formal writing, but *different than* is gradually gaining acceptance.

Disinterested, uninterested—*Disinterested* means *impartial, objective,* and *uninterested* means *lacking interest.*

Disremember—Dialectal expression for *do not remember,* not used in written English except to indicate dialect in conversation.

Double negative—Two or three negatives in one sentence are ordinarily unacceptable in formal writing unless the writer intends to arrive at a positive statement by using two negatives.

Elicit and *illicit*—*Elicit* means *to draw out; illicit* means *not permitted.*

Enthuse—Informal for *to become enthusiastic.*

Etc.—Latin abbreviation for *and so forth* should not be a vague substitute for the items which should be named specifically in a series. Since the *et cetera* means *and, and etc.* should not be used because the *and* is redundant. Common misspelling is *ect.*

Expect—Informal usage as a substitute for *suppose* or *suspect.*

Fix—Used as a noun, *fix* is informal for *predicament.* As a verb, it is colloquial for *punish. Fix* means *to make fast* or *to repair.*

Formally, formerly—*Formally* means in a formal manner; *formerly* means previously.

Guess—*Guess* is not a substitute for *believe.*

Had (hadn't) ought—The phrase should not be used for *ought to* or *should.*

Heap—Informal spoken word for *amount.*

Height, heighth—The first spelling is acceptable; the second is obsolete.

Holy, wholly—*Holy* means *sacred; wholly* means *entirely.*

In, into—*Into* shows movement from one place to another; *in* is static.

Infer, imply—*Infer* means to *draw a conclusion from evidence given; imply* means *to indicate* or *suggest.*

Invite—*Invite* used as a noun is an informal word for *invitation.*

Kind of, sort of—Informal expressions.

Later, latter—*Later* indicates *time; latter* is the second of a pair as in *the former* and the *latter.*

Leave, let—*Leave* should not be used for *let* to mean *allow* or *permit. Leave* means *depart from.*

Less, fewer—*Less* shows extent, amount, degree, but *fewer* refers to numbers.

Liable—See *Apt.*

Loose, lose—The first word is always an adjective; the second a verb.

Lots of—Informal for *many.*

Mad—Informal for *angry* or *annoyed* and slang for *enthusiastic.*

Mighty—Informal for *very.*

Most—Informal for *almost.*

Off of—Omit word *of* when using word *off*.

O.K. or *okay*—Informal for *endorse*.

Party—Informal for *person*. (Also legal terminology.)

Per—Used in business writing instead of *according to* or *concerning*.

Plan to—*Plan to* is preferable to *plan on*.

Pretty—Informal for *moderately*.

Quiet, quite—*Quiet* means *silent; quite* means *completely, entirely*.

Respectfully, respectively—*Respectfully* means *full of respect; respectively* means *each in turn*.

Same, such—Avoid using either word as a substitute for *it, this, that, them*.

Seldom ever—Omit *ever* when using *seldom*. It is redundant.

Shape—Informal for *condition*.

Show—Informal for *chance*.

Show up—Informal for *appear*.

Suit, suite—*Suit* means *clothes* or *series; suite* is *retinue* or *collection*.

Suspicion—This word is a noun. *Suspect* is the verb form.

Take and, try and, up and—Usually *take and* and *up and* can be omitted entirely from a sentence without losing meaning. *Try to* should be substituted for *try and*, which is colloquial.

Used to, didn't use to, used to could—Informal expressions.

Wait on—Dialectal for *wait for*.

Want in, out, off—Informal expressions which can be made formal by inserting infinitive: He wants *to go* out.

Ways—Informal for *way*.

Where . . . at, to—Omit *at* and *to* when using *where;* they are redundant.

-wise—Adding *-wise* to a noun creates informal expressions.

Without, on account of—Informal for *unless* or *because.*

EXERCISE 54A

Some of the following word groups are formal, and others are informal. Write F for formal and I for informal. Use your dictionary to find words you do not know.

1. bank on his strength _____
2. centripetal force _____
3. shell out money for expenses _____
4. polyphagia as one symptom _____
5. in good shape _____
6. real cool cat _____
7. extrasensory perception _____
8. plenty eats and drink _____
9. unsought adulation _____
10. the epitome of strength and power _____
11. awe-inspiring apparition _____
12. go for broke _____
13. a washout in the prelims _____
14. ravenous appetite _____
15. a patent prevarication _____
16. forced to declare bankruptcy _____
17. take it easy _____
18. seeking a special dispensation _____

21. up and died last night _____
22. in back of the old store _____
23. most everybody in town _____
24. hadn't ought to try _____
25. a judgment of the court _____
26. immediate apprehension _____
27. has got to stop _____
28. extentuating circumstances _____
29. sweat like a horse _____
30. disrespectful and overbearing _____
31. organized instruction _____
32. come home to roost _____
33. cocky as an old rooster _____
34. postreduction X-rays _____
35. release of tension _____
36. demand restitution _____
37. hood taken for a ride _____
38. jet propulsion system _____

19. tentatively scheduled for
    probation   _____

20. essence of propriety   _____

39. rudiments of a past age   _____

40. scale the heights   _____

EXERCISE 54B

Underline the words or phrases that are informal.
In the blank at the right write the word or phrase
that is appropriate for written English. If you
believe that no change should be made, write A
in the blank.

1. Will you wait on me while I finish this letter?   _____

2. He got himself into a terrible fix.   _____

3. She could of bought the dress if she had saved money for it.   _____

4. That is a mighty delicious cake you baked.   _____

5. He has a long ways to go before he reaches the top.   _____

6. Are you going to leave him go out of town alone?   _____

7. There are lots of novels Connie wants to read.   _____

8. Mr. Nelson insisted that he wants out of the responsibility.   _____

9. College students should plan on a lot of hard work before
   they get their degrees.   _____

10. Most every one talked about the game yesterday.   _____

11. Students should be quite in the library.   _____

12. The Martins are liable to think Jan does not like them if
    she does not attend the party.   _____

13. The ad for the new dictionary appeared in all the daily
    papers.   _____

14. Jim kind of wants to take part in the play.   _____

15. Tim has less arithmetic problems to do than his sister.   _____

16. He burst in the room and laughed hysterically.   _____

17. I guess you do not understand the story he told.   _____

18. Don told an incredulous story.   _____

19. Mark didn't used to like to play volley ball.   _____

20. Where did he go to with the moving van?   _____

IF YOU HAVE MISSED TWO OR MORE
SENTENCES in the first part, review the usage
glossary, and then continue with the second part.

21. The detective suspicioned that the old man had stolen the
money.   _____

22. He ordered two shirts and requested same be delivered to
him.   _____

23. The little boy was so mad that he smashed all his toys.   _____

24. She said that she could come to work latter in the day.   _____

25. Which party is responsible for rent collection?   _____

26. He can take and open the store if he has the energy.   _____

27. Nell seldom ever sees Susan in the library.   _____

28. He had ought to get a copy of the book for himself.   _____

29. Jack worked considerable hard to finish the project.   _____

30. Mrs. Otis does not know as she wants to be president
another year.   _____

31. This is all the farther the train runs.   _____

32. It seems to be alright for him to use the car.   _____

33. What affect did the rain have on the tomato crop?   _____

34. They received invites to the reception.   _____

35. If the house is in good shape, he might buy it.   _____

36. The shipment will be sent per the written instructions.   _____

37. They were enthused about winning the game.   _____

38. He disremembers the whole traumatic experience.   _____

39. The amount of people coming will have to be determined
     today.   _____

40. Mrs. Hudson formally lived in Wichita.   _____

lesson 55   **Parallelism**

To achieve a balanced harmony in writing, we use PARALLELISM: we pair IDENTICAL GRAMMAT-ICAL UNITS, whether they are WORDS, PHRASES, or CLAUSES:

Words: *open* and *close*

Phrases: *on the land* and *in the air*

Clauses: *after the game had ended* and *before the guests arrived*

Or we place these units in a series:

to want, to work, to win

She called, she cried, she screamed.

It is similar to writing about fruit, for example. *Fruit* is a general classification just like *vegetable*, *grain*, or *food*. The items of fruit we name can be *apples*, *pears*, and *cherries*. But we cannot include *carrots* or *bread*.

Similarly, if we are using infinitives, we cannot also include V-ing words:

NOT: *The artists wanted *to sketch* with charcoal, *to paint* with watercolors, and *enameling* copper jewelry.

BUT: The artists wanted *to sketch* with charcoal, *to paint* with watercolors, and *to enamel* copper jewelry

> Parellelism, however, refers to more than the single sentence. Several sentences can be parallel with one another. Or paragraphs—paragraphs of comparison, for example—can be patterned identically. These patterns within a written passage—like the patterns in music—give it rhythm, unity, and coherence. They involve the reader—or listener—and permit him to experience a sense of completeness at the end of the passage.

When we discussed Coordination in Lesson 25, we noted that the coordinating conjunctions *and*, *but*, *for*, *or*, and *nor* join two or more equal elements. In other words, the elements are parallel. Therefore, the following sentence is faulty because *and* joins a NOUN and an ADJECTIVE CLAUSE:

NOT: *Herb Jones, the actor, and who has visited us several times, will appear in a new movie.

We can revise this sentence by omitting the word *and;* the adjective clause then modifies *the actor*, an appositive (Lesson 28). The parallel structures in the revised sentence are *Herb Jones* and *the actor*.

BUT: Herb Jones, the actor who has visited us several times, will appear in a new
movie.

We can also achieve parallelism by combining the same kind of qualities or attributes. If we write about
a person, for example, we should discuss his physical appearance separately from his activities and interests. The following sentence is not parallel for two reasons: adjectives are combined with a noun in the
series, and the words discuss both physical characteristics and personal interests.

```
            ─────────── Parallel ───────────
      NS  LV Adj-c Adj-c      Adj-c                    Nsc
NOT: *Bill is tall, muscular, handsome, and a race car driver.
```

```
      ────────Parallel────────   ───────── Parallel ─────────
      NS              NS      LV Adj-c Adj-c      Adj-c
BUT:  Bill, a race car driver, is tall, muscular, and handsome.
```

In addition, terms used should be of the same classification. If we write about plants, for example, we
can include only the names of plants, not animals:

NOT: Jeremy proposed to analyze the structure of trees, shrubs, grass, and cows.

The word cows included in this list destroys the unity of the sentence. We have to explain in more
detail how the structure of cows is related to structure of plants—if there is a relationship.

SUBJECTS AND VERBS AND PREPOSITIONS IN PARALLEL STRUCTURES

If two verbs of different tenses appear in the same sentence, each verb should be complete. The word
offer cannot be used with has:

NOT: *He has and will offer again to help the family. (He has offer?)

BUT: He has offered and will offer again to help the family.

If one subject is singular and the other plural in a compound sentence, the verb should be stated for
each subject and agree with each subject:

NOT: The house was painted and   (Singular)
        the windows washed.   (Plural)

BUT: The house was painted and   (Singular subject and verb)
        the windows were washed.   (Plural subject and verb)

Each preposition that belongs idiomatically with a word should be stated even if one object is used
with both prepositions:

He argued with rather than shouted at the young executive.

PAIRED CONNECTORS

CORRELATIVE CONJUNCTIONS are another kind of connector used with coordinate elements to achieve parallelism. These are used in pairs:

both . . . and

not only . . . but also

either . . . or

neither . . . nor

whether . . . or

These correlative conjunctions, like the coordinating conjunctions, connect equal grammatical elements:

Nouns: He bought *not only the boat*   C Ndo
                          but also the boat trailer.   C Ndo

Adjectives: She was *both beautiful*   C Adj-c
                          and shapely.   C Adj-c

Phrases: They had to decide *whether to rent an apartment*   C Inf Ndo
                                          or to buy a house   C Inf Ndo

Clauses: *Either she arrives on time,*   C NS Vi Adv,
                    or we will leave without her.   C NS Vi Adv

PUNCTUATION

NO PUNCTUATION is needed between the words or phrases joined by correlative conjunctions. USE A COMMA before the second correlative conjunction that connects the second independent clause to the first, as in the last example above.

EXERCISE 55A

Rearrange the following sentences to show the parallel structures within them. Begin by underlining the same grammatical elements or parallel structures in each sentence. Then write the last element of the parallel structure under the first. See the pattern given in the example. If there are no parallel structures, write None in the space below the sentence.

-------------(1)-------------   -----------(2)----------
Example: Mary Lou *bought several dresses* and *ordered a red coat.*

Mary Lou *bought several dresses* (1) and
ordered a red coat (2).

1. He likes bacon and eggs.

2. Will you call her and tell her the time of the meeting?

3. She cleared the table, and then she washed dishes.

4. She can, however, comply with your instructions.

5. Jack and Tom bought an old car to repair and to rebuild.

6. Edison invented the light bulb, and Marconi invented the wireless.

7. The high school offers both sewing and cooking.

8. The boys can take wood shop, or they can take car repair.

9. Workers like their coffee break, but they do not care to pay for the coffee.

10. The acrobat flew to one trapeze and then swung back to the first one.

EXERCISE 55B

In the following sentences there may be a structure which is not parallel with other elements in the sentence. Underline it, and write the revised parallel form in the blank. If no revision is needed, write A for Acceptable in the blank. Begin by writing NS over each subject, V over each verb, and C over each conjunction. Then examine word groups joined by the conjunctions and determine whether they are parallel.

1. Jed sat there all day smoking and having a conversation.   _____

2. Mary can either wash the car, or she can clean the house.   _____

3. Miss Nelson is a teacher and who writes stories.   _____

4. She traveled in Europe not only to see the sights but also to study art.   _____

5. The art course included drawing, to paint, and sketching.   _____

6. The building designed by the architect and which John built has large cracks in the walls.   _____

7. The class has three projects: writing a term paper, to read three novels, and attending two plays.   _____

8. Mabel is not only attractive but also an intellectual.   _____

9. That painting is gaudy and without meaning.   _____

10. His suggestion is brilliant, original, and will work.   _____

EXERCISE 55C

Join these sentences by inserting correlative conjunctions: *either . . . or, neither . . . nor, not only . . . but also, both . . . and, whether . . . or.* You may omit words or add words. Be sure that the construction following one connector is parallel with the construction following the other. Begin by writing NS over each subject, V over each verb, and C over each conjunction.

Example: Charles will buy a horse.

         NS   C   Ndo C   Ndo
Charles will buy *either* a horse *or* a sports car.

OR

Charles will buy a sports car.

  C   NS   Vt--------   Ndo C NS Vt------   Ndo
Either Charles will buy a horse, *or* he will buy a sports car.

1. Sarah and Tom will buy the large white house in the center of town.
   They will consider living on her father's ranch.

2. He is a karate expert.
   He is an excellent wrestler.

3. The principal does not want to attend the convention.
   The teachers do not want to attend the convention.

4. George will repair the tractor and plow the field.
   He will hire Thomas to do the plowing.

5. Marshall will not give Ben a job.
   Marshall will not lend Ben any money.

lesson 56   **Sentence Editing**

After we have written one sentence or many sentences, we read what we have written and then edit or rewrite until the sentences express what we want to say. Sometimes rewriting a day or two after the original writing is the most productive way of any because we can read what we have written more objectively than if we try to revise immediately.

As editors, we must know how to eliminate unnecessary words, how to add words to clarify a point, how to combine ideas of equal importance, how to subordinate ideas of lesser importance to the main idea, how to create rhythm and balance with parallel structure—how to use the many writing techniques discussed in the preceding lessons.

In addition, we want variety in sentence patterns, emphasis to show importance of subjects, unity of thought, and economy.

VARIETY

In addition to using the word order of the basic sentence patterns, we have found that we can invert word order and use passive transformations. We can begin sentences with phrases or clauses for variety:

V-ed Phrase:	*Distressed because she had dropped her ring,* Ellen began to cry.
V-ing Phrase:	Joe, *wanting to help,* climbed down the ladder into the dry well.
Passive Verb:	His elbows *were skinned* as he hit the rough blocks of stone.
Prepositional Phrase:	*In the bottom of the well* Joe found the ring.
Adverbial Clause:	*When Joe handed it to Ellen,* she hugged and kissed him.
Inverted Sentence:	Never again would she lose it.

Sentences of various lengths relieve the monotony of a repeated pattern:

She arrived. She unlocked the door. As she entered the deserted cabin, she looked carefully into each dark corner of the room.

EMPHASIS

Emphasis shows our readers stress or importance of words and ideas. Choice of words and word position help the writer to emphasize particular parts. Examine the following techniques.

Well-chosen nouns and verbs in a sentence are usually more emphatic than clusters of ineffective modifiers. *Procedures* and *results* are nouns.

NOT: Indoctrination *procedures* guaranteed successful *results.*

BUT: Indoctrination guaranteed success.

The words *procedures* and *results* are vague and require modifiers. Omitting them and changing *successful* to *success* gives emphasis to the main ideas.

Position of the words to be emphasized is important also. The beginning and the end of the sentence are more emphatic than the middle of the sentence:

Beginning: *Finally* he decided to tell the truth.

Middle: He decided *finally* to tell the truth.

End: .   He decided to tell the truth *finally.*

We can use some mechanical devices for emphasis, but they should be used sparingly if they are to be effective:

Underlining or italics: Do *not* come unless you intend to work

Capitalizing all letters: Use RED ink to mark answers.

Increasing white space around words: Read   directions   carefully   before   answering.

NOTE: Question marks and commas are NOT used for emphasis.

UNITY

Each part of the sentence is related to the other:

NOT: Among tourist attractions in San Francisco are Fisherman's Wharf, Chinatown, Coit Tower, and *they have a city government.*

BUT: Among tourist attractions in San Francisco are Fisherman's Wharf, Chinatown, and Coit Tower.

The thought needed to complete a sentence is expressed, not omitted or understood:

NOT: *Trying to go out every night and working all day besides.

BUT: Trying to go out every night and working all day besides *take more energy than I seem to have.*

Ideas expressed are pertinent, not irrelevant strays which can creep into sentences:

NOT: Don Allen, who lived next door in my home town, *which is not too far from Chicago where we spent many enjoyable weekends when I was growing up,* is the new manager of a grocery chain.

BUT: Don Allen, who lived next door in my home town, is the new manager of a grocery chain.

ECONOMY

The shortest sentence is not always the best sentence, but elimination of unnecessary words saves the reader from wading through pages of meaningless prose.

One cause of REDUNDANCY is the unnecessary repetition of words similar in meaning. Improve the sentence by eliminating one word or word group:

NOT: *As a rule* he is *usually* on time.

BUT: *As a rule* he is on time.

NOT: He expects to arrive tomorrow *evening* about *midnight.*

BUT: He expects to arrive tomorrow about *midnight.*

PADDING is the use of vague, general words like *line, element, factor, situation, aspect,* and many others.

NOT: The important *factor* to consider in the news writing *situation* is the human interest *element.*

BUT: We should consider human interest in writing news stories.

FORMS OF THE VERB *TO BE* and expressions like *who was* or *which is* sometimes can be eliminated.

NOT: The coat *which is blue* is ten years old.

BUT: The *blue* coat is ten years old.

WORDY TRANSITIONS take up space but say very little:

NOT: *It goes without saying,* nevertheless, that they are unwilling to cooperate.

BUT: Nevertheless, they are unwilling to cooperate.

NOT: *Taking this factor into consideration,* they concluded that his findings were incomplete.

BUT: Therefore, they concluded that his findings were incomplete.

PRETENTIOUS WORDS do not give elegance to writing.

NOT: I can say with genuine veracity that my intentions to attain the pinnacle of success are of the most praiseworthy caliber.

BUT: Truthfully, I intend to succeed.

EXERCISE 56A

Rewrite the following sentences to remove colorless, unnecessary, and uninformative words. First,

cross out unnecessary words and add needed
words. Then arrange the remaining words into an
effective sentence. See Grading Guidelines at the
beginning of the book for the number of points
deducted for various kinds of writing problems.

1. The purpose of his lecture was to explain how one goes about giving artificial respiration to a person who has almost drowned.

2. The fact of the matter is that news which appears in newspapers is old by the time readers get their papers because television can give a report at the scene as it is happening.

3. It goes without saying that there are many reasons why the rules committee refuses to listen to Dwight Huston's grievances.

4. The man who was wearing a blue shirt made every attempt possible to rescue the dog which was small and brown and white as it perched precariously on a log in the river which was raging.

5. Getting down to the facts of the matter, it is increasingly evident to all concerned that the radical element in the college community is definitely, if not totally, responsible for the disquieting atmosphere that tends to exist hereabouts.

6. The different fields of occupation have intrigued me since I was in high school, and I am still contemplating carefully what course my future program of study will take.

7. The evidence at hand seems to point to the fact that Tim Elliott was not present at the time of the demise of the victim who had been put to rest by a bullet which penetrated his skull.

8. In all the careful considerations given to the problem at hand, Bob Richards has maintained an air of complete control and calm which is certainly admirable, to say the least.

9. There appears to be from time to time the expression of the feeling that there could be more efficiency in turning out products which are assembled on our assembly line.

10. In the course of the discussion of the possibilities for opening another unit in our extensive chain of operation across the country, Mark Hudson has appeared to be rather reluctant to embark on such a venture at this particular time which he considers not to be the most opportune.

EXERCISE 56B

Rewrite the following sentences to eliminate any ideas not directly related to the main thought in the sentence.

1. On his way home from work Dave crashed into an oncoming car, but he did not have time to get his homework done.

2. Mary Tyler, who operates the beauty shop and whose mother lives in Nebraska, won the award this year for an original hair style.

3. The history instructor announced that he would give a mid-term examination, but Dwight is having difficulty with several math problems.

4. If you like sea food, you will like Harvey's Haven, which serves delicious hamburgers.

5. Mrs. Watson, who has been living in Los Angeles where she operates a grocery for her nephew who is ill, and who has had a hard time all her life, is in the hospital now recovering from pneumonia.

6. The reference book John is using contains helpful information for three of his classes, but he finds he has little time to play baseball.

7. Rain came through the open window and ruined half the carpeting, and the furnace continued to operate efficiently.

8. Because Ellis dislikes working out details of a research project, he hired Ross who is a star athlete.

9. The dog, nose to the ground, ran wildly through the forest, and he likes to sleep by the open fire in the winter.

10. The geraniums bloomed all summer, and the evergreens thrived, but Lucy had no time to can peaches or pears.

lesson 57   Summary of Sentence Parts

All the lessons preceding this one have been about the sentence—sentence patterns, sentence parts, coordination, and subordination. How do we use these to understand sentences and to improve writing?

First, we know how to identify a word group as a sentence by recognizing a subject (NS) and verb (V):

NS   V
The small isolated island in the Pacific, north of Hawaii, had no landing strip for the plane with medical supplies and a doctor aboard.

As we examine this word group further, we are able to label *strip* as Ndo, the word that completes the verb, and recognize that the remaining words are mainly single-word or word-group modifiers. Each modifier and each word group functioning as a modifier have been italicized to show their relationship to the basic sentence pattern:

NS   Vt   Ndo
The small isolated island *in the Pacific, north of Hawaii,* had *no landing* strip *for the plane with medical supplies and a doctor aboard.*

We are also able to identify the two parts of the sentences: the subject—the noun with all its modifiers—and the predicate—the verb, its object and modifiers:

                    NS
Subject: The small isolated island in the Pacific, north of Hawaii,

                    Vt   Ndo
Predicate: had no landing strip for the plane with medical supplies and a doctor aboard.

Second, we are able to observe whether the subject-verb combination is introduced by a subordinator. If it is, the word group is a dependent clause which must either be rewritten as an independent clause or connected to an independent clause:

Before the plane could land to give help to the critically ill woman **(Dependent clause)**

Before the plane could land to give help to the critically ill woman, *men removed hundreds of palm trees to make a runway.* **(Independent clause is italicized.)**

Third, we are able to see whether the introductory word may function as a preposition. If it does, the word group needs words added, to make a prepositional phrase; or the word has to be attached to an independent clause:

P   P   P
After many hours   of strenuous work   in the hot, humid jungle-like area   **(A series of prepositional phrases.)**

After many hours of strenuous work in the hot, humid jungle-like area, *the men finally*
Vt   Ndo
cleared an adequate runway. **(The independent clause is italicized.)**

Last, we are able to analyze the relationship of ideas if we can recognize word groups and their function. Then we can decide whether we want to keep them as they are or rearrange them.

When we accomplish this last step, we can then say we are writers because we know what we want to say; and we are able to edit and revise what we write until it says what we want it to say.

EXERCISE 57A

Examine each word group. Write S in the blank if
it is an ACCEPTABLE SENTENCE and F if it is a
FRAGMENT; if it needs punctuation, a connector,
or punctuation and connector between two independent clauses, insert these in the appropriate
place and circle them. Begin by writing NS above
each subject and V above each verb.

1. Men's views of their relationship to the universe have changed many times
   throughout the centuries.   _____

2. At one time many thinking the sun revolved around the earth.   _____

3. Others believed that the earth is flat some still believe this.   _____

4. After Columbus had discovered the western hemisphere and Magellan had
   sailed around the world.   _____

5. Discovery of radio and the wireless improved communication.   _____

6. The advent of television connected people across continents and let them see
   how others live.   _____

7. Peoples of the world have been able to see an event simultaneously when the
   television broadcast is beamed by way of the communications satellite. _____

8. Improved telescopes with gigantic mirrors have opened new views of outer
   space and astronomers have been able to see stars and galaxies never viewed
   before.   _____

9. Astronauts have been able to make observations in the atmosphere-free void
   of space they have taken remarkable photographs which help scientists on
   earth.   _____

10. Finally, men's space flights have given them a view of the earth from a dis-
    tance and have let them see the earth sphere in its relationship to the rest of
    the universe.   _____

EXERCISE 57B

Identify the bold-faced word groups as the subject,
predicate, or modifier by writing the appropriate
word in the blank at the right. Begin by writing NS
above each subject and V above each verb.

Remember:

Subject: a noun or pronoun and its modifiers, or a word group functioning as a noun.

Predicate: a verb or verb phrase and its modifiers and complements.

Modifier: adjective or adverb, either single words or word groups functioning as modifiers.

1. Going abroad is an exciting experience for most people; **boarding a plane and
   flying across the Pacific to Hawaii** is thrilling beyond words.   _____

2. Because the islands have been idealized **in fiction and travel books,** they seem to
   be a refuge for relaxation on sunny beaches.   _____

3. The traveler is not disappointed **when he sees the blue Pacific hitting the beach
   at Waikiki,** but he learns that much of the natural beauty is threatened by man's
   destruction and pollution.   _____

4. The islands have their own identities, and even within each island **the contrast of
   areas** is very evident—a lush tropical growth next to lava-covered desolation.   _____

5. Other contrasts are the thirteen-thousand-foot volcanic mountains on Hawaii,
   where people may ski in the winter snow while **those on the sea-level coasts**
   enjoy the warm, sunny beaches.   _____

6. **Except for Oahu, where Honolulu and Waikiki are located,** the islands are not
   heavily populated.   _____

7. Land development is mainly on the outer edges of the islands because the inner
   portions **are used for crops like pineapple and sugar cane or are inaccessible.**   _____

8. Strange but beautiful Molokai, one of the smaller islands where Father Damien's
   leper colony is located, **is facing a new future since the federal government began
   installing irrigation lines.**   _____

9. Crops on Molokai have been limited mainly to pineapple **because strong winds
   blow down sugar cane and other tall plants.**   _____

10. **The meeting of East and West** is very evident in the islands where one sees a
    blending of many peoples and cultures.   _____

Now that you have completed the last exercise in this unit, YOU ARE READY FOR THE UNIT NINE
REVIEW. If you need additional practice, complete the X-TRAS which follow.

UNIT NINE

UNIT NINE REVIEW will consist of exercises like the ones in Lessons 53 through 57. To prepare for the REVIEW, read the lessons and go back over the exercises. Note any corrections you have made; if you do not understand any part of the exercises thoroughly, ask your instructor for help. Make sure that you understand the directions for each exercise because those on the REVIEW will be very similar.

Complete these exercises only if you want additional practice before you attempt the UNIT NINE REVIEW, Form A or Form B. Answers for these are in the Answer Key.

I.   Make point of view consistent by changing
     pronouns and verbs to appropriate forms.

Buying a house can be an exhausting experience. First, the prospective buyer must visit neighbor-

hoods within a city to decide where he wants to live. Then you had to find houses for sale. Some-

times we get the best results by working with a real estate agent. When he had finally found a suit-

able house, he can relax, but then you have to get ready for the big move.

II. Rewrite these sentences to make elements
     parallel. Begin by writing NS above each sub-
     ject and V above each verb. Then identify the
     elements to be made parallel.

   1. Dennis either will agree to the proposal or he will offer one of his own.

   2. Last month the Johnsons went to Italy, Austria, and Paris.

   3. Jackson has and will ask again for an assistant on the research project.

   4. Billy White, a juggler and who is also an acrobat, broke his arm last night.

5. The lock was broken and the tools stolen.

6. Jeff not only has a sailboat, but he also owns an airplane.

7. The sports car is well designed but without comfort.

8. The botanist could neither identify the plant pest, nor could he suggest an insecticide for it.

9. The notes about the experiment were clearly written and orderly but the laboratory equipment disorganized and dirty.

10. His teeth were discolored but without cavities.

III. Combine these sentence groups into single sentences by eliminating unnecessary words and by using coordinate and subordinate elements to show relationship of ideas. You may revise as much as you wish, but include all ideas expressed. See Grading Guidelines at the beginning of the book for the number of points deducted for various kinds of writing problems.

1. We may not think about our fears and wishes. We may not talk about them. They are often expressed in our dreams.

2. Marie had lost her surfboard. She spied a shark. She swam frantically toward shore.

3. Daryl finished ironing his shirts. He began to sweep the apartment. The telephone rang.

4. The child sniffed the air. She smelled the steak cooking on the barbecue. It was in the back yard. She felt hungry.

5. The play was about to begin. It was a premiere performance. The actors waited nervously back-stage. The audience became silent as the house lights dimmed. The curtain rose.

POSTTEST

The POSTTEST will consist of exercises like those in UNIT FOUR, UNIT EIGHT, and UNIT NINE. In addition, there will be sentences to combine, like the ones in UNIT NINE, and sentences like the following ones which reflect problems discussed throughout this book. These test your ability to proofread and to identify parts of sentences that need to be revised. To prepare for the POSTTEST, review all the lessons and exercises. Note any corrections you have made; if you do not understand any part of the exercises thoroughly, ask your instructor for help.

USAGE, PUNCTUATION, CAPITALIZATION, SPELLING. Read each sentence and examine each lettered, underlined segment. If you find an error in usage, punctuation, capitalization, or spelling in an underlined segment, note the letter printed under the part and record your answer in the blank to the right of the sentence. If there is no error, mark C in the blank. Numbers in parentheses refer to the units in this book.

1. The <u>wifes</u> of the employees <u>planned</u> the annual
       A   B
   picnic. (ONE)   C. NO CHANGE   1. _____

2. Only <u>familys</u> of company <u>employees</u> were eligible for
        A   B
   benefits. (ONE)   C. NO CHANGE   2. _____

3. The construction workers <u>raised</u> the steel girder <u>very easily</u>
                             A   B
   with a crane. (ONE)   C. NO CHANGE   3. _____

4. <u>Everyone want to</u> help the <u>Piersons</u> last year after their
      A   B
   house had burned. (ONE)   C. NO CHANGE   4. _____

5. The collection of old coins <u>had lain</u> unnoticed on the closet
                                  A

<u>shelf for</u> several years. (ONE)   C. NO CHANGE   5. _____
  B

6. Lynne <u>has drove</u> to New York several <u>times to</u> see Broad-
          A   B

way productions. (ONE)   C. NO CHANGE   6. _____

7. <u>In todays world</u> there is much suffering <u>despite rapid</u>
       A   B

<u>advances</u> in medicine. (TWO)   C. NO CHANGE   7. _____
  B

8. Michael <u>can't hardly see</u> where he <u>is going</u> in the
               A   B

fog. (TWO)   C. NO CHANGE   8. _____

9. Sheila <u>didn't get no money</u> for the <u>work she</u> did. (TWO) C. NO CHANGE   9. _____
             A   B

10. David was <u>pleased because</u> he did <u>fine</u> on his written
                 A   B

examination. (TWO)   C. NO CHANGE 10. _____

11. The engine <u>tune-up</u> made the car run <u>good</u> in cold
              A   B

weather. (TWO)   C. NO CHANGE 11. _____

12. <u>There are, moreover,</u> at least ten more pages to be written.
     A   B
(FOUR)   C. NO CHANGE 12. _____

13. Willis was determined to become <u>a Shakespearean</u>
                                A

<u>actor however,</u> he discovered he preferred to sing. (FOUR) C. NO CHANGE 13. _____
  B

14. Citrus <u>fruits need</u> more sunshine than many <u>plants; as a</u>
         A   B

result, they grow only in certain areas. (FOUR)   C. NO CHANGE 14. _____

15. Melinda <u>bought four</u> dresses, two <u>coats, and</u> three pairs of
           A   B

shoes. (FOUR)   C. NO CHANGE 15. _____

16. After Frank decided to spend a week <u>camping, he</u> ordered
                                  A

some <u>supplies; food,</u> tent, sleeping bag, and a
       B

canoe. (FOUR)   C. NO CHANGE 16. _____

17. Sarah and her bought ten yards of bright, flowered material
      A   B

    for bikinis. (FIVE)   C. NO CHANGE   17. _____

18. Roger gave Tom and I an explanation of the mystery that
              A   B

    we could not believe. (FIVE)   C. NO CHANGE   18. _____
         B

19. Vera and myself have been trying to build a sailboat for
      A   B

    two months. (FIVE)   C. NO CHANGE   19. _____

20. Mrs. Watson is the teacher whom, I believe, will teach the
                           A

    history class. (FIVE)   C. NO CHANGE   20. _____
    B

21. When each one replies to the invitation, send them a post-
                           A   B

    card to confirm reservations. (FIVE)   C. NO CHANGE   21. _____

22. All members of the committee has asked two witnesses to
                      A   B

    testify a third time. (FIVE)   C. NO CHANGE   22. _____

23. Where is the offices of the manufacturing plant which John
        A   B

    Holt and his partner purchased? (FIVE)   C. NO CHANGE   23. _____

24. Tiny is the largest of the two elephants in the circus. (SIX) C. NO CHANGE   24. _____
            A   B

25. Brian insists that I weigh much more than him. (SIX)   C. NO CHANGE   25. _____
               A   B

26. The statue, that stands near the entrance is a Barti
       A   B

    original. (SIX)   C. NO CHANGE   26. _____

27. The knight Sir Robert of York wore the colors of Lady
                A

    Katherine as he rode into the tournament area. (SIX) C. NO CHANGE   27. _____
    B

28. Jack Herbert who drives the blue limousine, discovered
         A   B

    three flat tires this morning. (SIX)   C. NO CHANGE   28. _____

29. Jack Brent owns the horse who won the last race. (SIX) C. NO CHANGE   29. _____
       A   B

30. <u>Sagging under the weight of the ice, we</u> decided to leave
                  A

    the cabin <u>immediately</u>. (SEVEN)   C. NO CHANGE 30. _____
                B

31. Jennifer <u>insists</u> no one can change her <u>mind — that</u> she is
            A   B

    always right. (EIGHT)   C. NO CHANGE 31. _____

32. "Dance of the Hours" is ballet music in the <u>opera</u>
                                          A

    <u>La Gioconda</u>. (EIGHT)   C. NO CHANGE 32. _____
      B

33. The graduate applied for several <u>jobs; even</u> with a degree
                                 A

    <u>you</u> find it hard to get the job that is available. (NINE)   C. NO CHANGE 33. _____
     B

34. <u>Incredulous</u> as it may seem, Nora is ten years <u>younger than</u>
          A   B

    <u>all the other members</u>. (NINE)   C. NO CHANGE 34. _____
          B

35. The <u>affect</u> of the <u>chlorine</u> gas was that it made several
          A   B

    people seriously ill.   C. NO CHANGE 35. _____

ANSWERS

EXERCISE 1A

1. V N	8. N	15. V N
2. V N	9. V N	16. N
3. V N	10. V N	17. V N
4. V N	11. V	18. V N
5. V N	12. V	19. V N
6. V N	13. V N	20. V N
7. V N	14. V N	

EXERCISE 1B

1. N	5. N	8. V
2. V	6. N	9. N
3. N	7. V	10. V
4. N		

EXERCISE 1C

   N   V   N
1. Vines covered the fence.

     N   V   N
2. The fence concealed the warehouse.

   N   V   N   N
3. Lightning struck the warehouse at midnight.

   N V
4. The fire spread rapidly.

       N   V   N
5. Quickly the flames enveloped the building.

    N   V
6. The firemen arrived promptly.

  N   V   N
7. They stretched hoses everywhere.

  N   V   N   V   N
8. They broke windows and entered the warehouse.

    N   N   N   N   V
9. The furniture, papers, books, and carpeting burned.

   N   V   N   V   N
10. A fireman found a cat and carried it outside.

   N V   V
11. The cat ran away and hid.

   N   V   N   V   N
12. Firemen climbed ladders and inspected the roof.

           N   V
13. Suddenly the roof collapsed and the

   N   V
walls caved in.

        N   V
14. Still the fire raged.

      N   N   V
15. At dawn the ruins still smoldered.

EXERCISE 2A

1. F
2. Butterflies and birds   fly
3. F
4. Fish   swim
5. (you)   Sit
6. Cocks   crow
7. F
8. Betty   phoned
9. Stars   twinkle
10. People   fish and hunt

EXERCISE 2B

1. Diane and Joe yawned.
2. The flowers blossomed and died.
3. The door and shutters banged.
4. Marilyn writes and paints.

EXERCISE 2C

Your instructor will check your sentences.

EXERCISE 3A

  NS   Vt   Ndo C NdoAdv
1. Maxine bought a coat and hat yesterday.

    NS   Vt   Ndo
2. The athletes carried torches.

  NS   C NS-------- Vt   Ndo
3. Robins and blue jays ate the cherries.

    NS   Vt   Ndo Adv
4. The bricklayer hurt his back badly.

  NS Vt   Ndo C Vt Ndo
5. Tim chews gum and eats popcorn.

296

EXERCISE 3B

      NS   **Vt**   **Ndo**   **Adv**
1. The wind tore the flag to shreds.

   NS C **NS**   **Adv**   **Vt**   **Ndo**
2. Ice and snow completely covered the road.

     NS   **Vi** **Adv**
3. Colors flashed brightly.

      NS **VI**   **C** **Vi**   **Adv----------**
4. The trees swayed and creaked in the wind.

    NS   **Vt**   **Ndo**
5. Paper littered the sidewalk.

   NS **C** **NS** **Vi**
6. Ellis and Brian agree.

     NS **Adv** **Vt**   **Ndo**
7. The collie quickly herded sheep.

    NS   **Vt**   **Ndo**   **C** **Ndo**
8. Ashley bought paints and brushes.

     NS   **Vi**
9. The pendulum swung.

    NS   **Vt** **Ndo**   **C** **Vt** **Ndo**
10. Sarah knits sweaters and sews skirts.

EXERCISE 3C

Your instructor will check your sentences.

EXERCISE 4A

1. committees	curricula	1,10
2. waitresses	dishes	2,2
3. geese	passers-by	6,11
4. quizzes	theses	2,10
5. men	valleys	6,3A
6. thieves	knives	4,4
7. children	toys	5,3A
8. women	r's	6,12
9. classes	larvae	2,10
10. mothers-in-law	crises	11,10

EXERCISE 4B

1. a soap   soaps
2. ____ information _____
3. ____ sincerity _____
4. a belief   beliefs
5. a position   positions
6. a wheel   wheels

EXERCISE 4C

1. emperor
2. waitress
3. blond
4. protégée

EXERCISE 4D

1. participation, participant
2. purity, purism, puritan, pureness
3. writer, writing
4. industry, industrialist, industrialization, industrialism
5. defendant, defense, defender
6. wisdom
7. reversal, reversion, reverser
8. profiteer or profit (n.)
9. government or governor
10. solvent, solvency, solver, solution

EXERCISE 5

1. was falling
2. had sprained
3. does like
4. are being painted
5. had been given
6. stalled
7. should have taken
8. ripped
9. have been blooming
10. had gathered

EXERCISE 6A

1. 1,2,5
2. 3,4
3. 3,4
4. 2
5. 5
6. Dictionaries and language books

EXERCISE 6B

1. R	6. R
2. R	7. I
3. R	8. I
4. I	9. I
5. I	

EXERCISE 6C

1. open	opens	opened	opened	opening
2. take	takes	took	taken	taking
3. buy	buys	bought	bought	buying
4. wash	washes	washed	washed	washing
5. see	sees	saw	seen	seeing
6. swim	swims	swam	swum	swimming
7. teach	teaches	taught	taught	teaching
8. drive	drives	drove	driven	driving
9. come	comes	came	come	coming
10. drag	drags	dragged	dragged	dragging
11. hop	hops	hopped	hopped	hopping
12. throw	throws	threw	thrown	throwing
13. write	writes	wrote	written	writing
14. give	gives	gave	given	giving
15. qualify	qualifies	qualified	qualified	qualifying
16. order	orders	ordered	ordered	ordering
17. run	runs	ran	run	running
18. blow	blows	blew	blown	blowing
19. go	goes	went	gone	going
20. freeze	freezes	froze	frozen	freezing

EXERCISE 6D

1. lengthen
2. operate
3. signify
   signal
   signalize
4. motorize
5. sicken
6. generate
7. simplify
8. solidify
9. colonize
10. populate

EXERCISE 7A

1. Parts 2 and 3
2. Parts 1 and 2
3. Parts 1 and 3
4. *-s* and *-es*
5. *-ed*

EXERCISE 7B

1. goes, went, *or* will go
2. doesn't
3. A
4. comes, came, *or* will come
5. finished *or* will finish
6. called
7. knew
8. A
9. began
10. doesn't

EXERCISE 7C

1. lives, can live, *or* lived
2. makes, made, *or* will make
3. stole
4. Doesn't . . . have *or* Does . . . have
5. flaps, flapped, *or* will flap
6. chose
7. Does . . . like *or* Doesn't . . . like
8. have *or* had
9. bought
10. does, did, *or* will do

EXERCISE 8A

1. hanged *or* will hang
2. had driven *or* drove
3. had drunk *or* drank
4. saw *or* had seen
5. did *or* had done
6. has . . . bought
7. Am . . . going
8. A
9. had written
10. were invited
11. has sung *or* sang
12. were awarded
13. was *or* has been
14. has spoken *or* spoke
15. were captured
16. went *or* have gone
17. wrote *or* had written
18. taught
19. tore *or* has torn
20. were offered

EXERCISE 8B

1. have woven
2. will wash
3. has ridden *or* had ridden
4. blew
5. had given
6. rang
7. burst
8. has hidden *or* had hidden
9. has lost *or* had lost
10. brought
11. cast
12. Has . . . blown *or* Had . . . blown
13. Do . . . avoid *or* Did . . . avoid
14. has fallen *or* had fallen
15. Had . . . mentioned
16. came
17. knew *or* knows
18. has frozen
19. drank
20. woke *or* waked

EXERCISE 9

1. prefers, preferred, *or* has preferred
2. will make *or* makes
3. left
4. will have completed
5. has opened
6. arrived *or* had arrived
7. tried, has tried, *or* will try
8. had prepared *or* prepared
9. will buy
10. will join, joined, has joined, *or* had joined
11. run, ran, have run, had run, *or* will run
12. swims, will swim, has swum, had swum, *or* swam
13. will participate *or* participates
14. has argued
15. traveled, had traveled, *or* will travel
16. will return *or* will have returned
17. meet
18. creep, crept, *or* will creep
19. plunged, has plunged, *or* will plunge
20. moved

EXERCISE 10A

       NS Vi   **Adv---------- Adv-------**
1. The hen <u>sat</u> (complete) on her eggs for three

   weeks.

            NS   **Vt**   **Ndo Adv--**
2. The farmer <u>raised</u> (incomplete) corn in his

  ----
  fields.

                NS Vi   **Adv Adv--**
3. The farmer's wife <u>rises</u> (complete) early every

  ----
  morning.

         NS   **Vi**   **Adv--- Adv---------**
4. She cannot <u>lie</u> (complete) in bed until noon.

             NS   **Vi**   **Adv--------------------**
5. The farmer <u>sits</u> (complete) in his favorite chair
  Adv--------------
  in the evening.

                NS Vt   **Ndo Adv**
6. The farmer's wife <u>set</u> (incomplete) the table for

  ----
  dinner.

            NS Vt   **Ndo Adv-----**
7. She <u>set</u> (incomplete) her hair at night.

EXERCISE 10B

1. lay (Vi)
2. had risen (Vi)
3. A *or* lie (Vi)
4. A (Vt)
5. had lain (Vi)
6. had sat (Vi)
7. Lay (Vt)
8. A (Vt)
9. A (Vi)
10. A (Vi)

EXERCISE 11

1. should not
2. cannot
3. will not
4. he is
5. I will
6. They would *or* They had

X-TRAS   UNIT ONE

I. 1. NS Vi
     2. NS Vt Ndo
     3. NS Vt Ndo
     4. NS Vi Adv
     5. NS Vi Adv
     6. NS Vt Ndo Adv

II. Ask your instructor to check your sentences.

             NS   **Vt**   **Ndo**
III. 1. The catalog listed equipment.

              NS Vi
     2. The car stalled.

```
        NS      Vt      Ndo C  Ndo
 3. The cowboy wore a gun and spurs.

          NS Vt      Ndo
 4. The cat licked its paws.

      NS  C  NS   Vt      Ndo
 5. Coins and jewels filled the chest.

        NS Vi      Adv
 6. The fire burned brightly.

      NS      Vi  C  Vi
 7. Children sang and hummed.

      NS  Vt     Ndo Adv
 8. Carl ordered shoes yesterday.

      NS  C  NS        Ndo   Adv------
 9. Bob and Jane visited Hawaii last year.

           NS  Vi Adv
10. The mule sat down.
```

IV. 1. waltzes   14. wolves
     2. media, mediums 15. feet
     3. mice   16. leaves
     4. mouthfuls   17. appendices
     5. parties   *or* appendixes
     6. data   18. formulas
     7. desperadoes   *or* formulae
        or desperados 19. nuclei
     8. papers   20. keys
     9. gulfs   21. memoranda
    10. alumni   *or* memorandums
    11. theories   22. pianos
    12. kisses   23. potatoes
    13. wreaths   24. cafeterias

V.   1. is . . . being helped

     2. has taken *or* took

     3. makes, will make, *or* made

     4. has stopped *or* stopped

     5. requires, required, *or* will require

     6. What did the man say . . . *or* has . . . said

     7. needs *or* will need

     8. was being cleaned

     9. has obtained *or* obtained

    10. have deposited *or* deposited

11. wants *or* wanted

12. has dragged *or* dragged

13. has *or* had

14. had purchased *or* purchased

15. carries, carried, *or* will carry

16. has memorized *or* memorized

17. has extracted, extracted, *or* had extracted

18. likes *or* liked

19. Has . . . mentioned *or* Had . . . mentioned

20. Has . . . called *or* did . . . call

VI. 1. began, have begun, *or* had begun

     2. will become

     3. could have been torn

     4. had known

     5. have . . . rung

     6. should be thrown

     7. has . . . chosen

     8. had broken

     9. dug

    10. blew *or* blows

    11. had dragged

    12. had ridden

    13. must have sunk

    14. saw *or* sees

    15. did *or* does

    16. dragged

    17. had eaten

    18. drew *or* draws

19. had risen

20. has taken

EXERCISE 12

1. readable
2. pleasant, pleased, pleasable
3. peaceful, peaceable
4. active, acted, acting
5. regional
6. fragmentary, fragmented
7. lovely, loveless, lovable, loved
8. foolish
9. rhythmic, rhythmical
10. prohibitory, prohibitive, prohibited, prohibiting

EXERCISE 13

1. Adj   5. Adj   8. Adj
2. N   6. Adj   9. N
3. Adj   7. Adj   10. Adj
4. N

EXERCISE 14A

1. children's   6. Charles' *or* Charles's
2. doctor's   7. men's
3. Bruce and Dick's   8. jury's
4. father-in-law's   9. fox's
5. dog's   10. Thomas' *or* Thomas's

EXERCISE 14B

1. Jay's sister and Susan's brother
2. skiers' equipment
3. kitten's paws
4. Bert Jones's house *or* Bert Jones' house
5. Burton and Washborn's store
6. many children's dreams
7. small boy's energy
8. attorney's response
9. father-in-law's boat
10. football coaches' conference

EXERCISE 15A

1. D (Num)   5. Poss   8. Adj
2. NA   6. V-ing   9. D (Num)
3. V-ed   7. NA   10. Adj
4. D

EXERCISE 15B

1. five brawny truck drivers
2. the magnificent snow-covered fir trees or the fir trees, magnificent and snow-covered,
3. blue, pink, purple African violet blossoms or African violet blossoms, blue, pink, purple,
4. a sunny, warm Hawaiian beach, inviting and secluded, (*A, sunny, warm, inviting, secluded* can precede or follow *Hawaiian beach* in almost any order.)
5. several hundred hungry chickens, cackling and pecking, (*Cackling, pecking,* and *hungry* can precede or follow *chickens.*

EXERCISE 15C

1. The short, fat, the creaking cabin
2. Little, big, custard, chocolate
3. His dark, dingy, bright
4. The gray stone, entire city
5. The church, well-trained, poised, the difficult
6. The American, three
7. The four-year-old, the valuable antique
8. The exhausted, an overwhelming
9. Orange, red, yellow, the antique
10. The fourteen, satisfied, relaxed, an outstanding

EXERCISE 15D

Your instructor will check your sentences.

EXERCISE 16A

1. badly, loudly   6. slowly, precisely
2. Gradually, higher, higher 7. carefully
3. silently   8. hesitatingly
4. Quickly   9. Apprehensively
5. aromatically, very   10. carefully

EXERCISE 16B

Your instructor will check your sentences.

EXERCISE 17

Your instructor will check your choices.

EXERCISE 18

1. real   really, very
2. can't hardly   can hardly
3. most   almost
4. sure   surely, very
5. real   really, very
6. bad   badly, threateningly, discontentedly
7. good   badly, viciously
8. most   almost

EXERCISE 19A

Your instructor will check your phrases.

EXERCISE 19B

Your instructor will check your sentences.

EXERCISE 19C

1. aboard   ship
2. over   X
3. within   circle
4. under   bridge
5. of   boys
6. between   you and me
7. round   bend
8. at   nine o'clock
9. inside   X
10. from   point
11. out   X
12. into   lake
13. across   town
14. below   X
15. after   dark
16. amid   confusion
17. like   him
18. at   fair
19. to   house
20. for   horsemen

EXERCISE 19D

1. of the club   Adj   members
2. of his friends   Adj   two
3. into the well   Adv   fell
4. at night   Adv   late
5. in abundance   Adv   grew
6. from New York   Adv   arrived

7. in the blue dress   Adj   woman
8. across the street   Adv   helped
9. out the window   Adv   Look
10. of hay   Adj   load
11. with the dog   Adj   girl
12. with the dog   Adv   fell
13. before   X
14. around the block   Adv   walked
15. of apples   Adj   baskets
16. like that   Adj   car
17. to the bank   Adv   took
18. of silence   Adj   moment
19. After heavy rains   Adv   was flooded
20. of brick   Adj   house

EXERCISE 19E

1. on the back porch   fell
2. on a scrap of paper   wrote
3. with great fury   broke
4. in a small boat   transferred
5. with carved legs   piano
6. with a knowledge of furniture   people
7. with one leg gone   table

X-TRAS   UNIT TWO

I.   1. few, Mark's last

2. Recent, many, unidentified, contaminating

3. sterilized, surgical, disease-producing

4. Unidentified, flying, many, people's

5. trained, flying

6. the, fear-ridden, trembling, his, recent

7. Any, new, complex, keen

8. The, hungry, thirsty, two-year-old

9. the, colonel's, owned, damaged, scorched

10. weekly, field, good, travel

II. 1. Very   4. frequently

    2. quickly   5. Reliably

    3. Thoroughly, not

6. Unfortunately, not   9. privately, safely

7. radically   10. unusually

8. eagerly, home

III. Ask your instructor to check your sentences.

IV. 1. of the skaters—Most
        around the campfire—huddled

     2. of the cabins—All
        with snow—high

     3. down the steep driveway—backed
        into the fence—swerved

     4. of the teams—captains
        at each other—shouted

     5. of the chairs—Two
        of paint—coat

     6. at the window—stood
        out—X

     7. By nightfall—had returned *or* modifies
        sentence
        to camp—had returned
        of the hunters—most

     8. in the field—Lilies
        in the gentle wind—swayed

     9. of geese—flock
        in formation—flew
        over the quiet forest—flew

    10. of concrete—Tons
        for the bridge pillars—forms

    11. At home—waited *or* modifies sentence
        for a telephone call—anxiously *or* waited

    12. at the end—greeted *or* modifies sentence
        of the play—end
        of the audience—members

    13. from New York—soloist
        on the stage—collapsed and fainted

    14. of ice cream—dish

    15. from one corner—moved

of the room—corner
to the other—moved

V. Ask your instructor to check your phrases and
    sentences.

VI. Ask your instructor to check your phrases and
    sentences.

EXERCISE 20

   Adj NS   Vt   Nio Adj Adj Ndo
1. The florist sold Brian a white orchid.

   NS Vt   Ndo   C Adj Adj   Ndo
2. He raised orchids and other tropical flowers.

   NS   Vt   Adj Adj Adj   Ndo
3. Maria enjoyed her first orchid corsage.

   NS Vt Nio Adj Ndo
4. She gave Brian a kiss.

   NS   Vt Ndo   C   Ndo Adv-----------
5. They met Barbara and Ken at the dance.

   Adv   NS Vt Adj Adj   Ndo
6. Afterward they had a midnight supper
   Adv----------------
   at Petit Pierre's.

EXERCISE 21

   Adj Adj NS   Vi   Adv-------
1. The sales manager resigned last week.

   NS----------- Vt   Adj Ndo   Adv
2. Myron Holt wanted the position desperately,

   NS---------------- Vt   Ndo   Adj Noc
3. Mr. Farnsworth considered Myron a candidate.

   NS Adv Vt   Ndo   C Ndo
4. He also considered Evan Watts and Joe Steele.

   Adv   NS Vt   Ndo ---------- Adj Noc
5. Finally he named Ruth Olson sales manager.

   Adj NS Vt   Adj Ndo   Adv
6. The men opposed his decision angrily.

   NS---------------- Vt   Adv Vt   Adj Ndo
7. Mr. Farnsworth would not change his mind.

EXERCISE 22A

1. Vt   5. Vi
2. Nio   6. NS
3. Vt   7. Ndo
4. Ndo   8. NS

303

EXERCISE 22B

1. ruler   Nio
2. babies   Nio
3. king   Noc
4. X
5. Ruth   Noc
6. Margaret   Nio
7. bridesmaid   Noc
8. X
9. Jenny   Nio
10. boy   Nio
11. winner   Noc
12. voters   Nio

EXERCISE 22C

Your instructor will check your sentences.

EXERCISE 23A

   NS   LV Adv-c
1. Dale is home.

   Adj NS LV   Adj-c
2. The sea appears calm.

   Adj NS   LV   Adj-c
3. The music sounds pleasant.

   Adj NS   LV   Adj-c   Adj-c
4. The fabric feels soft and warm.

   Adj NS LV   Adj-c
5. The sky looks threatening.

   Adj NS   LV   Adj-c
6. The sailor seems apprehensive.

       LV Adj NS
7. There is the champion.

   Adj NS   LV Adj-c
8. The mansion was elegant.

   NS   LV Nsc
9. Margery is a pianist.

   Adj NS LV   Adj-c
10. The bear looked vicious.

EXERCISE 23B

   Adj NS Vi----------- Adv--------
1. The cart is standing in the hall.

   Adj NS   LV Adj-c
2. The paintings look restful.

   Adj NS   Vt   Adj Ndo
3. The fawn tasted the milk.

   NS----------- LV   Adj Nsc
4. Mr. Danton became a counselor.

   Adj NS   LV   Adj-c
5. The runner appeared exhausted.

   Adj NS   Vi   Adv
6. The watchman appeared suddenly.

EXERCISE 24A

   NS   LV Adj Nsc
1. Louis Agassiz was a naturalist.

   NS Vt   Adj   C Adj   Ndo
2. He studied European and American animals.

   NS Vt   Adj   Ndo
3. He observed many species.

   NS Vi   Adv
4. He worked constantly.

   NS Vt   Adj   C Adj Adj Ndo
5. He described recent and fossil fish forms.

   Adj   NS   LV   Adj-c
6. These descriptions were invaluable.

   NS   Vt   Adj   Ndo   Adj
7. Agassiz labeled Darwin's theories false.

   NS Vt   Adj Adj   Ndo
8. He established a zoological laboratory.

   Adj NS   LV Adj Nsc
9. An island was the site.

   NS   Vt   Ndo Adj   Noc
10. Harvard appointed him zoology professor.

EXERCISE 24B

   Adj NS   Vi
1. The gypsy danced.

   Adj NS   Vt   Adj Ndo
2. The marshal arrested the thief.

   NS   Vt   Nio Adj Ndo
3. Gilbert presented Jonas the medal.

   NS   LV Adj Nsc
4. Douglas is an instructor.

   Adj NS   Vi Adv
5. The antenna fell down.

   Adj NS   LV Adj-c
6. The food is delicious.

Adj NS Vt Ndo
7. The truck lost a wheel.

Adj NS LV Adj-c
8. The hostess looked attractive.

Adj NS Vi Adv
9. The hawk swooped downward.

NS LV------- Adv-c
10. Malcolm has been here.

X-TRAS UNIT THREE

I.
1. LV	5. Nio	9. NS
2. Vi or LV	6. Vt	10. Vt
3. Noc	7. Adv	11. Ndo
4. Nsc	8. Adj	12. Ndo

II.
1. NS Vt Ndo
2. NS Vt Ndo
3. NS LV Nsc
4. NS Vt Ndo
5. NS LV Nsc
6. NS LV Adj
7. NS Vt Nio Ndo
8. NS Vi Adv
9. NS Vt Ndo Noc
10. NS Vt Ndo
11. NS Vt Nio Ndo
12. NS Vt Ndo Noc
13. NS Vt Nio Ndo
14. NS Vt Ndo Noc
15. NS Vt Ndo
16. NS Vt Ndo
17. NS Vi Adv
18. NS LV Adj
19. NS Vt Ndo
20. NS Vt Ndo

III. Ask your instructor to check your sentences.

IV.
1. Adj	6. Vi-Vt-LV
2. Ndo	7. Adv
3. LV	8. Nsc, Adj, Adv
4. Adj	9. NS
5. NS, Ndo	10. Whom? What?

EXERCISE 25

1. C	6. C
2. C	7. S
3. S	8. S
4. S	9. S
5. F	10. C

EXERCISE 26A

1. None
2. rusty, broken screen door
3. dedicated, trustworthy attorney
4. meek, anxious patient
5. none
6. brilliant, flashing neon sign

EXERCISE 26B

1. house; they	5. artistically, but
2. none	6. coat, or
3. shade, and	7. none
4. none	8. none

EXERCISE 26C

Your instructor will check your sentences.

EXERCISE 26D

1. . . . season, and For . . .
2. . . . fall; as a result, He
   ; consequently,
   ; therefore,
3. . . . party; Only . . .
4. . . . motorcycles, but They . . .
5. . . . course; nevertheless, It . . .
   ; however,
6. . . . forest, but We . . .
7. . . . brother, but She . . .
8. . . . work; She . . .
9. . . . hike; in addition, He . . .
   ; besides
10. . . . horse; She . . .

EXERCISE 26E

1. men, moreover, wanted
2. aspect; however, they
3. Finally, Bob
4. refused; consequently, the
5. Tom, as a result, lost

EXERCISE 26F

1. wood, groceries,
2. following: bandages, splints, antiseptic, and
3. Adams, sister; James, father; Owens,

4. banquet, picnic
5. thread, **needles**, fabric
6. First,
7. office: first, **draperies**; next, chairs; finally, efficient, **gray-haired**,
8. trunks, clothes, furniture; wood, tools, food;
9. chair, door,

EXERCISE 27

1. A	11. ; he
2. A	12. ; Marie
3. ; consequently,	13. ; then
4. A	14. A
5. ; the room	15. A
6. A	16. ; in addition,
7. A	17. ; it
8. ; as a result,	18. ; consequently,
9. A	19. ; small bouquets
10. Omit comma.	20. ; millions

EXERCISE 28

1. Mrs. Martin, our next-door neighbor, teaches sculpturing.
   OR: Our next-door neighbor Mrs. Martin . . .
   (No punctuation in the second version.)

2. Margaret's boy friend Bob is the winner of several golf trophies.
   OR: Bob, winner of several golf trophies, is Margaret's boy friend.
   OR: Bob, Margaret's boyfriend, is the winner of several golf trophies.

3. Stanley Blank, the violinist, is concertmaster of the orchestra.

4. Deep in the mountain is a huge cave, formerly a hiding place for rustlers. (You may omit *formerly*.)

5. The plane, a new supersonic jet, flew for several hours through a raging storm.

6. The Blakes' house, a Victorian mansion, burned down last night.

7. Ted's books, textbooks and novels, lay on the desk.

8. The knight, one of King Arthur's men, charged wildly through the castle.

9. The speaker's report, ten ways to prevent water pollution, was lively and informative.

10. The high fence concealed the old house, formerly the residence of an eccentric millionaire.

X-TRAS   UNIT FOUR

I. Ask your instructor to check sentences for 1, 3, 5, 6.

2. It has a subject (NS) and predicate (V).
4. The sentence consists of two independent clauses and has two NS-V combinations with appropriate punctuation between them.
7. Semicolon (;)
8. Comma (,) and *and, but, or, for*

II.
1. sun;
2. Ranch: horseback riding, hunting, and fishing.
3. kites, paddle canoes, dive for fish, and collect rocks.
4. cliffs, flowers, ridges, (No comma after *beaches*.)
5. fires;
6. close; seats,
7. skis; bare,
8. cheese, cookies, canned meats, bag;
9. bicycles; touring, park,
10. reasons: first, gasses; second, noise; third, automobiles; fourth,

EXERCISE 29A

1. Myron bought *her* (Nio) a ticket for the play.

2. Carol gave *them* (Nio) *their* (Adj) keys.

3. *Who* (NS) attended *your* (Adj) meeting?

4. *They* (NS) told *us* (Nio) the details of the accident.

5. Are *you* (NS) the chairman of the dance committee?

6. Mary and *she* (NS) received *their* (Adj) awards.

7. *She* (NS) sent *him* (Nio) a part of *mine* (Nop).

8. A part of *his* belongs to *them.*

    NS   Adj
9. *Mary* likes *his* cooking.

    NS LV Nsc
10. *I* am *I.*

EXERCISE 29B

1. him	he
2. I	me
3. A	
4. I	me
5. I	me

EXERCISE 30

1. He bought himself it.
2. They liked ours better than his (or hers).
3. They called me, not you.
4. We scoured the hills for her.
5. He ordered steak for them.

EXERCISE 31

1. Each one	S
2. Few	P
3. Several	P
4. Anything	S
5. One	S
6. both	P
7. anybody	S
8. Neither	S
9. Others	P
10. Many	P

EXERCISE 32A

1. bird	its
2. Tom	his
3. plants	they
4. convertible	its
5. Owen	his
6. Mary, play	she, it
7. jury	it
8. Cora and Bob	themselves
9. team	its
10. children	they

EXERCISE 32B

1. Virginia	she
2. X	who
3. X	him
4. Dick	he
5. I	myself
6. antiques	Those
7. X	This
8. X	myself
9. X	they
10. X	one
11. Bill and Joe	they
12. X	They
13. committee	it
14. Mark	himself
15. Sue and Sandy	they
16. X	This
17. X	it
18. X	myself
19. X	It
20. Judy	She

EXERCISE 32C

These are suggested revisions. Discuss your revisions with your instructor if you need help.

1. Donna suggested that her mother buy new bed sheets.
   OR: Donna told her mother, "You need new bed sheets."

2. . . . and he himself would get hurt.
   OR: . . . and his brother would get hurt.
   OR: . . . and one of them would get hurt.

3. . . . techniques; the discussion covered . . .
   OR: . . . the men covered . . .

4. . . . every night, a routine which every secretary should follow.

5. . . . to visit Germany after graduation.

6. . . . countries; the new merchandise made . . .
   OR: . . . countries; as a result, they had to rent . . .

7. . . . to examine the design of a car which has a maximum speed of . . .

8. The map of the United States is good because it shows all the state capitals, but the map

makers did not include the main highways.

OR: . . . it does not include the main highways.

EXERCISE 33

1. one	his/her
2. Each	his
3. children	themselves
4. Everyone	him
5. Each piece or piece	its
6. someone	him
7. Everyone	his
8. houses	them
9. Dick	himself
10. mothers	their
11. a customer	him
12. Dogs and cats	their
13. man	his
14. Everyone	he
15. nobody	his
16. boy	him
17. everybody	his
18. no one	his
19. actor	his
20. reporters	their

EXERCISE 34

1. Each	has
2. Meg and Tom	are
3. Bill or John	is coming
4. group	intends
5. people	are
6. Peggy and Anne	conduct
7. Neither the man nor his son	has
8. surgeon	attends
9. *The Skyfighters*	is
10. team	go
11. One	has registered
12. Ten dollars	seems
13. None	is or are
14. guns	are
15. boys	are
16. mathematics	is
17. treasures	are
18. Everyone	needs
19. Dick, Bob, and Joe	are
20. cars	are
21. corners	are
22. You and John	are
23. Robin or Jane	is
24. Each one	has

25. any	is or are
26. collection	contains
27. jury	announces
28. (each) man	has
29. Dog	makes
30. news	is
31. twenty-five dollars	is
32. this	is
33. Joe and Mike	are
34. none	is or are
35. art objects	are
36. houses	are
37. stars	seem
38. neither Joe nor Ted nor Bill	intends
39. Nobody	likes
40. rooms	need

X-TRAS UNIT FIVE

I.   . . . Some really enjoy . . . *groups* . . . *They might choose* plays or movies . . . Or *they prefer* to stay . . . Still others *want* to . . . *They* participate in sports . . . . . . college classes. *They can also enjoy* hobbies . . .

II. 1. boxes *are* lying

2. Ice, snow, wind make

3. alumni are

4. Neither the chair nor the desk is

5. Each has flown

6. bids are

7. carton is

8. None is or are

9. The alumni plan

10. Twenty dollars is

III. 1. Brian told Richard, "I will get the new job."
OR: Brian told Richard, "You will get the new job."
OR: Brian learned he would get the new job and told Richard about it.
(Other revisions are also possible.)

308

2. Nancy saw a dress which she thought her sister would like. (Other revisions, like the examples for No. 1, are also possible.)

3. . . . money. The offer made Tom happy. OR: Bill's generosity made Tom happy. (Substitute a noun for *this*.)

4. . . . not Ben. The betting made Tom nervous. Getting married made Tom nervous. The speculation made Tom nervous. (Clarify by using a noun in place of *which*.)

5. The dentist pulled the decayed tooth. OR: the abcessed tooth OR: the aching tooth . . .

EXERCISE 35A

1. X
2. Although Bob was engaged to Nan,
3. X
4. While waiting for the test results,
5. X
6. X
7. where he placed it two years before.
8. X
9. Because he likes his job,
10. while enjoying the gentle rocking motion of the waves.
11. Until he agrees to cooperate,
12. When the truck had a flat tire,
13. As the plane descended,
14. when it landed on the race track.
15. when he tried to leave the store.
16. X
17. when the shipment arrives
18. After talking for five hours,
19. because he wanted to improve his comprehension
20. as she watched the horror movie.

EXERCISE 35B

1. D	6. P	11. I	16. D
2. P	7. P	12. D	17. I
3. I	8. D	13. D	18. D
4. I	9. D	14. P	19. P
5. P	10. P	15. P	20. P

EXERCISE 35C

These are suggested revisions. There may be other ways to combine the sentences.

1. Max Thompson donated five hundred dollars although he could have used the money himself.

2. He stayed here for the convention although he should be in Boston now.

3. After they had driven all night, they finally found a motel with a vacancy.

4. He enjoys writing stories even though he has never sold one.

5. Since Jack has chosen medicine for his profession, he faces many years of arduous study and work.

6. As the sun rose over the horizon, John felt he could hardly face the day.

7. Before he decided to buy the new car, he talked with several friends.

8. After the prom was over, everyone went to the drive-in.

9. While Bill waited for Cora outside the school, he saw two cars collide.

10. When the wind slammed the door closed, the shivering girl could not get back into the house without her key.

EXERCISE 36

Here are some suggested revisions.

1. Dick is the *taller* of my two sons.
2. Mrs. Smith hates weddings more than her husband *does.*
   OR: Mrs. Smith hates weddings more than *she hates* her husband.
3. A light blue dress is more becoming than a yellow *one.*
4. Martha says that her frog can jump farther *than mine.* (or his, or hers)
5. Jim is a more powerful weight lifter than any *other* man in the neighborhood.
6. Jerry already weighs more than *he.*

7. Brad's camping equipment is more complete than *Tom's* (equipment).
8. Mr. Hollis says that Meg is the best typist of the four girls in the office.
9. I do believe that this new arm chair is *more* comfortable than the old one.
10. Jim likes Paul better than *he likes* Bob.
    OR: Jim likes Paul better than *Bob does.*
11. Students in large classes often get lower grades *than students in small classes.*
12. An intern's monthly salary is usually lower than *that of* an unskilled worker.
13. Riding comfort in a modern car is far superior to *that of* a stagecoach.
14. Sacramento is closer to Auburn than San Francisco *is.*
    OR: Sacramento is closer to Auburn than *it is to* San Francisco.
15. The *loyalty of a dog* to his master is unlike *that of any other* animal.
16. The *physical endurance of a mountain climber* is probably greater than *that of an executive* sitting at his desk all day.
17. Does *a pound of potatoes* weigh more than *a pound of feathers?*
18. *Storms in Florida* seem more violent than *those in Ohio or Indiana.*
19. The Empire State Building is *so tall that one can scarcely see the top from the ground.*
20. This restaurant serves delicious food, but it is *much less expensive than I thought it would be.*

EXERCISE 37A

1. who or that	6. who or that
2. which or that	7. C or that
3. C or which	8. C or which
4. C or who	9. who or that
5. C or which	10. who or that

EXERCISE 37B

1. which he bought two months ago	radio
2. who was lost in the department store	girl
3. that would bring the contract	letter
4. whom he despised	those
5. (that) Sue showed at school	puppy
6. X	
7. which turned the corner	car
8. that had been brown	fields
9. who viewed it	those
10. X	

EXERCISE 37C

These are suggested revisions. Ask your instructor to examine what you have written if it is different from sentences given here.

1. Many men dislike mowing lawns, an attitude which irritates their wives.
   OR: Many men dislike mowing lawns. Their indifference irritates their wives.
2. The promotion which he had earned came after many years.
3. Marie was disappointed because the trip to Australia cost more than she had saved.
4. The *No Smoking* signs that had been placed on the classroom walls were fluorescent red.
5. The news magazine that contained depressing reports lay on the living room table.

EXERCISE 37D

1. Brown, yacht,	6. none
2. none	7. Hill, bakery,
3. none	8. none
4. none	9. honor, Evans,
5. Oakes, before,	10. none

EXERCISE 37E

These are suggested revisions. Ask your instructor to check other versions.

1. The magician who is appearing at the Rialto has performed in many cities.
2. The menu which (or that) consists of beef, fish, and pork did not appeal to the vegetarians.
3. The red sports car, which (or that) was her graduation gift last June, has dents in all the fenders and a smashed headlight.
4. We consulted Jeff Williams, who recently opened his interior decorating shop, before we bought this carpeting.
5. My sister, who has always enjoyed operas, will attend the opening night with me.
6. Daisy, who lives next door, will finally get married tomorrow after a seven-year engagement.
7. The cat which (or that) is wearing a jeweled collar is sitting high in the oak tree.
8. The rain, which (or that) is the heaviest in years, flooded all the downtown streets.

9. She threw into the incinerator an empty hair spray can, which (or that) exploded with a bang.
10. Willoughby owns a German shepherd, which (or that) nipped the leg of an intruder last night.

EXERCISE 38A

1. None
2. (that) he would operate the mill next year — Ndo
3. Why the accident happened — NS
4. None
5. whoever signed it — Nop
6. None
7. that he has no time for sleep — Ndo
8. that unexpected guests arrived last night — Nsc
9. whoever calls — Nio
10. that he cannot dissect frogs — Nsc

EXERCISE 38B

These are suggested revisions. Discuss your revisions with your instructor if you need help.

1. The reason you do not trust me is that I told your mother about your accident.
   OR: You do not trust me because I told your mother about your accident.

2. Imagination is forming pictures in one's mind of objects or people not present.

3. Mark disappeared from home last night because he thinks his parents are unreasonable.

4. The reason the college team won the football trophy is that every player worked to win.
   OR: The college team won the football trophy because every player worked to win.

5. Homework consists of assignments from every class to do at home.
   OR: Homework is having assignments . . . .

6. He failed in school because he never took time to study.

7. Remuneration is the money a person receives for work he has done.

8. An art collection is a group of paintings on display for examination or sale.

9. The reason he did not earn much money picking apples is that he slept under the tree most of the time.
   OR: He did not earn much money picking apples because he slept under the tree most of the time.

10. Baptism under fire is the movement of new troops into battle for the first time.
    OR: . . . is new troops going in to battle . . .

EXERCISE 39

1. who attends a private school — Adj
   that he will not go back — N
   when the fall semester begins — Adv

2. After Cleo had finished her father's portrait, — Adv
   (that) she would paint a picture of a mountain cabin — N
   (that) she remembered — Adj

3. which was full that night — Adj
   that lay at the edge of town — Adj

4. (that) she had visited Switzerland — N
   while she was in Europe last year — Adv

5. which greeted Dawson's guests when he opened the dining-room doors. — Adv

EXERCISE 40A

1. The	organ.	6. Oxygen	lungs.
2.		7. The	heart.
3. The	pump.	8.	
4. The	dioxide.	9.	
5.		10. The	body.

EXERCISE 40B

1. The	mammal.	6. The	foot.
2.		7.	
3. The	bill.	8. The	swimmer.
4.		9.	
5.		10. The	Tasmania.

EXERCISE 40C

Your instructor will check your sentences.

I.

	Clauses	Phrases

1. After most of the boys had delivered their papers,

of the boys
at the corner soda fountain

2. who manages a small nursery

for rose bushes   with Mr. Hall

3. as heat pushed water up the stem and over the coffee in the basket.

up the stem   over the coffee
in the basket

4. where the stuffed owl perched

with flowers and leaves

5. (that) Neil valued most

in the den

6. (that) Gretchen wore
that crisscrossed up her legs to her knees

up her legs
to her knees

7. which hung loosely from her shoulders

from her shoulders
in soft folds to her feet

8. after the young bacteriologist concluded his report about his research project

of scientists
about his research project

9. Although Michael and Sandra Holmes were both experienced race-car drivers, after they were married

10. that the man . . . was now incompetent
(that) he had trusted for years

II.   1. Omit *Most*

2. than Tom's *or* than Tom's car

3. the high*er*

4. X

5. farthest south

III.   1. The reason . . . . is that he fears . . . OR
Greg hesitates to fly the plane alone because . . .

2. Sympathy is understanding, even sharing, another's . . .

3. The reason . . . is that . . . OR Sally likes Jeremy because he makes . . .

IV.   Ask your instructor to check these sentences.

V.   1. As (while) Miguel waited in a long line in front of the theater, he watched the girls pass by.

2. The house was unbearably hot because the airconditioner had stopped working.

3. As the Sacramento Valley was cooled by ocean breezes, the temperature dropped forty degrees in an hour.

4. Some students study night and day as (while) they prepare for final exams.

5. Mr. Hughes' secretary typed the mailing list which represented all the customers in two cities.

VI.   1. Sarah felt a cold chill (as Ben told her
Adv

N
abruptly) (that he was too busy to talk with her.)

2. (As the temperature climbed to 100
Adv

degrees,) people traveled to the beaches
Adj   **N**
(where they hoped) (they would get cool)
Adv   **Elliptical**
(while swimming in the lakes and rivers)
Adj
(which skirted the large city.)

3. (After Dan had purchased the plans for
   the sailboat,) he bought a table saw
   Adj
   (which he needed), and then he cleaned
   the garage and organized the tools
   Adv
   (before he began construction).

VII. Ask your instructor to check your sentences.

EXERCISE 41

1. From all over the world come the travelers.
2. What city do most people enjoy?
3. Do the house-covered hills please sightseers?
4. Down steep hills suddenly roll cable cars.
5. Does the earthquake threat frighten residents?
6. What is a serious threat to San Francisco?
7. Is water pollution a serious threat to San Francisco?
8. Does the new subway system relieve traffic congestion?
9. In the Bay Area live millions of people.
10. Do several bridges link the Bay Area lands?

EXERCISE 42A

1. A	6. P
2. P	7. P
3. A	8. A
4. A	9. A
5. A	10. A

EXERCISE 42B

1. Mount Everest was conquered in 1953 by Edmund Hillary and Tensing Norgay.
2. The climbers were surrounded by towers of ice.
3. Goggles, padded clothes, and oxygen masks were worn by the men.
4. Camps were set up by the climbers on the way up the mountain.
5. The last camp at 25,850 feet was erected by Hillary, Norgay, and the other men.
6. A stormy night was spent in a tent 1,200 feet from the peak by Hillary and Norgay.
7. In the morning the steep slopes were climbed by them.
8. At one point they were stopped completely by a ridge of ice.

9. Fortunately a passage to the top was found by them.
10. The top was finally reached by them just before noon.

EXERCISE 42C

1. Builders are constructing houses of nonwood products.
2. Manufacturers can mold urethane foam into beams and columns.
3. They manufacture easily assembled door frames among other urethane products.
4. Manufacturers have hardly scratched the future uses of urethane.
5. Two inches of foam achieve more insulation than six inches of traditional insulation.
6. The workman can spray insulating foam on the surfaces.
7. The foam insulation blocks out dusty air and moisture.
8. Some builders are using the sprayed foams in place of shingles.
9. Foam plastics offer all kinds of freedom in design.
10. Urethane building materials present an exciting new concept in building.

EXERCISE 43

1. barking	Adj	11. to help	N
2. injured	N	12. wiring	N
3. Eating	N	13. boating	Adj
4. Exercising	N	14. fishing	N
5. to resign	Adv	15. to fly	N
6. boiling	Adj	16. Swinging	N
7. to cooperate	N	17. torn	Adj
8. flying	N	18. Thinking	N
9. forgotten	Adj	19. winnings	N
10. Writing	N	20. to cooperate	Adv

EXERCISE 44A

1. Opening the door (verbal)
2. had torn (verb)
3. streaking along the highway (verbal)
4. to win the track meet (verbal)
5. to earn recognition (verbal)
6. was filled (verb)
7. buying a new car (verbal)
8. to accompany him (verbal)
9. arranging artificial flowers (verbal)
10. has been considering (verb)

EXERCISE 44B

1. to help his father	Adv
2. Washing dishes	NS
3. finding a treasure	Nsc
4. sitting very still	Adj
5. was painting	V
6. Playing the piano	NS
7. has been making	V
8. laughing and yelling at the townspeople	Adj
9. to buy more land	Adj
10. built by my grandfather	Adj

EXERCISE 45

These are suggested revisions. There may be other acceptable ways to combine the sentences. Ask your instructor to look at any sentence you would like to have checked.

1. The young woman prepared the dinner auto-matically, her mind fixed on her handsome dinner guest.
2. The mission having been accomplished, the astronauts were able to return to earth.
3. He relaxed in his large chair, the fire blazing in the fireplace, the wind blasting the trees and shrubs outside.
4. The new owners moved eagerly into the old house, the rooms newly painted and carpeted.
5. The heir having been located, the attorney was able to settle the old man's estate.

EXERCISE 46

These are suggested revisions. There may be other acceptable ways to combine the sentences. Ask your instructor to look at any sentences you would like to have checked.

1. Omaha, a city with thousands of residents subject to transfer, needs furnished apartments.
OR: Having thousands of residents subject to transfer, Omaha needs furnished apartments.
2. Scholarships, donated by businessmen in the community, have helped many college students.
3. Marcia typed the letter rapidly, her fingers scarcely touching the keys.
4. Trying hard to look sophisticated, the little old lady puffed nervously on the cigarette.
OR: Puffing nervously on the cigarette, the little old lady tried hard to look sophisticated.
5. Overloaded with cargo, the airplane barely missed the tree tops at the end of the runway.
6. To appear well-informed, he tried to use words he could scarcely pronounce.
7. The girl combine her hair is Dave's friend. (No punctuation)
8. Barbara, sobbing uncontrollably, paid no attention to the strolling musicians singing beneath her window.
9. Sportsmen from all over the world gathered in the small mountain town for a week of celebration.
10. The statue of Jacob Lester, standing near the main entrance of the museum, was donated by his admirers.
OR: The statue of Jacob Lester, donated by his admirers, stands in the museum near the main entrance.

X-TRAS   UNIT SEVEN

I.	1.	Operating a laundromat	NS
	2.	to do his lessons alone	Ndo
	3.	sending letters every day	Ndo
	4.	filled with spring flowers	Adj
	5.	Informed about her appointment as representative	Adj
	6.	to speak with the probation officer	Adv
	7.	guarding visiting diplomats	Nop
	8.	Chopping the vegetables carefully	Adj
	9.	labeled an outstanding chemist	Adj
	10.	carrying three cartons	Nop
	11.	Appalled by the sight	Adj
	12.	to present the recently completed wildlife film	Ndo
	13.	Not knowing anything about San Francisco	Adj

14. to show every one his first
    published novel   Adv

15. Coming together from all parts
    of the country   Adj

II.   1. The new rotary mower, *engineered to
    protect its users,* has a blade guard and
    rear protector shield.

2. Now available is a torch lamp, *designed to
    project 80 degrees of heat for a wide
    variety of uses.*

3. The volunteer fire fighters will meet for
    four days next week *to examine new
    equipment and to discuss fire fighting
    techniques.*

4. Michael awoke suddenly and saw in the
    hotel room five men *all peering out the
    door and down the hall.* (Watch place-
    ment of *room* and *peering.*) Another
    possibility: . . . five men in the hotel
    room all peering out the door . . . (If the
    word *all* is expressed following *room,*
    peering then modifies the pronoun *all.*)

5. *Hoping to teach small deaf children some
    day,* the young veteran has been studying
    lip reading at the hospital.

III. 1. Nora's husband delivered a bouquet of
    yellow roses to her.

2. Shippers blamed transportation problems
    for the spoilage of frozen fish. (The orig-
    inal sentence is weak because the person
    or group doing the blaming has not been
    identified. As a result, the sentence can
    be revised several ways.) The fish spoiled
    because they were not shipped quickly
    enough. The fish market managers blamed
    transportation problems . . .

3. The treasurer's report has encouraged
    Judson and Tomkins.

IV. Ask your instructor to check these sentences.

EXERCISE 47

1. . . . experience!
2. . . . Conqueror.

3. . . . execution.
4. . . . request?
5. Dr.   Mrs.   7 a.m.
6. . . . travel
7. . . . initials T.E.M.,   . . . luggage.
8. . . . me!   . . . that?
    OR: . . . that!

EXERCISE 48A

1. . . . River, but (1)
2. No comma (1a)
3. No comma (6a)
4. . . . feet, grotesque, satanic faces with bulging
    eyes and sharp pointed teeth, and unreal com-
    binations of different kinds of animals.
    (8 and 9)
5. However, the . . . (7)
6. No comma (1b)
7. . . . Tower, built . . . (6)
8. . . . Tower, they . . . (3)
9. . . . them, the massive network . . . (6)
10. levels; consequently, the lines . . . (2)
11. No comma (5a)

EXERCISE 48B

1. . . . Budapest, the capital of Hungary,
    situated . . . (10)
2. No comma (10a)
3. No comma (11a)
4. . . . Parliament building, which still . . . bomb
    fragments, lends . . . (11)
5. . . . heightened, moreover, when these . . . (13)

EXERCISE 48C

1. "Tod, the Colosseum . . . (15)
2. . . . Tod explained, "It's a movie set . . . (16)
3. . . . in Rome, Italy, on a movie set . . . (19)
4. . . . Mother and Dad," Ellen said excitedly,
    "and tell . . . (17)
5. Dear Mother and Dad, (22)
6. . . . Love from both of us, (21)

EXERCISE 49

1. C3	4. D1
2. C2	5. D2
3. C3	6. C4

EXERCISE 50A

1. or-gan-ize
2. syl-lab-i-ca-tion
3. ab-so-lute
4. cre-a-tiv-i-ty
5. light-ning
6. math-e-mat-ics

EXERCISE 50B

1. The fifty-year-old lighthouse—the one on Bard's point—is no longer used.
2. The black-haired villain—but why talk about him now?
3. The Anglo-American treaty is still in effect.
4. Ted had his newest suits dry-cleaned.
5. The sad-faced clown—Tom and Sue saw him yesterday—delighted the children.

EXERCISE 51

1. Italics: *Times-Herald*
2. Double quotation marks: . . . part, "The . . . season."
3. Parentheses: . . . rang (it seemed to ring constantly), the . . .
4. Italics or double quotation marks: *libel liable* or "libel" "liable"

5. Brackets: [Editor's note: Medina, Ohio]
6. Single quotation marks: . . . soliloquy 'To be, or not to be . . .'
7. Double quotation marks and single quotation marks: "The song 'Happy Days . . . Again' seemed . . . little," Tom's grandmother recalled.
8. Parentheses: . . . heard (I really should not say this) that . . .
9. Double quotation marks and italics: "When will the tenth volume of *History of the World* be published?" the book . . .
10. Italics or double quotation marks: *biblos book* or "biblos" "book"

EXERCISE 52

1. Juan Garcia, Spanish
2. Harold Radcliff *Car Repair Is a Challenge*
3. Last Sunday,   Bob
4. His, Wild Oak Street
5. People, New York City, Lake Tahoe
6. Last March Terry, Eugene, Oregon
7. Jeff, Life Science 2A or 2a
8. Martha, English
9. The French
10. Judge Walters

X-TRAS   UNIT EIGHT

I. 1.   "L '   F   N   D   C   ," T   E [;]
           let s have dinner at the french restaurant near notre dame cathedral   tod suggested to ellen
           "I '   F   I   ."
           i ll find out how much french i remember

    2.   T   ,   ,   —   [; . F]   ,
           they walked down the dark narrow shop lined street finally they found the entrance to the

           restaurant .

    3.   S
           seated on benches at a rustic table in the crowded dimly lit room they waited for the waiter

           to bring the menu [: ;] but he set a large basket of bread on the table without saying a word .

    4.   A   . T   ,
           a short time later he brought another basket to the table this one was filled with raw unpeeled
           vegetables tomatoes peppers onions cucumbers cauliflower and celery . A again he said

           nothing .

    5.   "I   '   ," E   T
           i wonder what we ll get next   ellen said as she chewed on a stalk of celery while tod cut a

           tomato and a pepper into pieces

316

6. they did not have to wait long the waiter brought a third basket and it was filled with a large assortment of sausages he smiled as he watched ellen s surprised expression

7. tod i don t believe it ellen exclaimed which one should i try first

8. a short time later the waiter brought the menu when he returned to take orders tod quickly discovered that he had to order in french because the waiter knew no english

9. after tod and ellen had finished the main course the waiter brought a large basket of cheeses and then he brought the menu for dessert

10. as they left the restaurant at 11 15 p m ellen asked tod plaintively do you suppose you could take me back to the hotel in a wheelbarrow i m not sure i can walk

---

II. 1. . . . story "The End of Something"
. . . novel *For Whom the Bell Tolls.*

2. The *Wall Street Journal* . . .

3. . . . inefficiency—what else can he call it— cost . . . Commas or parentheses may also be used.

4. "Pretend that . . . father," the counselor . . . "Try to show . . . he acts."

5. . . . words *whether* and *weather* in . . .

EXERCISE 53A

Because there can be more than one way to rewrite these sentences, the revisions below are suggested as possibilities. If you have a question about any of your revisions, ask your instructor to check your sentences.

1. The artist should clean his brushes each time he finishes painting. *He* will find the brushes ready to use the next time *he decides* to paint.
2. Americans must vote for the men they want to run their government. *They* have no one to blame but *themselves* if *they* get officials whom *they* do not want.
3. The student usually applies himself to his school work the first month of classes. Then *he relaxes* and *neglects his* assignments.

4. Many partygoers seem to enjoy a game of charades. *They like* dramatizing clues for *their* partners.
5. The youth of the nation should be given an opportunity to prove that he can be responsible. *He* sometimes *acts* unwisely because *he is* rebelling against what *he* believes *is* unreasonable domination. ("Youth" is singular; "youths" is plural.)
6. When preparing to write an essay, one should select a topic which *he* (or "one") can understand thoroughly. If *he* has only general information, *he* cannot write a convincing paper.
7. The newspaper is sometimes considered to be the voice of the people. But when *it contains* news stories against the best interests of the people, *one begins* to wonder whether *it speaks* for the people or for *its* own personal interests.
8. If everyone *wants* to do *his* part to help others, *he* should work with volunteer service organizations and not expect to get paid for every minute *he spends* working.
9. A person who buys this car receives a guarantee which says *the owner will not be charged* for parts which have to be replaced, but *he will be charged* only for the labor for replacing them.
10. When a person fills out an application for a position, *he* should try to fill out every blank to indicate to the interviewer that *he has* tried to give all the information requested.

EXERCISE 53B

Because it is possible to rewrite sentences acceptably in more than one way, the revisions below are suggested as possibilities. If you have a question about any of your revisions, ask your instructor to check your sentences.

1. As the clumsy waitress served the four-course meal, she dropped bits of food on each of the diners.
2. New drivers make many mistakes, but experienced drivers can make just as many if they are not careful.
3. Because Matt *had* lost his keys, he could not drive his car, he could not get into the house, and he could not unlock his office desk. Just as he decided to try to escape his troubles by going fishing, he realized that he could not get his fishing gear out of the locked garage.
4. Although the Johnson brothers had built many beautiful homes, they had also erected "cracker boxes" (OR flimsy structures) which looked as if they would fall down in a strong breeze.
5. The horse, wearing all his trappings, carried the knight, dressed in a heavy suit of armor, and could scarcely get out of the mud puddle he backed into accidentally.
   OR: Weighted down by decorative trappings and a knight in heavy armor, the horse could hardly pull himself out of the spongy mud puddle.
   OR: The knight in heavy armor, riding his elaborately decorated horse, could hardly maneuver the burdened animal out of the spongy mud puddle.
6. Jim, neatly dressed in a new suit, felt disgusted when he saw Nan wearing dungarees and shirt for the senior dance.
7. Ted Owen and I never realized how much work we would have when we agreed to organize the football parade.
8. Veteran producer Clyde Thornton demonstrated his ability and talent when he produced that movie.
   OR: Veteran producer Clyde Thornton has produced an outstanding movie, evidence of his unique ability to produce one success after another for many years.
9. Because a big game hunter in Africa never knows when an enraged beast might attack him, he should be an excellent marksman.
10. The farmer who had helped his neighbors harvest crops in previous years asked them to help him harvest the wheat which he had raised.
    OR: Neighbors who had received the farmer's help in past harvest seasons came to help him harvest the wheat which he had raised.

EXERCISE 54A

1. I	11. F	21. I	31. F
2. F	12. I	22. I	32. I
3. I	13. I	23. I	33. I
4. F	14. F	24. I	34. F
5. I	15. F	25. F	35. F
6. I	16. F	26. F	36. F
7. F	17. I	27. I	37. I
8. I	18. F	28. F	38. F
9. F	19. F	29. I	39. F
10. F	20. F	30. F	40. F

EXERCISE 54B

1.	wait on	wait for
2.	fix	situation *or* predicament
3.	could of	could have
4.	mighty	very
5.	ways	way
6.	leave	let
7.	lots	a lot *or* many
8.	wants out	wants to be relieved
9.	plan on	plan to do
10.	most	almost
11.	quite	quiet
12.	liable	likely
13.	ad	advertisement
14.	kind of wants	thinks he may want
15.	less	fewer
16.	in	into
17.	guess	believe
18.	incredulous	incredible
19.	didn't like to	did not prefer to
20.	to	omit *to*
21.	suspicioned	suspected
22.	same	that they
23.	mad	angry
24.	latter	later
25.	party	person
26.	take and	omit "take and"
27.	ever	omit "ever"
28.	had ought	ought
29.	considerable	very
30.	as	that *or* does not know whether she wants

31. all the farther   as far as
32. alright   all right
33. affect   effect
34. invites   invitations
35. shape   condition
36. per   according to
37. enthused   enthusiastic
38. disremembers   does not remember
39. amount   number
40. formally   formerly

EXERCISE 55A

1. He likes bacon and
       eggs.

2. Will you call her and
       tell her the time of the meeting.

3. She cleared the table, and then
she washed the dishes.

4. none

5. Jack and
Tom   bought an old car to repair and
           to rebuild.

6. Edison invented the light bulb, and
Marconi invented the wireless.

7. The high school offers both sewing and
       cooking.

8. The boys can take wood shop, or
     they can take car repair.

9. Workers like their coffeebreak, but
they do not care to pay for the coffee.

10. The acrobat flew to one trapeze and then
     swung back to the first one.

EXERCISE 55B

1. having a conversation   conversing *or* talking
2. Mary can either   Either Mary can *or*
                      Mary can either wash
                        the car or clean the
                        house
3. who writes stories   a writer *or* a story
                          writer
4. C

5. to paint   painting
6. which John built   built by John
7. to read three novels reading three novels
8. an intellectual   intellectual (Omit "an")
9. without meaning   meaningless
10. will work   workable

EXERCISE 55C

1. Either Sarah and Tom will buy . . . , or they
will consider . . .
Sarah and Tom will either buy . . . or consider
. . . (No punctuation)
Sarah and Tom either will buy . . . or will
consider . . . (No punctuation)

2. He is both a karate expert and an excellent
wrestler.

3. Neither the principal nor the teachers want to
attend the convention.

4. Either George will repair . . . , or he will hire . . .
George will either repair or hire . . .
(No punctuation)

5. Marshall will neither give Ben a job nor lend
him money.

EXERCISE 56A

These are suggested revisions, not necessarily the
only ones possible.

1. He explained how to give artificial respiration
to a drowning victim.
2. Because television can give on-the-spot cover-
age, newspaper stories by comparison are old
when readers receive their papers.
3. The rules committee refuses to listen to
Dwight Huston's grievances for many reasons.
4. The man in the blue shirt tried valiantly to
rescue the small brown and white dog perched
precariously on a log in the raging river.
5. Some college radicals seem to be causing cam-
pus unrest.
6. I still cannot decide what job I would like to
have.
7. Evidence suggests that Tim Elliott was not
present when the man was shot through the
head.
8. Bob Richards is to be admired for his control
and calm in handling the problem.

9. Our assembly line efficiency could be increased.
10. Mark Hudson hesitates at this time to open another store in our cross-country chain.

EXERCISE 56B

These are suggested revisions, not necessarily the only ones possible.

1. On his way home from work Dave crashed into an oncoming car.
2. Mary Tyler, who operates the beauty shop, won the award this year for an original hair style.
3. The history instructor announced that he would give a mid-term examination.
4. You will like Harvey's Haven, which serves delicious hamburgers.
   OR: If you like sea food, you will like Harvey's Haven.
5. Mrs. Watson, who lives in Los Angeles where she operates a grocery for her sick nephew, is in the hospital now, recovering from pneumonia.
6. The reference book John is using contains helpful information for three of his classes.
7. Rain came through the open window and ruined half the carpeting.
8. Because Ellis dislikes working out details of a research project, he hired Ross.
9. The dog, nose to the ground, ran wildly through the forest.
10. The geraniums bloomed all summer, and the evergreens thrived.

EXERCISE 57A

1. S	6. S
2. F	7. S
3. flat; some	8. space, and
4. F	9. space; they
5. S	10. S

EXERCISE 57B

1. Subject	6. Modifier
2. Modifier	7. Predicate
3. Modifier	8. Predicate
4. Subject	9. Modifier
5. Subject	10. Subject

X-TRAS   UNIT NINE

I. . . . to live. Then *he has* to find houses . . . Sometimes *he gets* the best . . . When *he has* finally found . . . but then *he has* to get ready . . .

II.
1. Either Dennis will agree . . . (Place *either* before the subject.)

2. Italy, Austria, and France. (Paris is a city; Austria and Italy are countries.)

3. Jackson has *asked* and will ask again . . .

4. Billy White, a juggler and an acrobat, . . .

5. The *lock was* broken and the *tools were* stolen. (*Tools* is plural.)

6. Not only does Jeff have a sailboat . . .

7. . . . well designed but uncomfortable.

8. Neither could the botanist identify . . .

9. The *notes . . . were* clearly written . . . , but the laboratory *equipment was* disorganized . . .

10. . . . discolored but not decayed.

III. These are suggested revisions. If your sentences are different, ask your instructor to check them for you.

1. We may not think about our fears and wishes or talk about them, but they are often expressed in our dreams.
   OR: Although we may not think about our fears . . . talk about them, they are . . .

2. After Marie had lost her surfboard, she spied a shark and swam frantically toward shore.

3. Daryl had finished ironing his shirts and had begun to sweep the apartment, when the telephone rang.
   OR: After Daryl had . . . apartment, the telephone rang. (Watch sequence of tenses.)

4. The child sniffed the air and smelled steak cooking on the barbecue in the back yard; she felt hungry.
OR: As the child sniffed . . .
OR: When the child sniffed . . .

5. The play, a premiere performance, was about to begin, and the actors waited nervously backstage; the audience became silent as the house lights dimmed and the curtain rose.

X-TRAS POSTTEST

1. A—wives
2. A—families
3. C
4. A—wants
5. C
6. A—has driven
7. A—today's
8. A—can hardly
9. A—didn't get money
10. B—well (Adv)
11. B—well, efficiently (Adv)
12. C—*Moreover* is parenthetical.
13. B—actor; however,
14. C
15. C
16. B—supplies: (colon)
17. A—Sarah and she (NS)
18. A—Tom and me (Nio)
19. A—Vera and I (NS)
20. A—who (NS)
21. B—him (refers to *each one*)
22. A—have asked (*Members* is plural.)
23. A—are (*Offices* (NS) is plural.)
24. A—larger (two elephants)
25. B—he (elliptical clause)
26. A—statue that (Modifier identifies *statue.*)
27. C
28. A—Herbert, who (Modifier is extra.)
29. B—horse that (*Horse* is an animal.)
30. A—Dangling modifier (Sagging roof)
31. C
32. B—title of opera should be italicized
33. B—one or he (refers to *graduate*)
34. A—Incredible
35. A—effect

Index